THE GUILD™

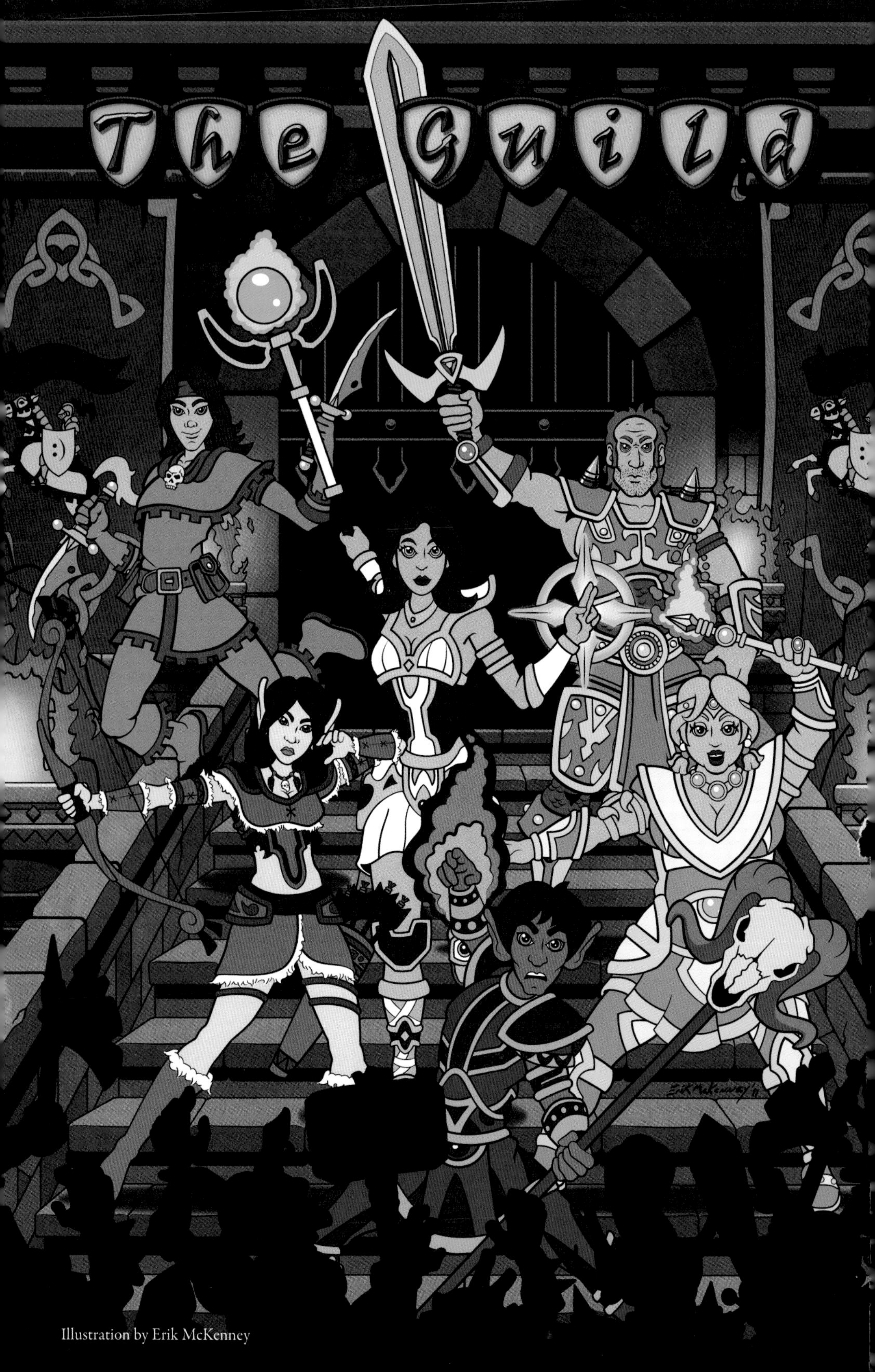
The Guild

Illustration by Erik McKenney

KNIGHTS OF GOOD

Script
FELICIA DAY
JEFF LEWIS
SEAN BECKER
KIM EVEY
SANDEEP PARIKH

Art

DARICK ROBERTSON	**RON CHAN**	**WELLINTON ALVES**
RICHARD P. CLARK	**BECKY CLOONAN**	**JASON GORDER**
KRISTIAN DONALDSON	**DAVE STEWART**	**TIM SEELEY**
EVAN BRYCE	**MICHELLE MADSEN**	**ADAM WARREN**
ANDREW CURRIE	**JEREMY BASTIAN**	**EMILY WARREN**

Letters
BLAMBOT®'S NATE PIEKOS

Cover Art
**GEORGES JEANTY WITH DEXTER VINES
AND TARIQ HASSAN**

Back Cover Art
BLAIR SHEDD

DARK HORSE BOOKS

President & Publisher
MIKE RICHARDSON

Editor
SCOTT ALLIE

Assistant Editor
BRENDAN WRIGHT

Collection Designer
KAT LARSON

This story takes place before the events of season 1 of the web series *The Guild*, created by Felicia Day.

Special thanks to the cast and crew of *The Guild*; the donors for season 1 of *The Guild*; Kim Evey; Joss Whedon; Pat Duncan; George Ruiz; and most importantly, my parents.

NEIL HANKERSON Executive Vice President TOM WEDDLE Chief Financial Officer RANDY STRADLEY Vice President of Publishing MICHAEL MARTENS Vice President of Book Trade Sales ANITA NELSON Vice President of Business Affairs DAVID SCROGGY Vice President of Product Development DALE LAFOUNTAIN Vice President of Information Technology DARLENE VOGEL Senior Director of Print, Design, and Production KEN LIZZI General Counsel MATT PARKINSON Senior Director of Marketing DAVEY ESTRADA Editorial Director SCOTT ALLIE Senior Managing Editor CHRIS WARNER Senior Books Editor DIANA SCHUTZ Executive Editor CARY GRAZZINI Director of Print and Development LIA RIBACCHI Art Director CARA NIECE Director of Scheduling

THE GUILD™ VOLUME 2: KNIGHTS OF GOOD

This volume reprints the Dark Horse comic books The Guild: Vork, The Guild: Tink, The Guild: Bladezz, The Guild: Clara, *and* The Guild: Zaboo.

Published by Dark Horse Books, a division of Dark Horse Comics, Inc., 10956 SE Main Street, Milwaukie, OR 97222

DarkHorse.com

Library of Congress Cataloging-in-Publication Data

The guild volume 2 : knights of good / script, Felicia Day ... [et al.] ; art, Darick Robertson ... [et al.]. -- 1st ed.
p. cm.
ISBN 978-1-59582-900-9
1. Internet games--Comic books, strips, etc. 2. Graphic novels. I. Day, Felicia, 1979- II. Robertson, Darick. III. Title: Knights of good.
PN6728.G79G85 2012
741.5'973--dc23
2012002858

To find a comics shop in your area, call the Comic Shop Locator Service toll-free at (888) 266-4226.

First edition: July 2012

1 3 5 7 9 10 8 6 4 2
Printed at Midas Printing International, Ltd., Huizhou, China

CONTENTS

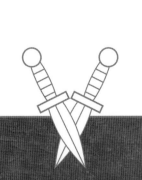

CHAPTER ONE
VORK

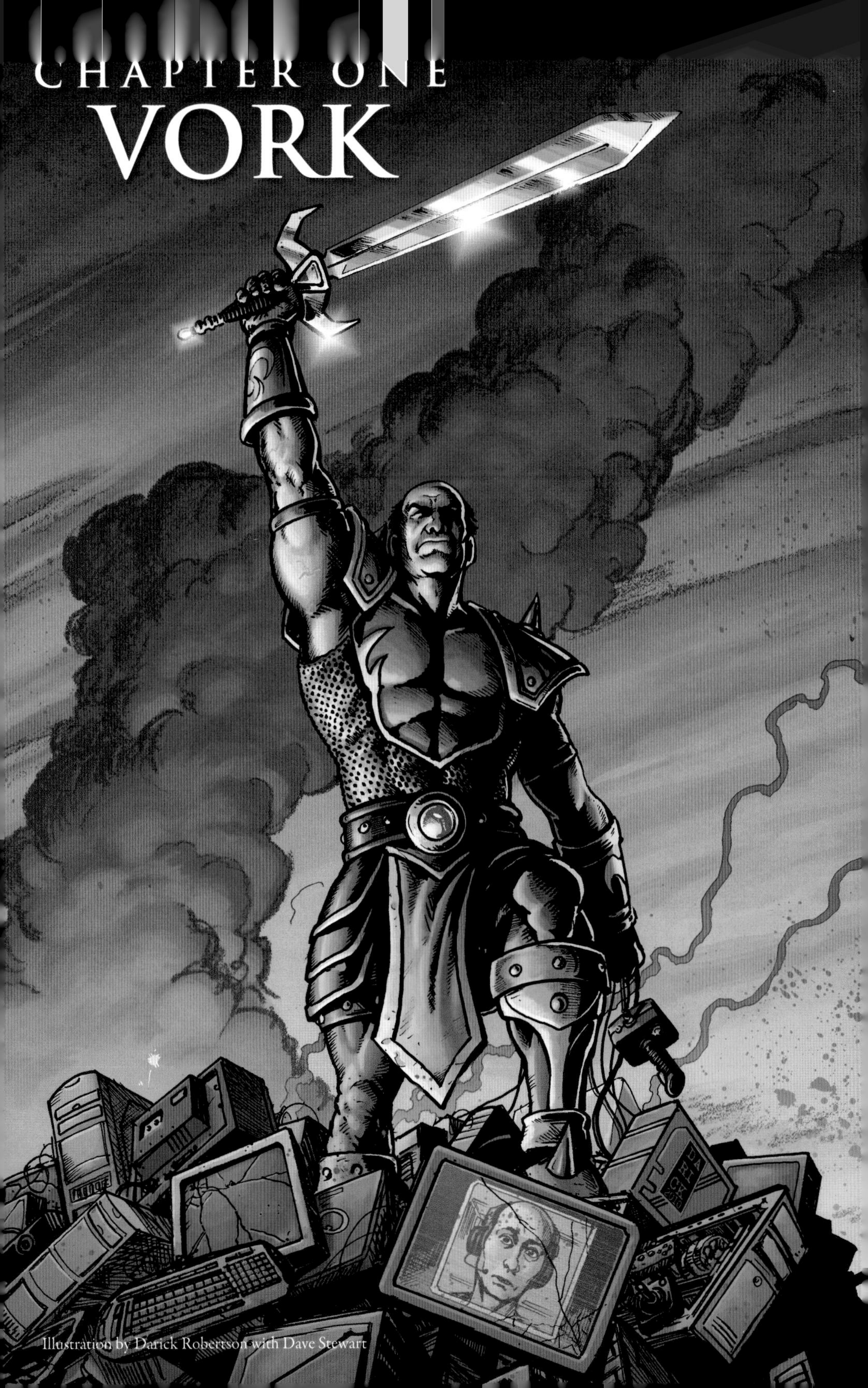

Illustration by Darick Robertson with Dave Stewart

Illustration by Gilbert Hernandez

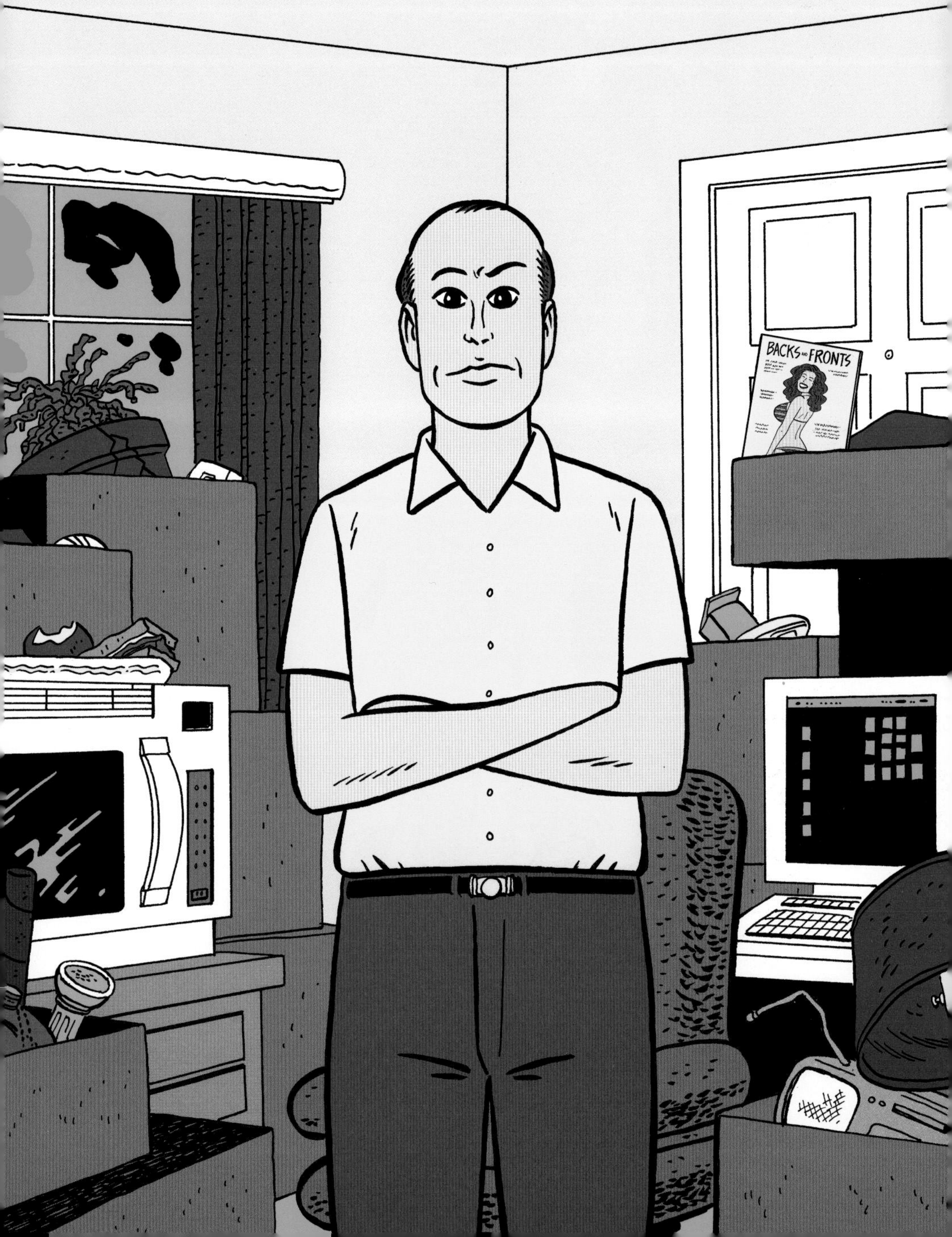
BACKS AND FRONTS

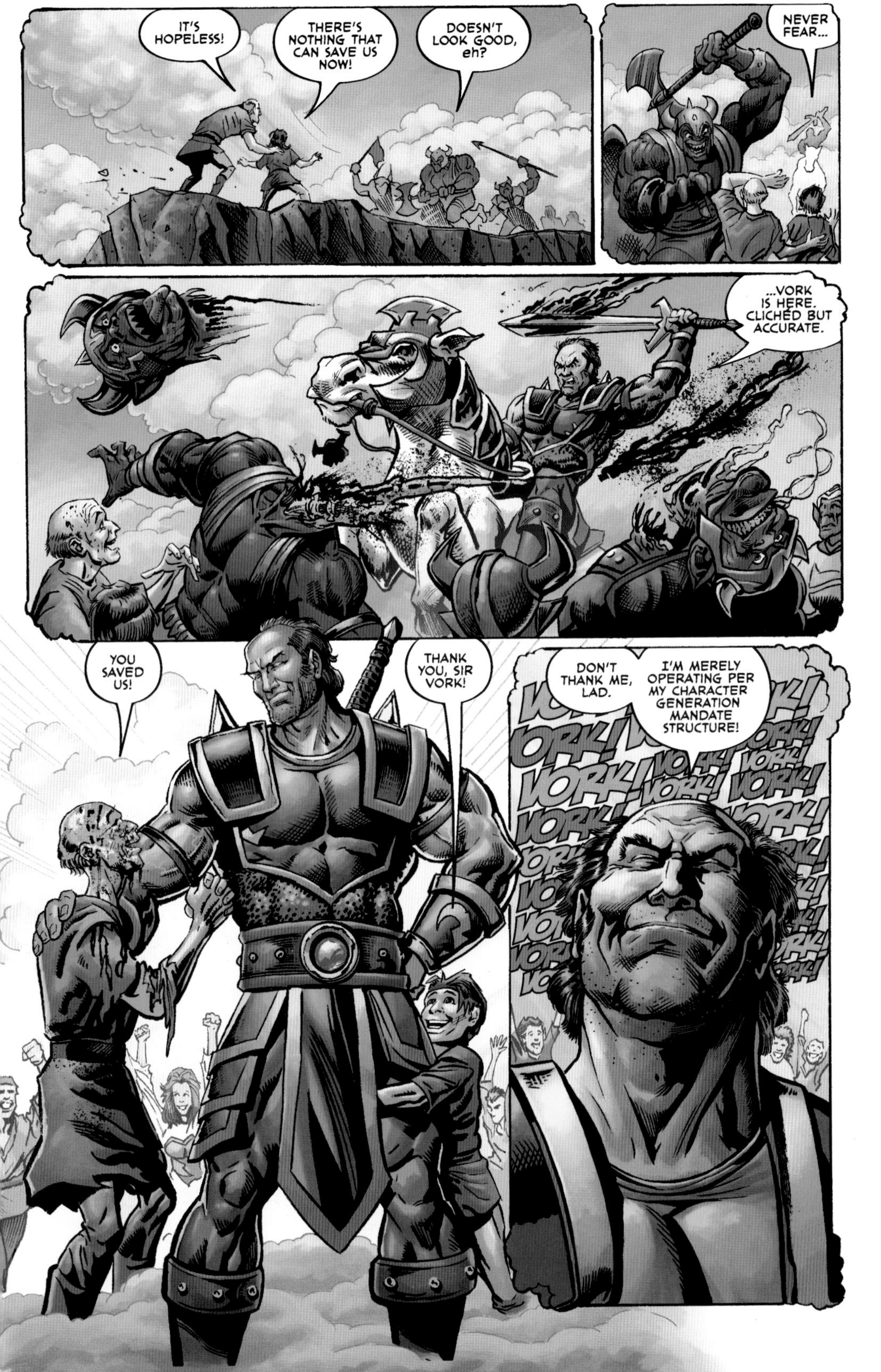
IT'S HOPELESS!
THERE'S NOTHING THAT CAN SAVE US NOW!
DOESN'T LOOK GOOD, eh?
NEVER FEAR...
...VORK IS HERE. CLICHED BUT ACCURATE.
YOU SAVED US!
THANK YOU, SIR VORK!
DON'T THANK ME, LAD.
I'M MERELY OPERATING PER MY CHARACTER GENERATION MANDATE STRUCTURE!
VORK! VORK! VORK! VORK! VORK! VORK!

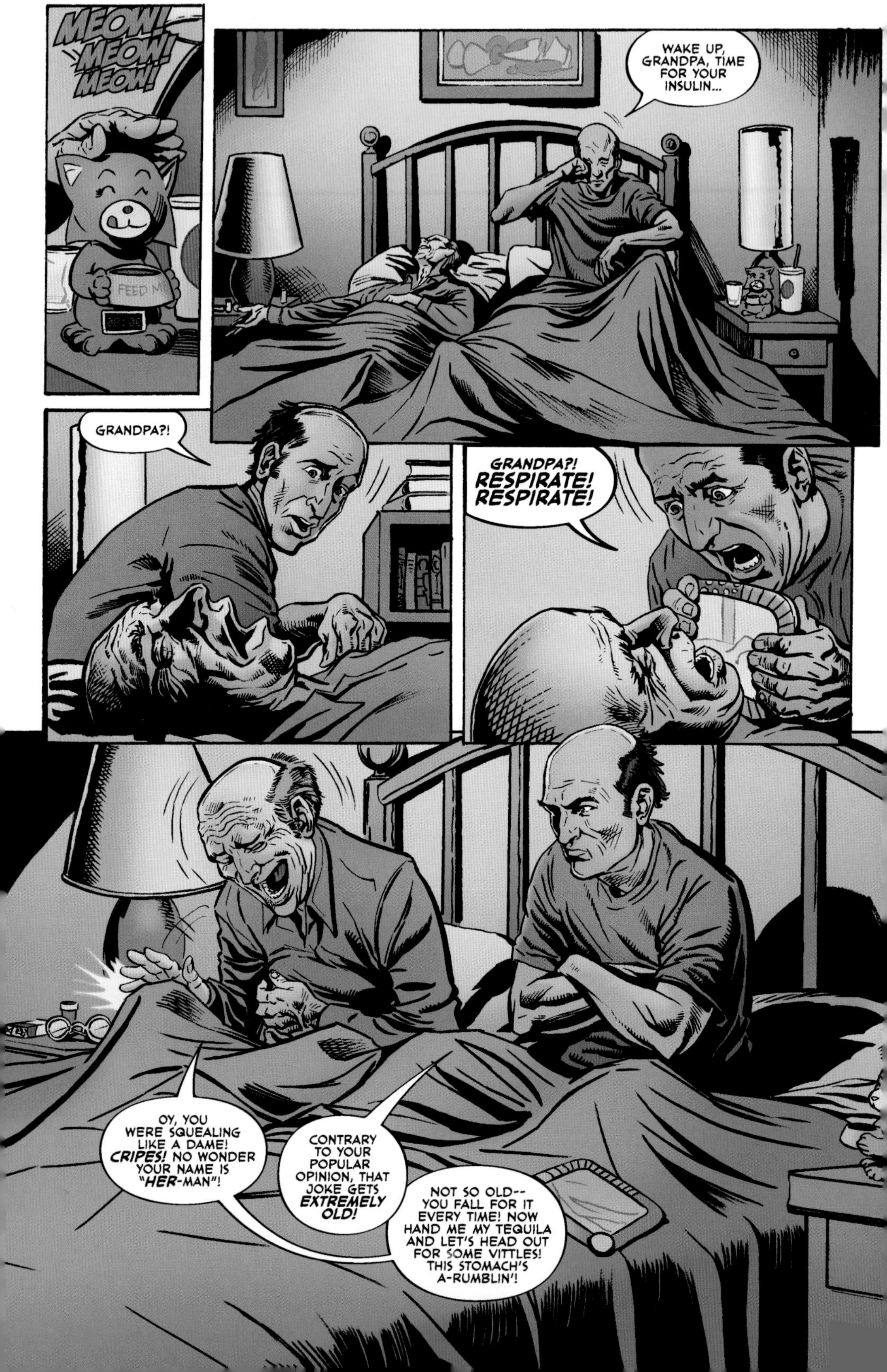
MEOW! MEOW! MEOW!
FEED ME
WAKE UP, GRANDPA, TIME FOR YOUR INSULIN...
GRANDPA?!
GRANDPA?! RESPIRATE! RESPIRATE!
OY, YOU WERE SQUEALING LIKE A DAME! CRIPES! NO WONDER YOUR NAME IS "HER-MAN"!
CONTRARY TO YOUR POPULAR OPINION, THAT JOKE GETS EXTREMELY OLD!
NOT SO OLD-- YOU FALL FOR IT EVERY TIME! NOW HAND ME MY TEQUILA AND LET'S HEAD OUT FOR SOME VITTLES! THIS STOMACH'S A-RUMBLIN'!

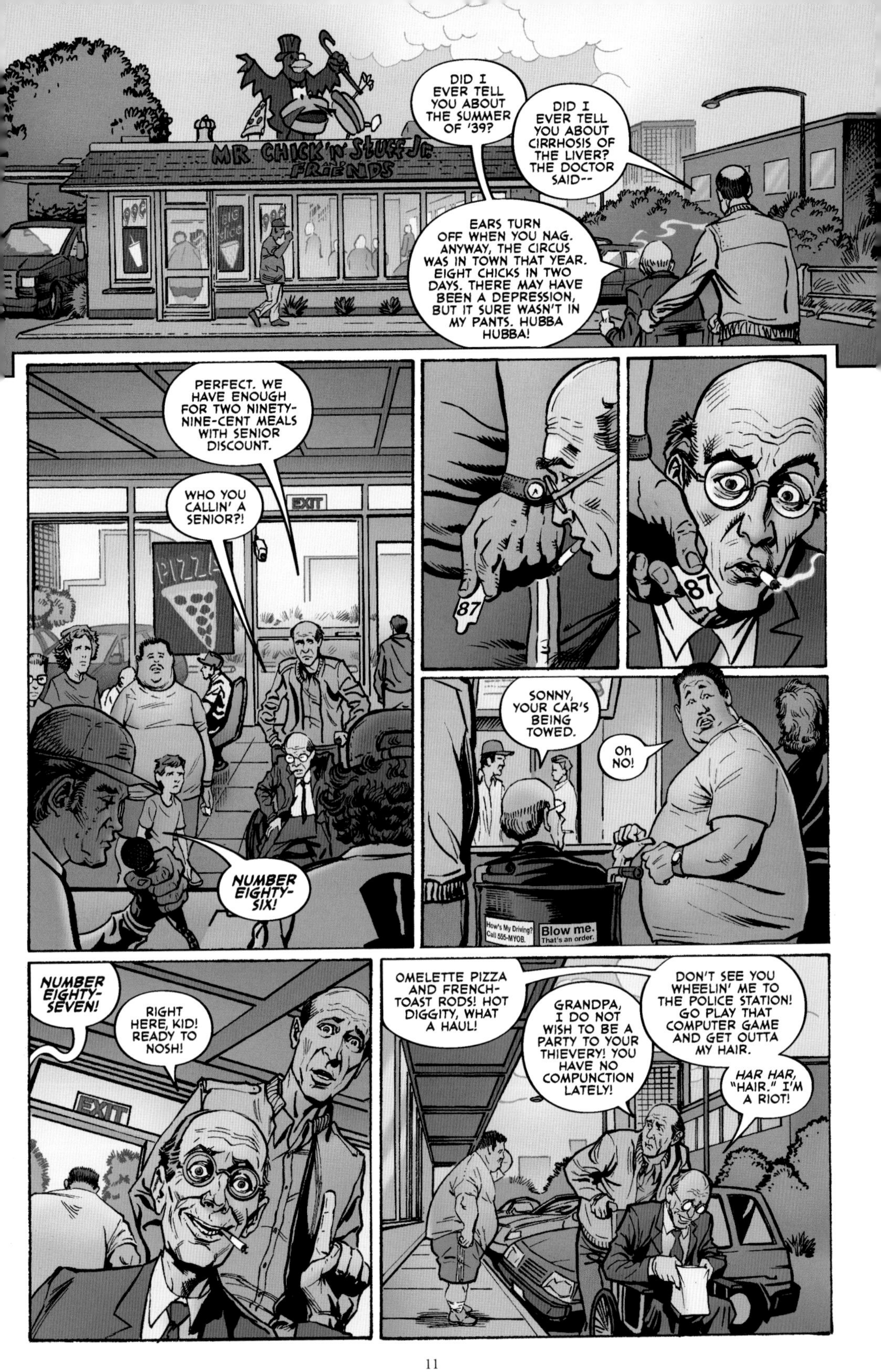
MR. CHICK 'N' STUFF JR. FRIENDS
DID I EVER TELL YOU ABOUT THE SUMMER OF '39?
DID I EVER TELL YOU ABOUT CIRRHOSIS OF THE LIVER? THE DOCTOR SAID--
EARS TURN OFF WHEN YOU NAG. ANYWAY, THE CIRCUS WAS IN TOWN THAT YEAR. EIGHT CHICKS IN TWO DAYS. THERE MAY HAVE BEEN A DEPRESSION, BUT IT SURE WASN'T IN MY PANTS. HUBBA HUBBA!
PERFECT. WE HAVE ENOUGH FOR TWO NINETY-NINE-CENT MEALS WITH SENIOR DISCOUNT.
WHO YOU CALLIN' A SENIOR?!
EXIT
PIZZA
NUMBER EIGHTY-SIX!
87
87
SONNY, YOUR CAR'S BEING TOWED.
Oh NO!
How's My Driving? Call 555-MYOB.
Blow me. That's an order.
NUMBER EIGHTY-SEVEN!
RIGHT HERE, KID! READY TO NOSH!
EXIT
OMELETTE PIZZA AND FRENCH-TOAST RODS! HOT DIGGITY, WHAT A HAUL!
GRANDPA, I DO NOT WISH TO BE A PARTY TO YOUR THIEVERY! YOU HAVE NO COMPUNCTION LATELY!
DON'T SEE YOU WHEELIN' ME TO THE POLICE STATION! GO PLAY THAT COMPUTER GAME AND GET OUTTA MY HAIR.
HAR HAR, "HAIR." I'M A RIOT!

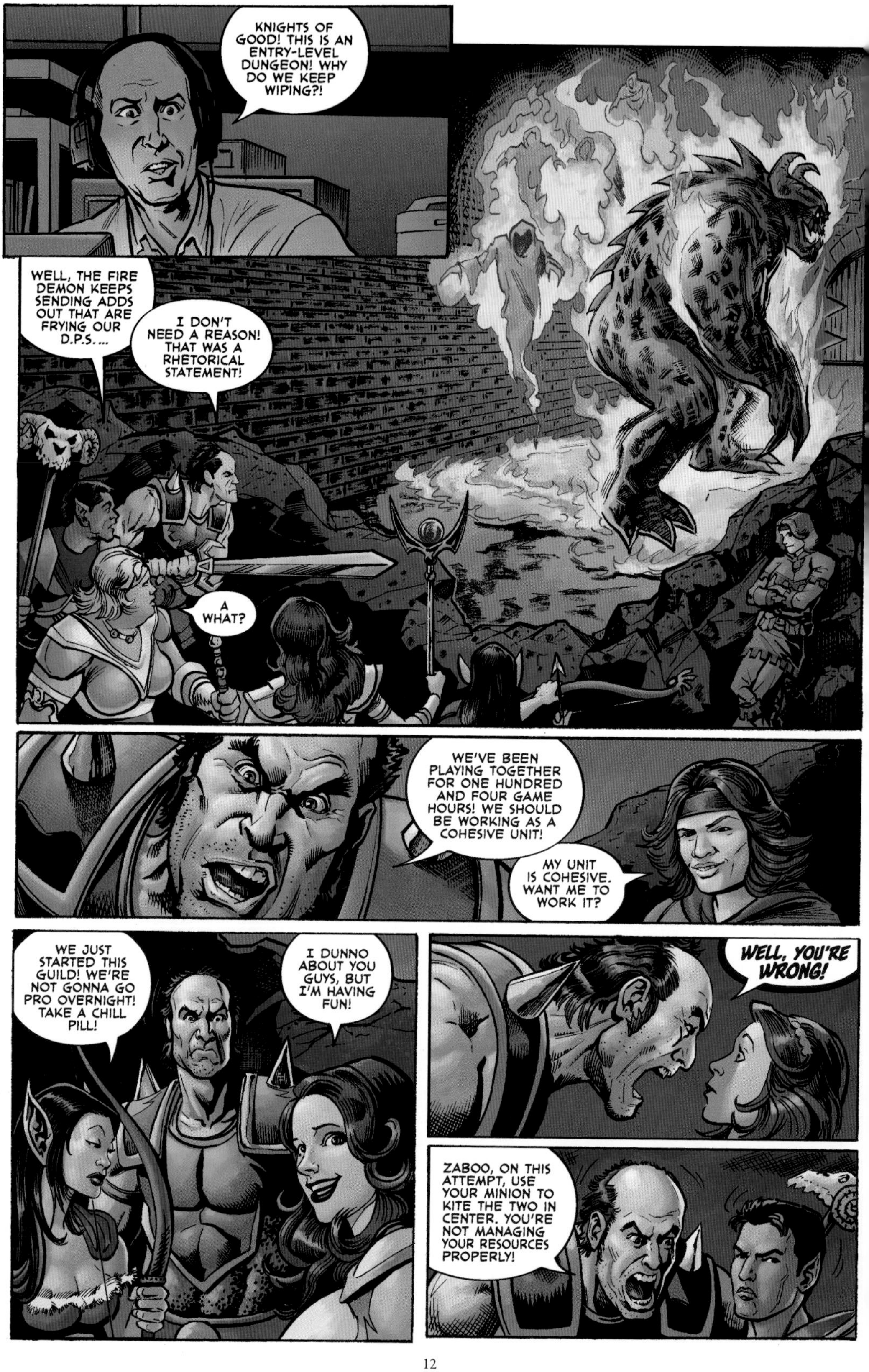
KNIGHTS OF GOOD! THIS IS AN ENTRY-LEVEL DUNGEON! WHY DO WE KEEP WIPING?!
WELL, THE FIRE DEMON KEEPS SENDING ADDS OUT THAT ARE FRYING OUR D.P.S....
I DON'T NEED A REASON! THAT WAS A RHETORICAL STATEMENT!
A WHAT?
WE'VE BEEN PLAYING TOGETHER FOR ONE HUNDRED AND FOUR GAME HOURS! WE SHOULD BE WORKING AS A COHESIVE UNIT!
MY UNIT IS COHESIVE. WANT ME TO WORK IT?
WE JUST STARTED THIS GUILD! WE'RE NOT GONNA GO PRO OVERNIGHT! TAKE A CHILL PILL!
I DUNNO ABOUT YOU GUYS, BUT I'M HAVING FUN!
WELL, YOU'RE WRONG!
ZABOO, ON THIS ATTEMPT, USE YOUR MINION TO KITE THE TWO IN CENTER. YOU'RE NOT MANAGING YOUR RESOURCES PROPERLY!

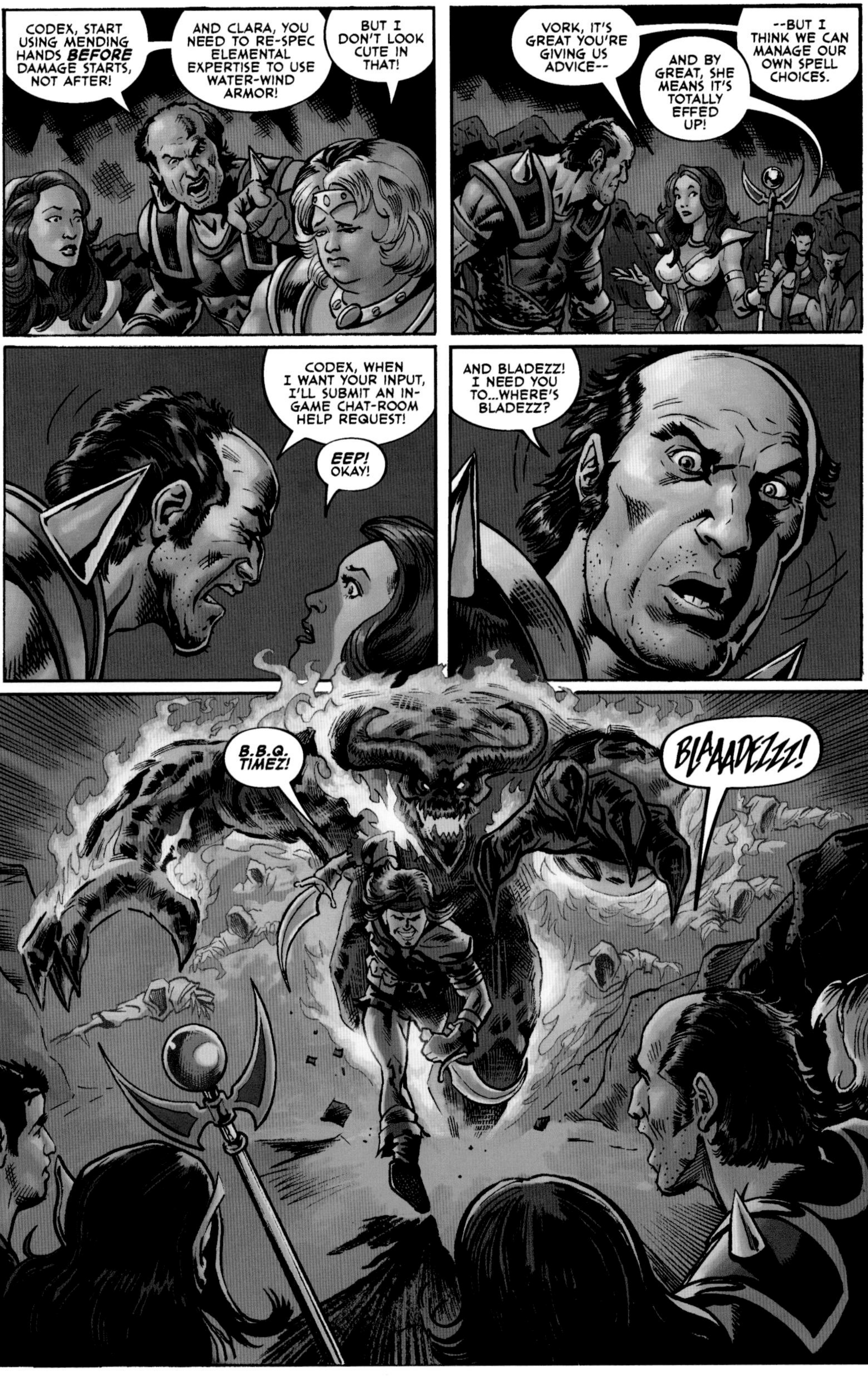
CODEX, START USING MENDING HANDS *BEFORE* DAMAGE STARTS, NOT AFTER!
AND CLARA, YOU NEED TO RE-SPEC ELEMENTAL EXPERTISE TO USE WATER-WIND ARMOR!
BUT I DON'T LOOK CUTE IN THAT!
VORK, IT'S GREAT YOU'RE GIVING US ADVICE--
AND BY GREAT, SHE MEANS IT'S TOTALLY EFFED UP!
--BUT I THINK WE CAN MANAGE OUR OWN SPELL CHOICES.
CODEX, WHEN I WANT YOUR INPUT, I'LL SUBMIT AN IN-GAME CHAT-ROOM HELP REQUEST!
EEP! OKAY!
AND BLADEZZ! I NEED YOU TO...WHERE'S BLADEZZ?
B.B.Q. TIMEZ!
BLAAADEZZZ!

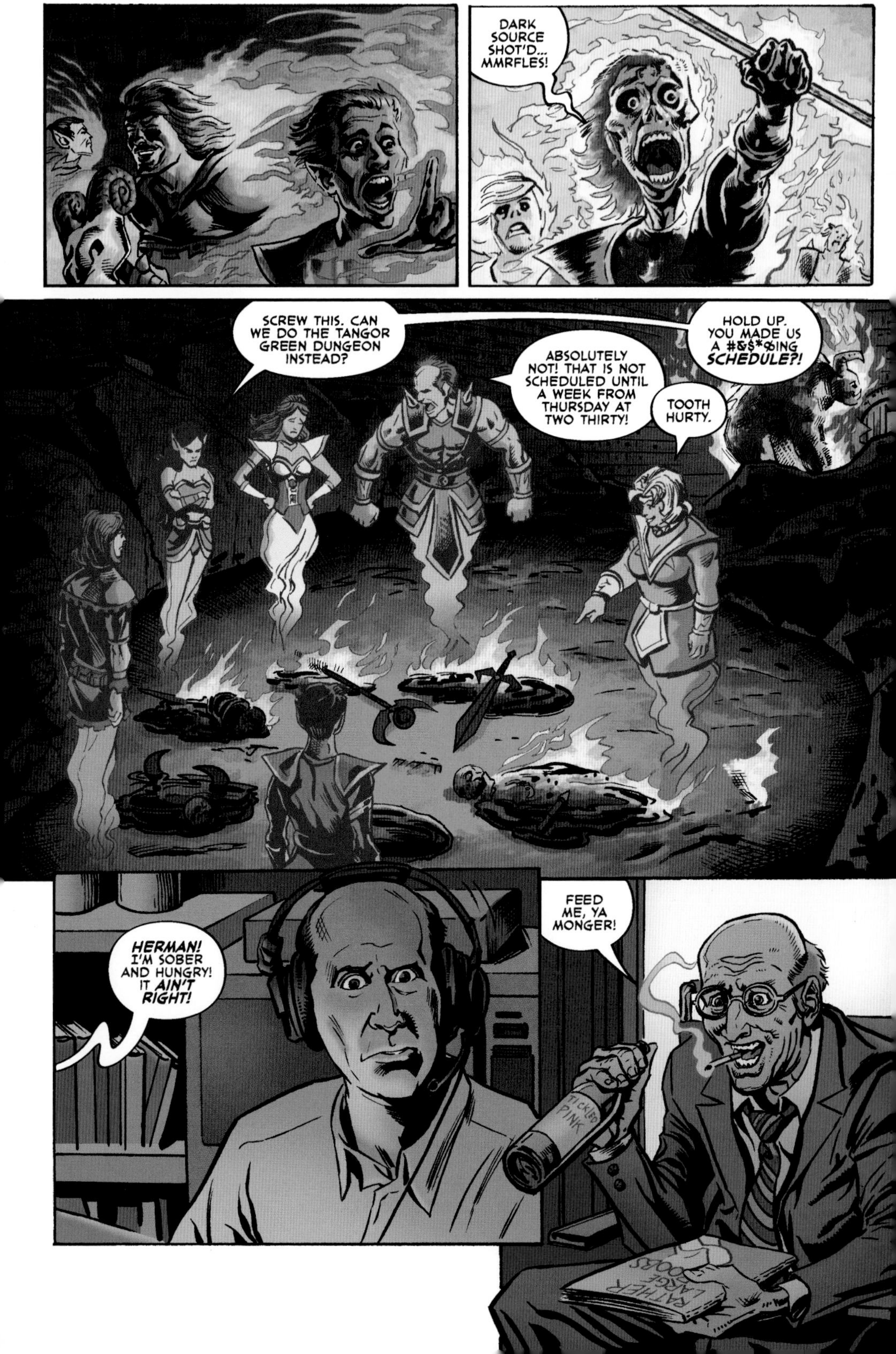
DARK SOURCE SHOT'D... MMRFLES!
SCREW THIS. CAN WE DO THE TANGOR GREEN DUNGEON INSTEAD?
ABSOLUTELY NOT! THAT IS NOT SCHEDULED UNTIL A WEEK FROM THURSDAY AT TWO THIRTY!
HOLD UP. YOU MADE US A #&$*%ING SCHEDULE?!
TOOTH HURTY.
HERMAN! I'M SOBER AND HUNGRY! IT AIN'T RIGHT!
FEED ME, YA MONGER!
TICKLED PINK
RATHER LARGE BOOKS

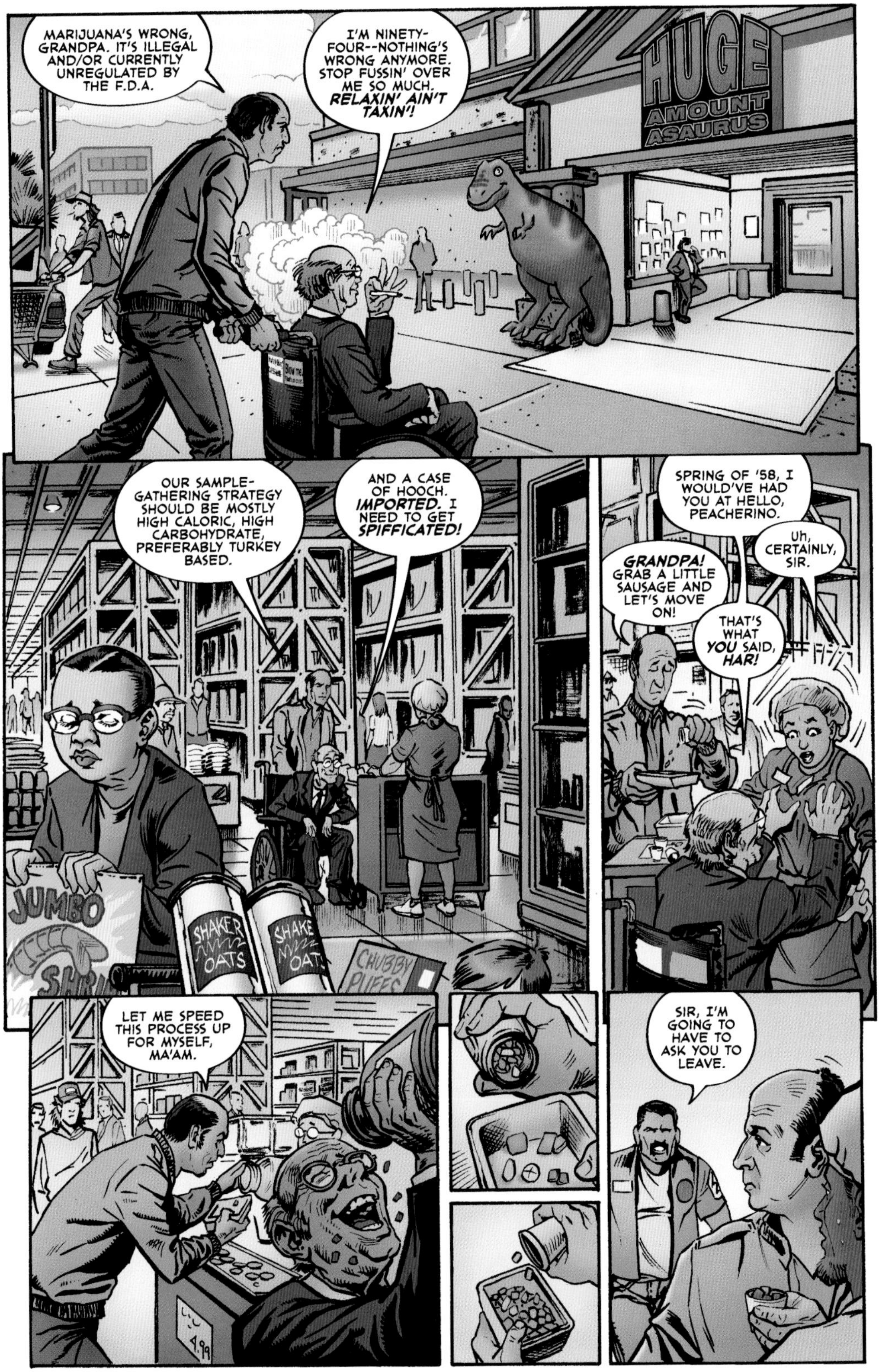
MARIJUANA'S WRONG, GRANDPA. IT'S ILLEGAL AND/OR CURRENTLY UNREGULATED BY THE F.D.A.
I'M NINETY-FOUR--NOTHING'S WRONG ANYMORE. STOP FUSSIN' OVER ME SO MUCH. RELAXIN' AIN'T TAXIN'!
HUGE AMOUNT ASAURUS
OUR SAMPLE-GATHERING STRATEGY SHOULD BE MOSTLY HIGH CALORIC, HIGH CARBOHYDRATE, PREFERABLY TURKEY BASED.
AND A CASE OF HOOCH. IMPORTED. I NEED TO GET SPIFFICATED!
JUMBO
SHAKER OATS
SHAKE OATS
CHUBBY PUFFS
SPRING OF '58, I WOULD'VE HAD YOU AT HELLO, PEACHERINO.
GRANDPA! GRAB A LITTLE SAUSAGE AND LET'S MOVE ON!
UH, CERTAINLY, SIR.
THAT'S WHAT YOU SAID, HAR!
LET ME SPEED THIS PROCESS UP FOR MYSELF, MA'AM.
4.99
SIR, I'M GOING TO HAVE TO ASK YOU TO LEAVE.

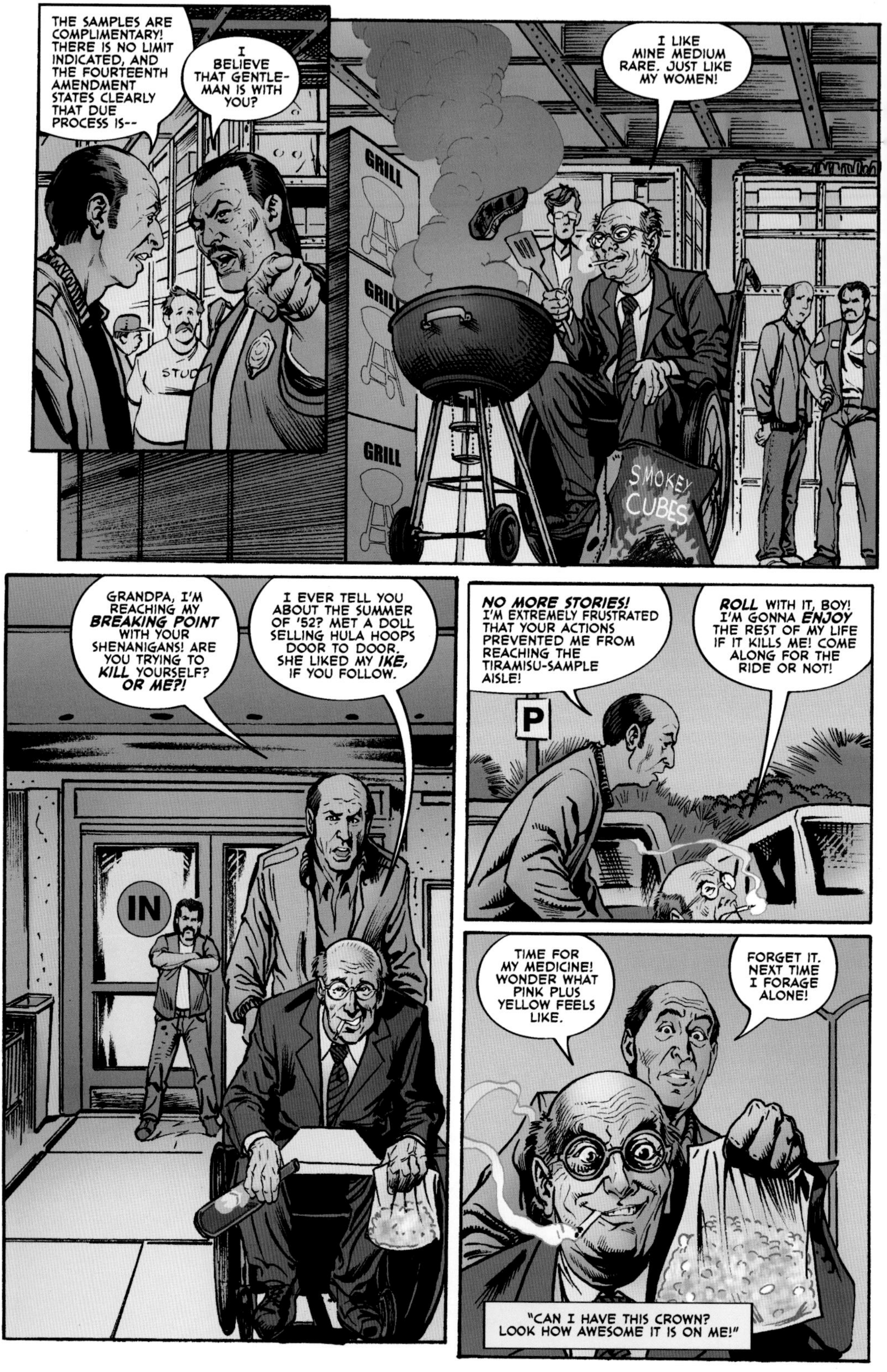
THE SAMPLES ARE COMPLIMENTARY! THERE IS NO LIMIT INDICATED, AND THE FOURTEENTH AMENDMENT STATES CLEARLY THAT DUE PROCESS IS--
I BELIEVE THAT GENTLEMAN IS WITH YOU?
STUD
GRILL
GRILL
GRILL
I LIKE MINE MEDIUM RARE. JUST LIKE MY WOMEN!
SMOKEY CUBES
GRANDPA, I'M REACHING MY BREAKING POINT WITH YOUR SHENANIGANS! ARE YOU TRYING TO KILL YOURSELF? OR ME?!
I EVER TELL YOU ABOUT THE SUMMER OF '52? MET A DOLL SELLING HULA HOOPS DOOR TO DOOR. SHE LIKED MY IKE, IF YOU FOLLOW.
IN
NO MORE STORIES! I'M EXTREMELY FRUSTRATED THAT YOUR ACTIONS PREVENTED ME FROM REACHING THE TIRAMISU-SAMPLE AISLE!
ROLL WITH IT, BOY! I'M GONNA ENJOY THE REST OF MY LIFE IF IT KILLS ME! COME ALONG FOR THE RIDE OR NOT!
P
TIME FOR MY MEDICINE! WONDER WHAT PINK PLUS YELLOW FEELS LIKE.
FORGET IT. NEXT TIME I FORAGE ALONE!
"CAN I HAVE THIS CROWN? LOOK HOW AWESOME IT IS ON ME!"

CLARA! THAT'S FOR A HUNTER! LOOK AT THE STATS!

YOU THINK STATS TRUMP LOOKS? AS IF!

BEFORE WE DESCEND INTO OUR POSTFIGHT FRENZY OF GREED, WE MUST DISCUSS OUR ABYSMAL PERFORMANCE DURING THIS FIGHT!

WHY TALK? WE KILLED Z'CHOU'T'RECK THE REBORN DEMON PHOENIX! DANCE PARTY'D!

WE COULD HAVE DEFEATED HIM SOONER HAD YOU DEPLOYED A SOUL SYPHON BEAM AT THE FORTY-SIX-SECOND MARK! INSTEAD YOU WERE AN IMBECILE AND USED SKULL THRUST! TWENTY DEMERITS!

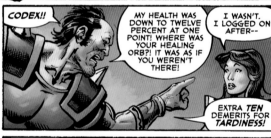

CODEX!!

MY HEALTH WAS DOWN TO TWELVE PERCENT AT ONE POINT! WHERE WAS YOUR HEALING ORB?! IT WAS AS IF YOU WEREN'T THERE!

I WASN'T. I LOGGED ON AFTER--

EXTRA TEN DEMERITS FOR TARDINESS!

AND BLADEZZ! YOUR AGGRESSIVE AGGRO-PULLING LED TO A FOURTEEN PERCENT THREAT INCREASE--

I GOT SOMETHING YOU CAN PULL THAT'LL INCREASE...

TEN DEMERITS FOR TECHNIQUE, FIVE FOR INNUENDO!

OKAY, ASSNUT, WHAT IS THIS DEMERIT CRAP?!

DEMERITS ARE MY WAY TO ADMINISTER PUNISHMENT AND ESTABLISH ORDER! WELCOME TO FIVE OF THEM FOR BACK TALKING!

WELCOME TO "MOTION TO KICK VORK OUT OF THE GUILD"!

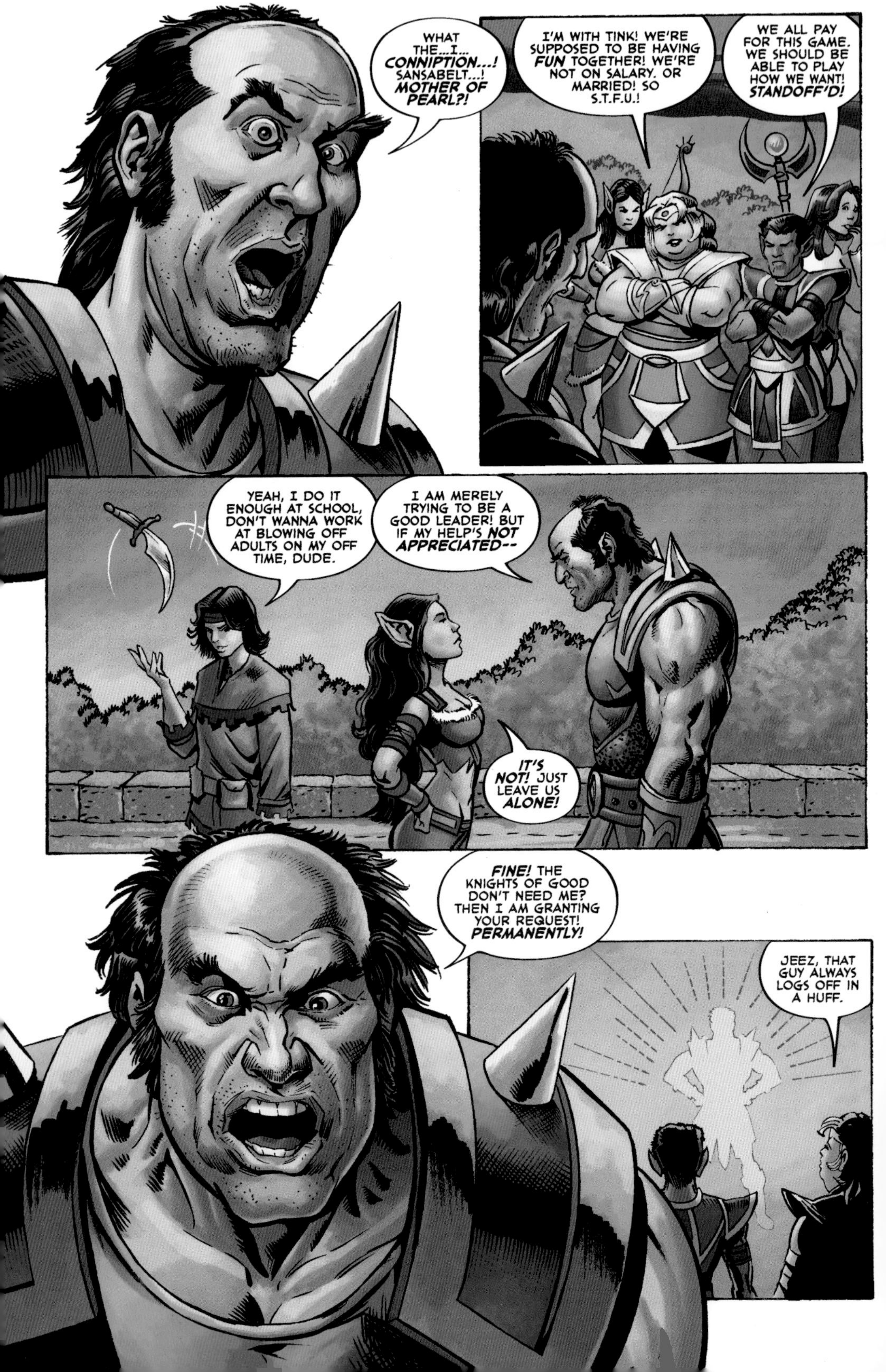
WHAT THE...I... CONNIPTION...! SANSABELT...! MOTHER OF PEARL?!
I'M WITH TINK! WE'RE SUPPOSED TO BE HAVING FUN TOGETHER! WE'RE NOT ON SALARY. OR MARRIED! SO S.T.F.U.!
WE ALL PAY FOR THIS GAME. WE SHOULD BE ABLE TO PLAY HOW WE WANT! STANDOFF'D!
YEAH, I DO IT ENOUGH AT SCHOOL, DON'T WANNA WORK AT BLOWING OFF ADULTS ON MY OFF TIME, DUDE.
I AM MERELY TRYING TO BE A GOOD LEADER! BUT IF MY HELP'S NOT APPRECIATED--
IT'S NOT! JUST LEAVE US ALONE!
FINE! THE KNIGHTS OF GOOD DON'T NEED ME? THEN I AM GRANTING YOUR REQUEST! PERMANENTLY!
JEEZ, THAT GUY ALWAYS LOGS OFF IN A HUFF.

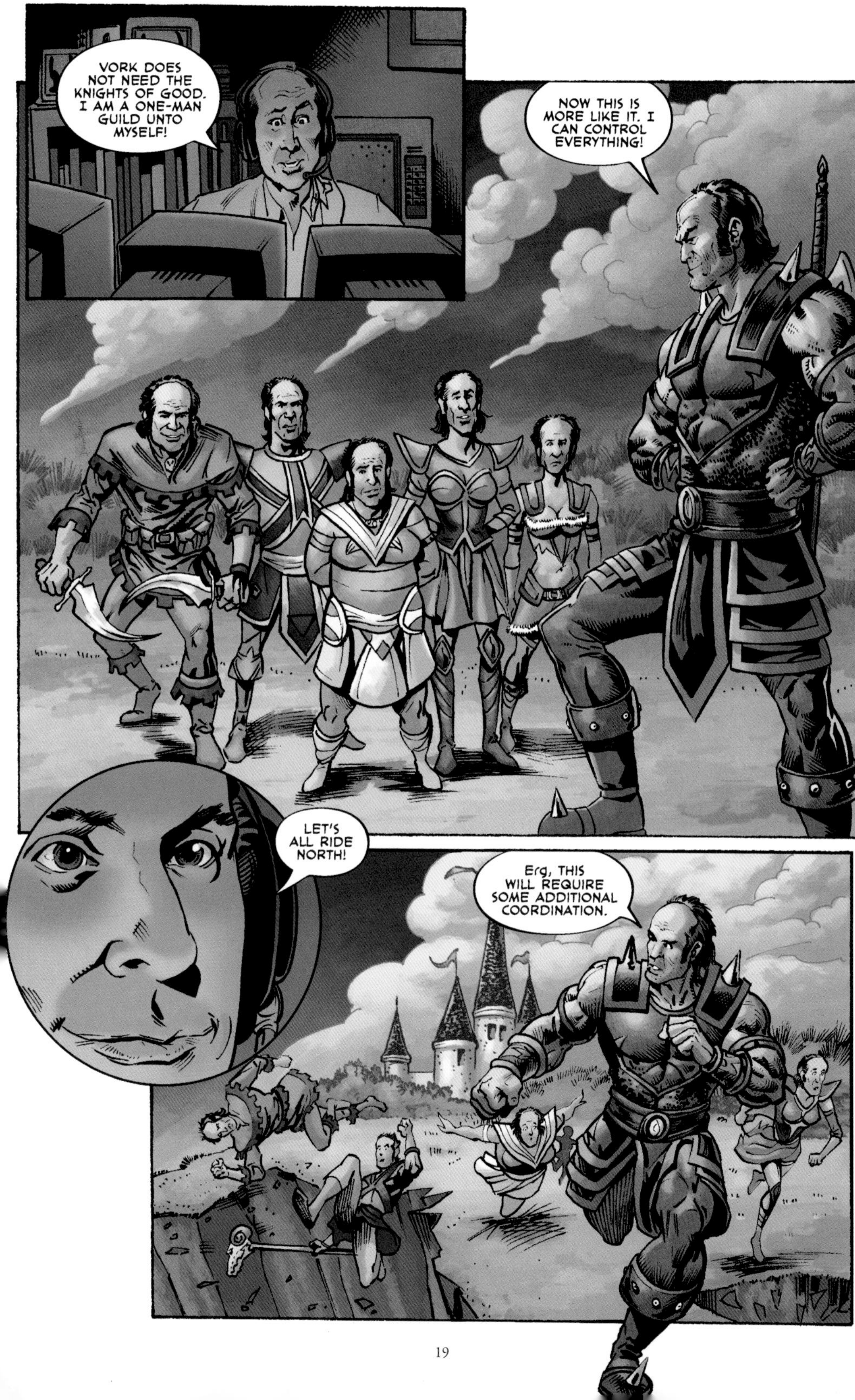
VORK DOES NOT NEED THE KNIGHTS OF GOOD. I AM A ONE-MAN GUILD UNTO MYSELF!
NOW THIS IS MORE LIKE IT. I CAN CONTROL EVERYTHING!
LET'S ALL RIDE NORTH!
Erg, THIS WILL REQUIRE SOME ADDITIONAL COORDINATION.

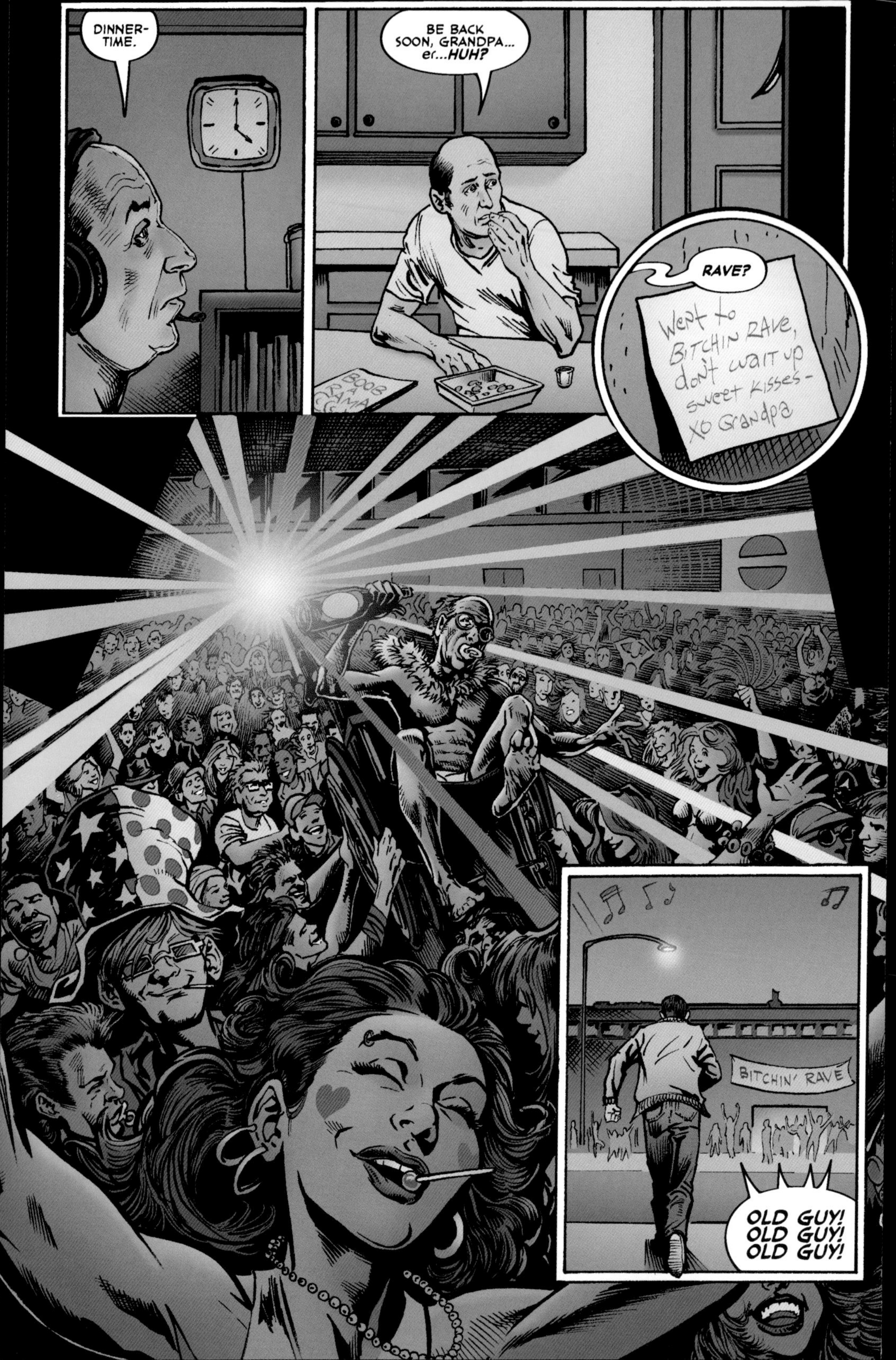
DINNER-TIME.
BE BACK SOON, GRANDPA... er...HUH?
RAVE?
Went to BITCHIN RAVE, don't wait up sweet kisses - XO Grandpa
BITCHIN' RAVE
OLD GUY! OLD GUY! OLD GUY!

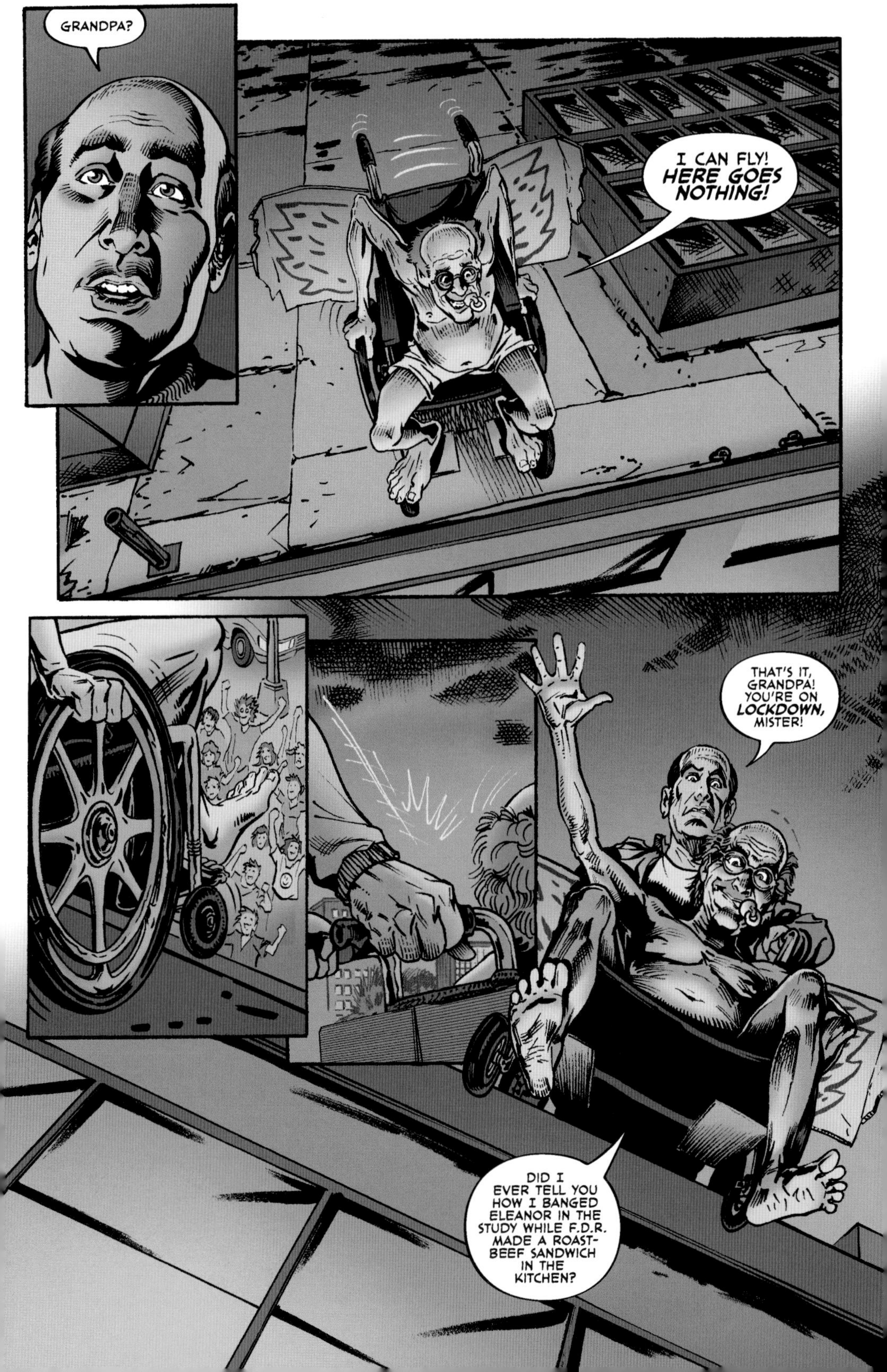
GRANDPA?
I CAN FLY! HERE GOES NOTHING!
THAT'S IT, GRANDPA! YOU'RE ON LOCKDOWN, MISTER!
DID I EVER TELL YOU HOW I BANGED ELEANOR IN THE STUDY WHILE F.D.R. MADE A ROAST-BEEF SANDWICH IN THE KITCHEN?

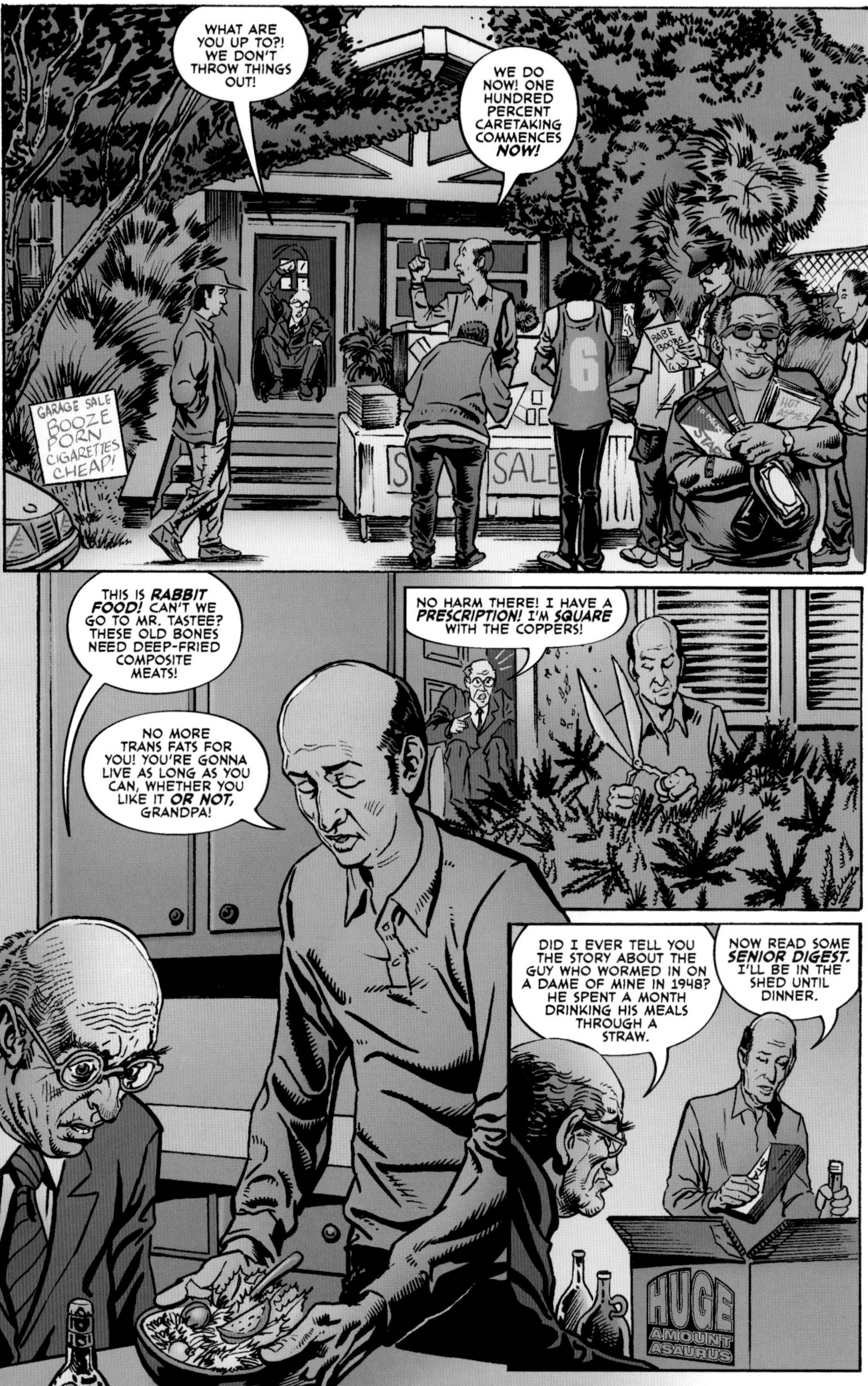
WHAT ARE YOU UP TO?! WE DON'T THROW THINGS OUT!
WE DO NOW! ONE HUNDRED PERCENT CARETAKING COMMENCES **NOW!**
GARAGE SALE BOOZE PORN CIGARETTES CHEAP!
SALE
BABE BOOBS
HOT ASSES
THIS IS **RABBIT FOOD!** CAN'T WE GO TO MR. TASTEE? THESE OLD BONES NEED DEEP-FRIED COMPOSITE MEATS!
NO MORE TRANS FATS FOR YOU! YOU'RE GONNA LIVE AS LONG AS YOU CAN, WHETHER YOU LIKE IT **OR NOT,** GRANDPA!
NO HARM THERE! I HAVE A ***PRESCRIPTION!*** I'M ***SQUARE*** WITH THE COPPERS!
DID I EVER TELL YOU THE STORY ABOUT THE GUY WHO WORMED IN ON A DAME OF MINE IN 1948? HE SPENT A MONTH DRINKING HIS MEALS THROUGH A STRAW.
NOW READ SOME ***SENIOR DIGEST.*** I'LL BE IN THE SHED UNTIL DINNER.
HUGE AMOUNT ASAURUS

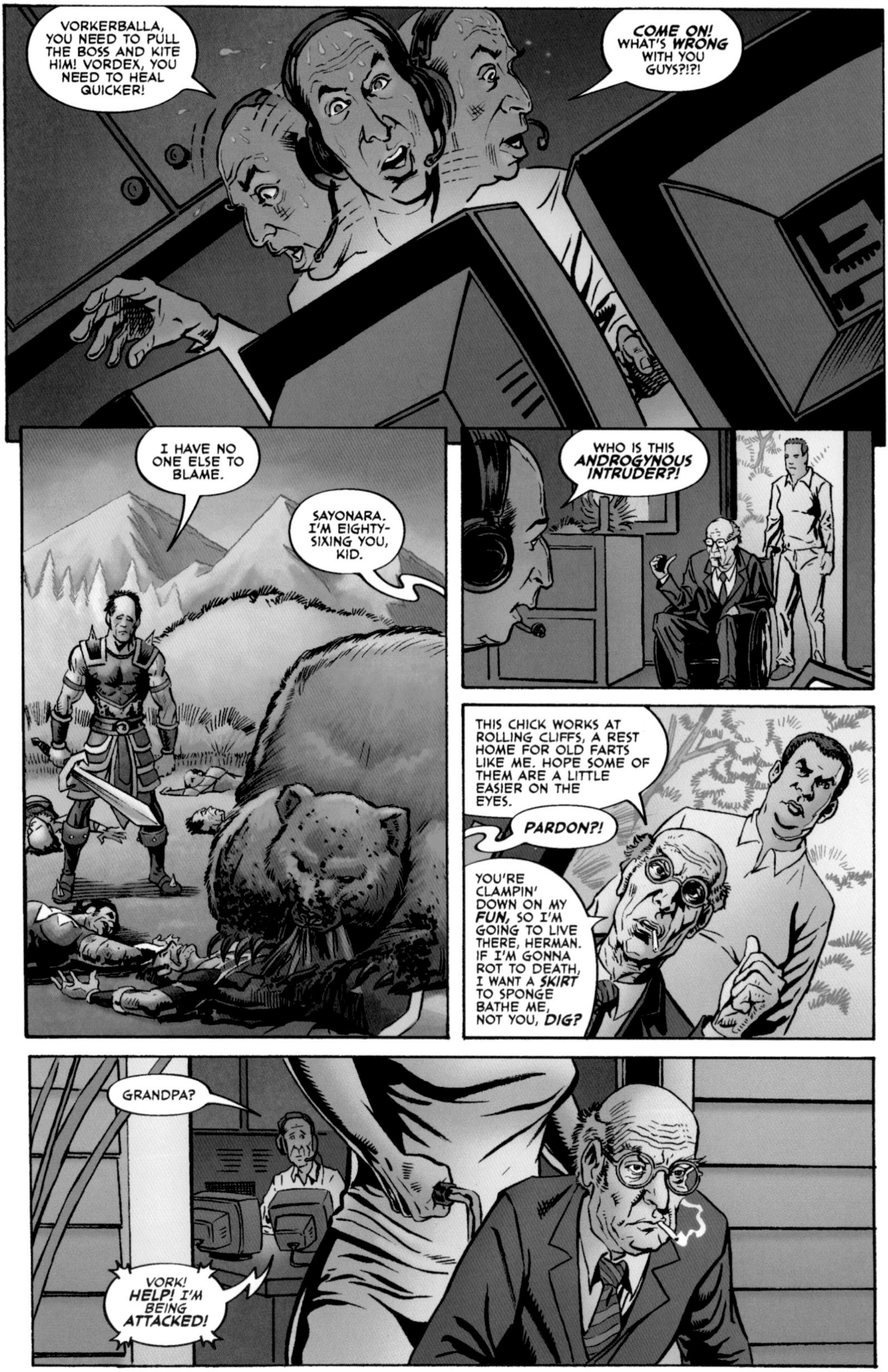
VORKERBALLA, YOU NEED TO PULL THE BOSS AND KITE HIM! VORDEX, YOU NEED TO HEAL QUICKER!
COME ON! WHAT'S WRONG WITH YOU GUYS?!?!
I HAVE NO ONE ELSE TO BLAME.
SAYONARA. I'M EIGHTY-SIXING YOU, KID.
WHO IS THIS ANDROGYNOUS INTRUDER?!
THIS CHICK WORKS AT ROLLING CLIFFS, A REST HOME FOR OLD FARTS LIKE ME. HOPE SOME OF THEM ARE A LITTLE EASIER ON THE EYES.
PARDON?!
YOU'RE CLAMPIN' DOWN ON MY FUN, SO I'M GOING TO LIVE THERE, HERMAN. IF I'M GONNA ROT TO DEATH, I WANT A SKIRT TO SPONGE BATHE ME, NOT YOU, DIG?
GRANDPA?
VORK! HELP! I'M BEING ATTACKED!

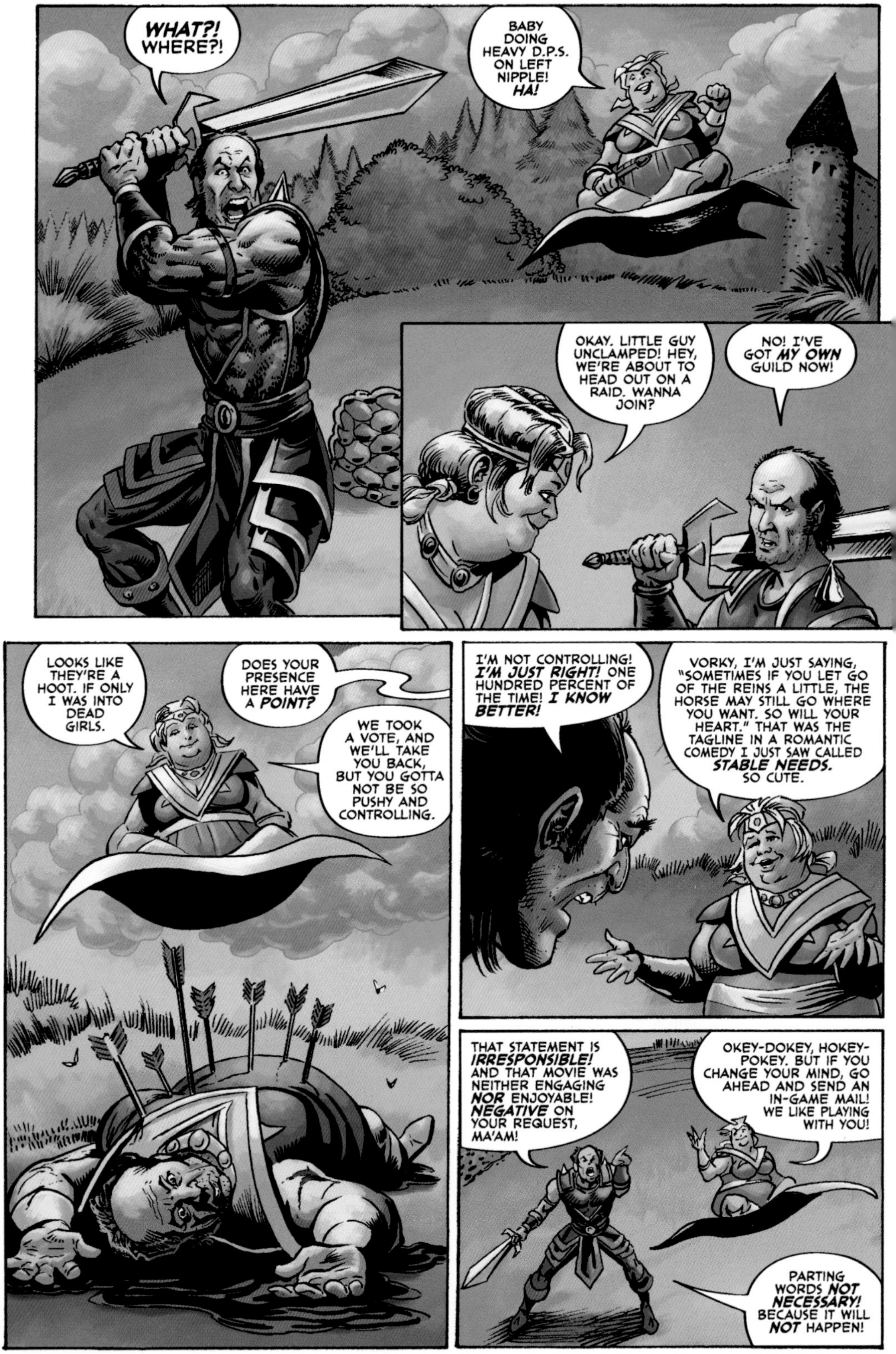
WHAT?! WHERE?!
BABY DOING HEAVY D.P.S. ON LEFT NIPPLE! HA!
OKAY. LITTLE GUY UNCLAMPED! HEY, WE'RE ABOUT TO HEAD OUT ON A RAID. WANNA JOIN?
NO! I'VE GOT MY OWN GUILD NOW!
LOOKS LIKE THEY'RE A HOOT. IF ONLY I WAS INTO DEAD GIRLS.
DOES YOUR PRESENCE HERE HAVE A POINT?
WE TOOK A VOTE, AND WE'LL TAKE YOU BACK, BUT YOU GOTTA NOT BE SO PUSHY AND CONTROLLING.
I'M NOT CONTROLLING! I'M JUST RIGHT! ONE HUNDRED PERCENT OF THE TIME! I KNOW BETTER!
VORKY, I'M JUST SAYING, "SOMETIMES IF YOU LET GO OF THE REINS A LITTLE, THE HORSE MAY STILL GO WHERE YOU WANT. SO WILL YOUR HEART." THAT WAS THE TAGLINE IN A ROMANTIC COMEDY I JUST SAW CALLED STABLE NEEDS. SO CUTE.
THAT STATEMENT IS IRRESPONSIBLE! AND THAT MOVIE WAS NEITHER ENGAGING NOR ENJOYABLE! NEGATIVE ON YOUR REQUEST, MA'AM!
OKEY-DOKEY, HOKEY-POKEY. BUT IF YOU CHANGE YOUR MIND, GO AHEAD AND SEND AN IN-GAME MAIL! WE LIKE PLAYING WITH YOU!
PARTING WORDS NOT NECESSARY! BECAUSE IT WILL NOT HAPPEN!

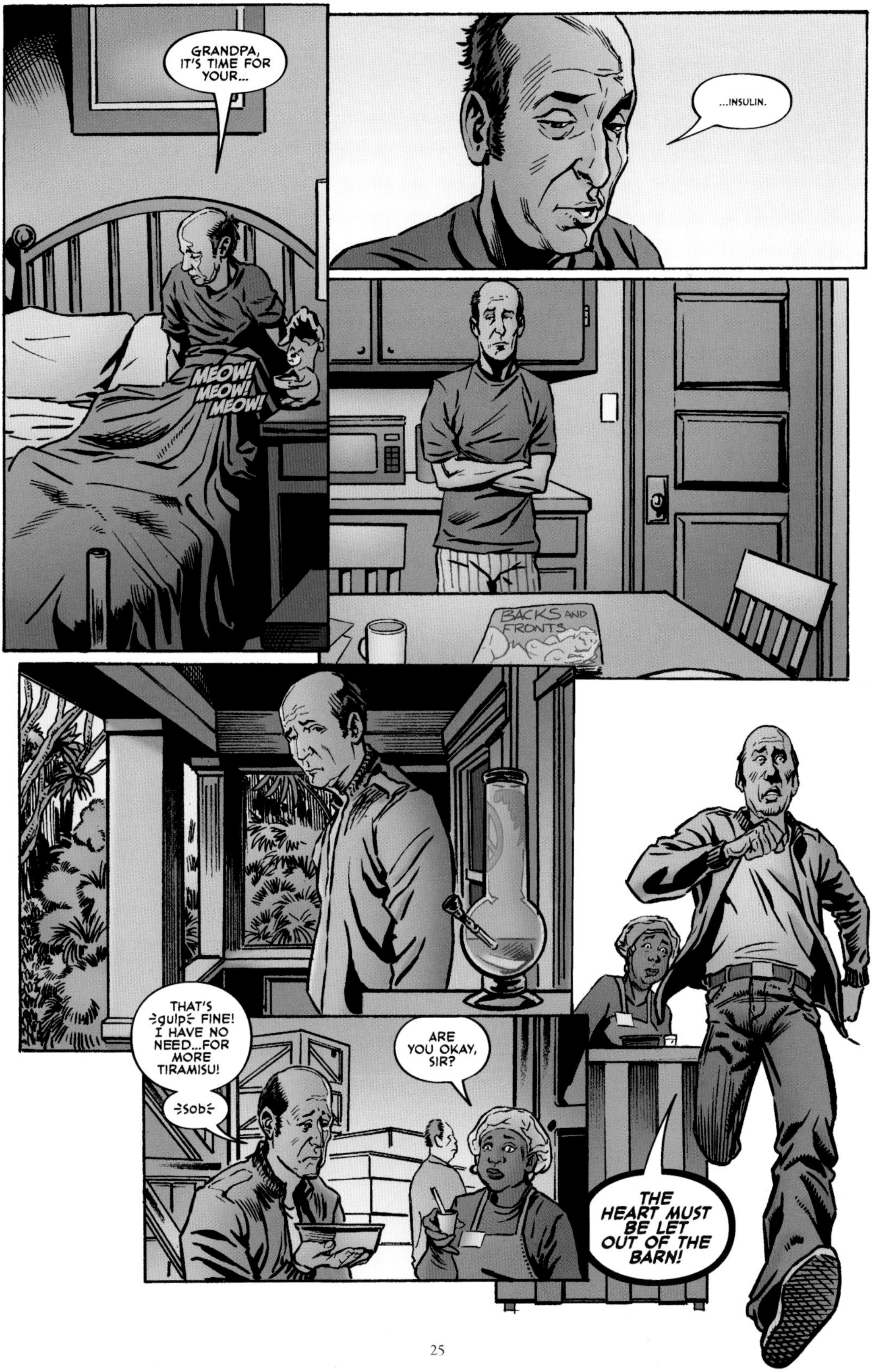
GRANDPA, IT'S TIME FOR YOUR...
MEOW! MEOW! MEOW!
...INSULIN.
BACKS AND FRONTS
THAT'S ≈gulp≈ FINE! I HAVE NO NEED...FOR MORE TIRAMISU!
≈Sob≈
ARE YOU OKAY, SIR?
THE HEART MUST BE LET OUT OF THE BARN!

WELCOME TO
ROLLING CLIFFS
SENIOR HOME

C-7.

THEY GOT NO BOOZE, SERVE NOTHING BUT DECAF, AND NOW EVEN *MY POOPS* ARE BORING. IF THERE'S A HELL, *THIS* IS THE ZIP CODE.

COME HOME!

NO WAY, *HOSE HEAD!*

IF THAT'S YOUR DECISION.

HEY! WHERE YOU GOIN'?! DO SOME MORE *BEGGING* SO WE CAN DITCH THIS JOINT!

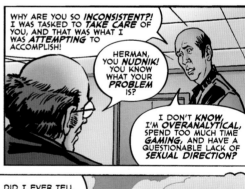

WHY ARE YOU SO *INCONSISTENT?!* I WAS TASKED TO *TAKE CARE* OF YOU, AND THAT WAS WHAT I WAS *ATTEMPTING* TO ACCOMPLISH!

HERMAN, YOU *NUDNIK!* YOU KNOW WHAT YOUR *PROBLEM* IS?

I DON'T *KNOW*, I'M *OVERANALYTICAL*, SPEND TOO MUCH TIME *GAMING*, AND HAVE A QUESTIONABLE LACK OF *SEXUAL DIRECTION?*

DID I EVER TELL YOU THE STORY OF HOW I STORMED THE BEACH AT NORMANDY?

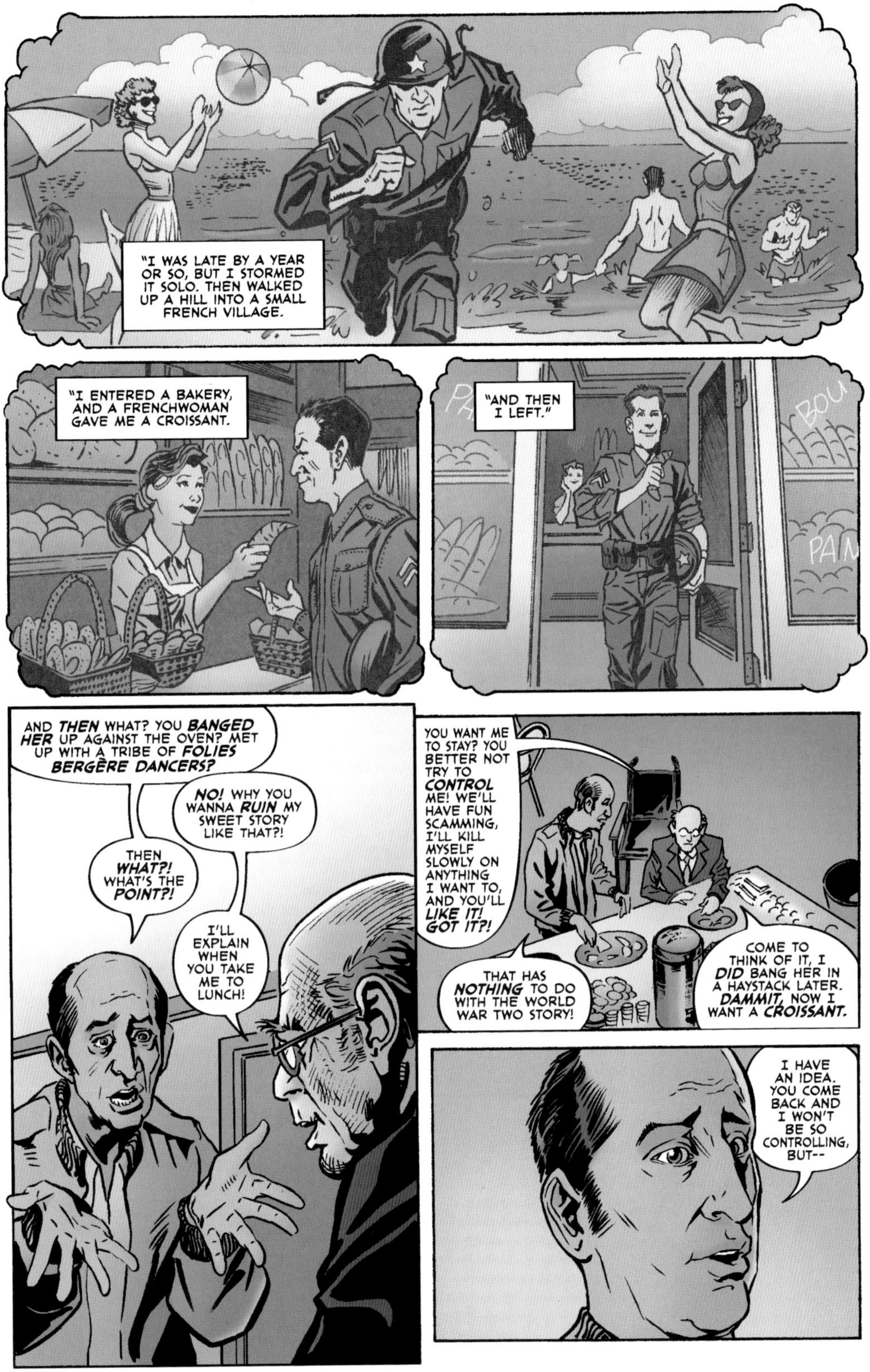
"I WAS LATE BY A YEAR OR SO, BUT I STORMED IT SOLO. THEN WALKED UP A HILL INTO A SMALL FRENCH VILLAGE.
"I ENTERED A BAKERY, AND A FRENCHWOMAN GAVE ME A CROISSANT.
"AND THEN I LEFT."
AND THEN WHAT? YOU BANGED HER UP AGAINST THE OVEN? MET UP WITH A TRIBE OF FOLIES BERGÈRE DANCERS?
NO! WHY YOU WANNA RUIN MY SWEET STORY LIKE THAT?!
THEN WHAT?! WHAT'S THE POINT?!
I'LL EXPLAIN WHEN YOU TAKE ME TO LUNCH!
YOU WANT ME TO STAY? YOU BETTER NOT TRY TO CONTROL ME! WE'LL HAVE FUN SCAMMING, I'LL KILL MYSELF SLOWLY ON ANYTHING I WANT TO, AND YOU'LL LIKE IT! GOT IT?!
THAT HAS NOTHING TO DO WITH THE WORLD WAR TWO STORY!
COME TO THINK OF IT, I DID BANG HER IN A HAYSTACK LATER. DAMMIT, NOW I WANT A CROISSANT.
I HAVE AN IDEA. YOU COME BACK AND I WON'T BE SO CONTROLLING, BUT--

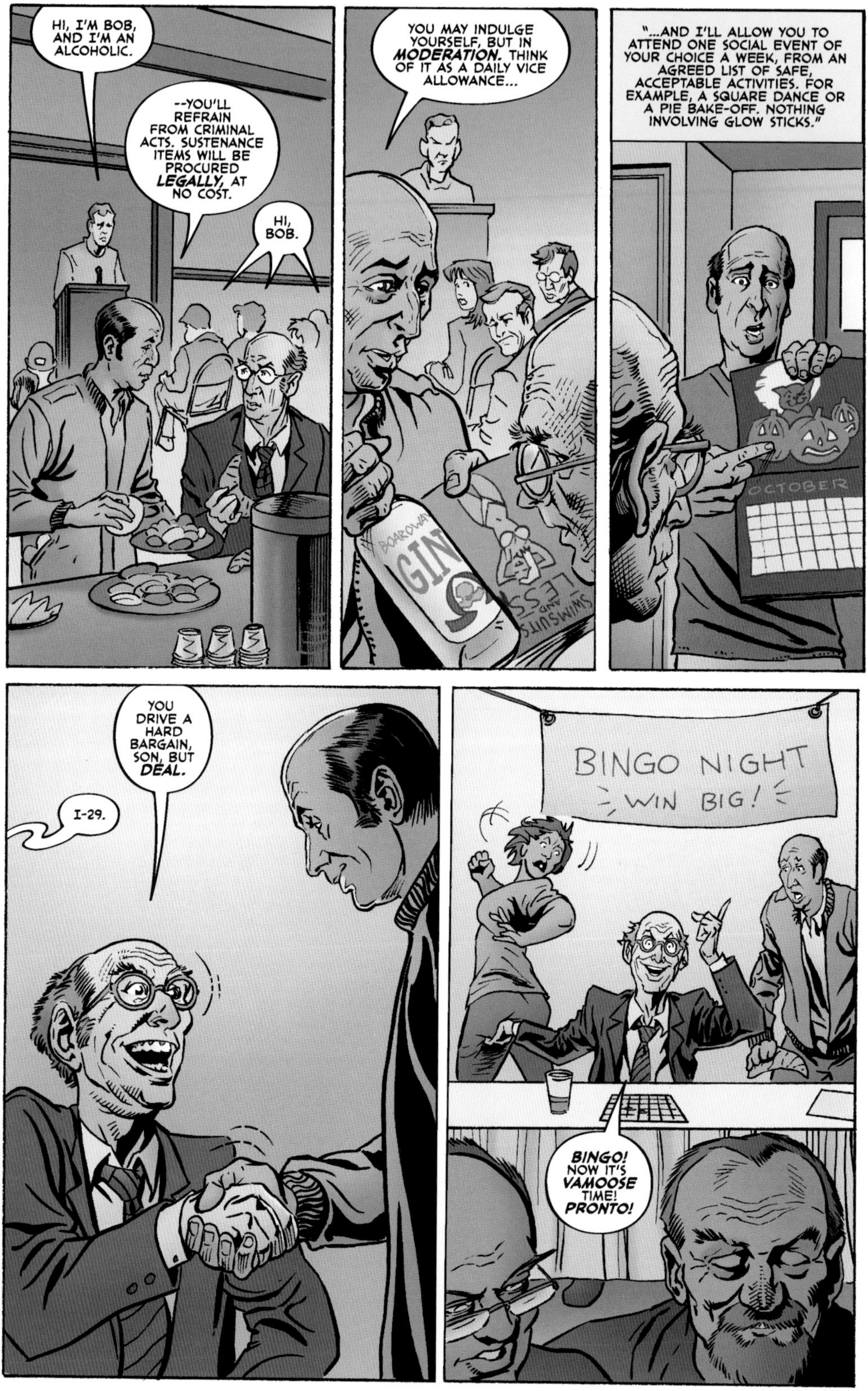
HI, I'M BOB, AND I'M AN ALCOHOLIC.
--YOU'LL REFRAIN FROM CRIMINAL ACTS. SUSTENANCE ITEMS WILL BE PROCURED *LEGALLY,* AT NO COST.
HI, BOB.
YOU MAY INDULGE YOURSELF, BUT IN *MODERATION.* THINK OF IT AS A DAILY VICE ALLOWANCE...
BOAROWAY GIN
SWIMSUITS AND LESS
"...AND I'LL ALLOW YOU TO ATTEND ONE SOCIAL EVENT OF YOUR CHOICE A WEEK, FROM AN AGREED LIST OF SAFE, ACCEPTABLE ACTIVITIES. FOR EXAMPLE, A SQUARE DANCE OR A PIE BAKE-OFF. NOTHING INVOLVING GLOW STICKS."
OCTOBER
YOU DRIVE A HARD BARGAIN, SON, BUT *DEAL.*
I-29.
BINGO NIGHT
WIN BIG!
BINGO! NOW IT'S *VAMOOSE* TIME! *PRONTO!*

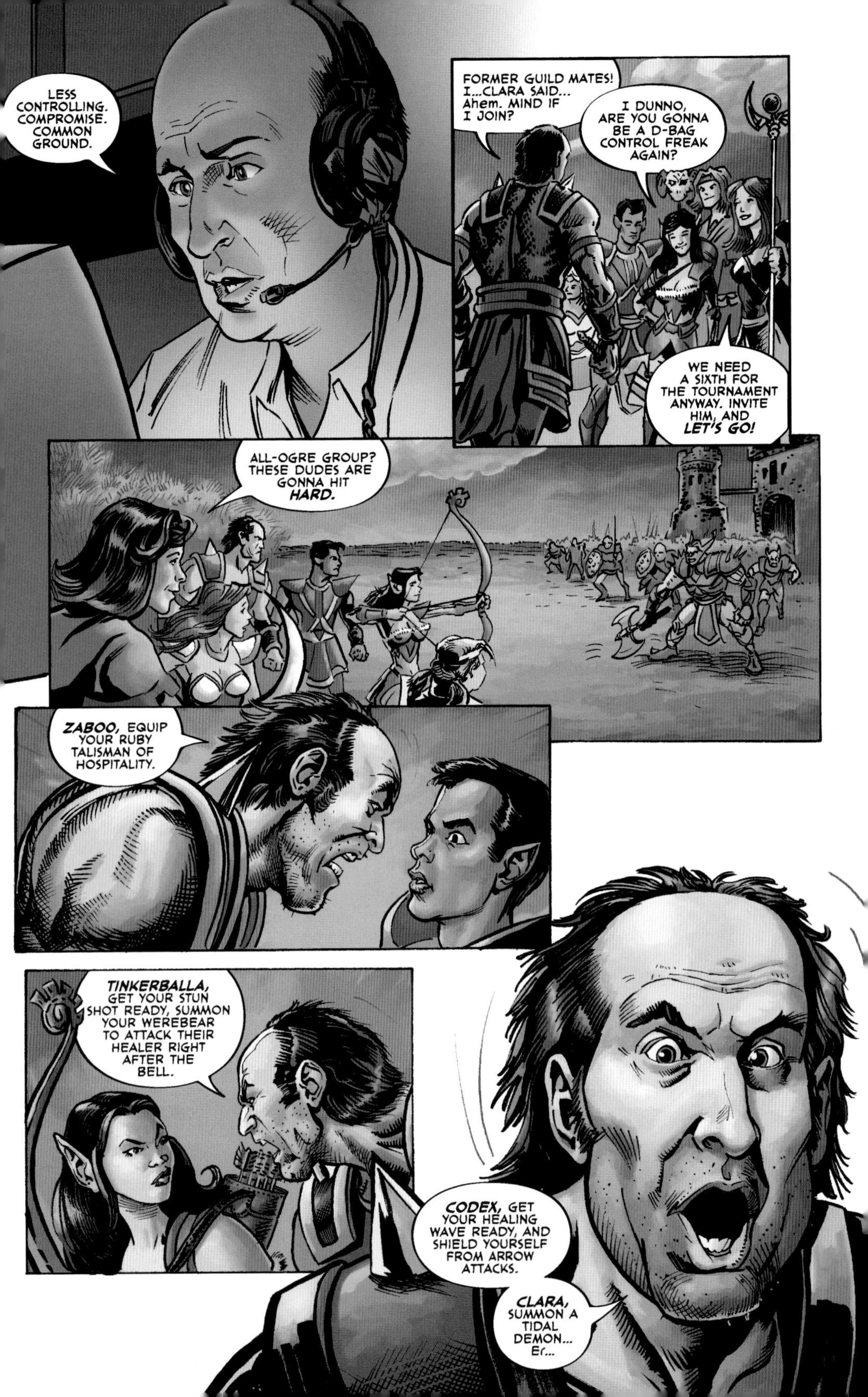
LESS CONTROLLING. COMPROMISE. COMMON GROUND.
FORMER GUILD MATES! I...CLARA SAID... Ahem. MIND IF I JOIN?
I DUNNO, ARE YOU GONNA BE A D-BAG CONTROL FREAK AGAIN?
WE NEED A SIXTH FOR THE TOURNAMENT ANYWAY. INVITE HIM, AND LET'S GO!
ALL-OGRE GROUP? THESE DUDES ARE GONNA HIT HARD.
ZABOO, EQUIP YOUR RUBY TALISMAN OF HOSPITALITY.
TINKERBALLA, GET YOUR STUN SHOT READY, SUMMON YOUR WEREBEAR TO ATTACK THEIR HEALER RIGHT AFTER THE BELL.
CODEX, GET YOUR HEALING WAVE READY, AND SHIELD YOURSELF FROM ARROW ATTACKS.
CLARA, SUMMON A TIDAL DEMON... Er...

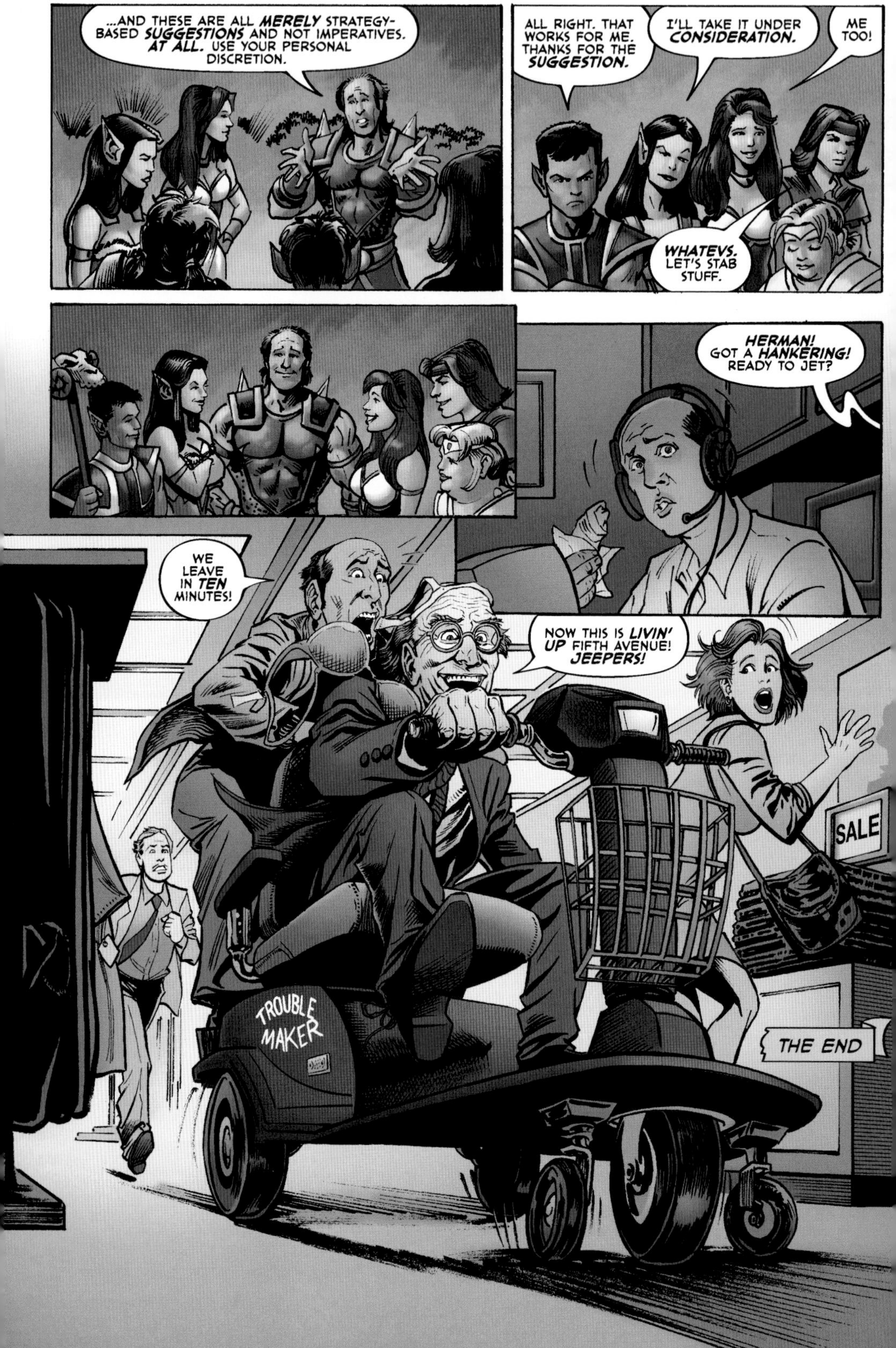
...AND THESE ARE ALL MERELY STRATEGY-BASED SUGGESTIONS AND NOT IMPERATIVES. AT ALL. USE YOUR PERSONAL DISCRETION.
ALL RIGHT. THAT WORKS FOR ME. THANKS FOR THE SUGGESTION.
I'LL TAKE IT UNDER CONSIDERATION.
ME TOO!
WHATEVS. LET'S STAB STUFF.
HERMAN! GOT A HANKERING! READY TO JET?
WE LEAVE IN TEN MINUTES!
NOW THIS IS LIVIN' UP FIFTH AVENUE! JEEPERS!
SALE
TROUBLE MAKER
THE END

Illustration by Ron Chan

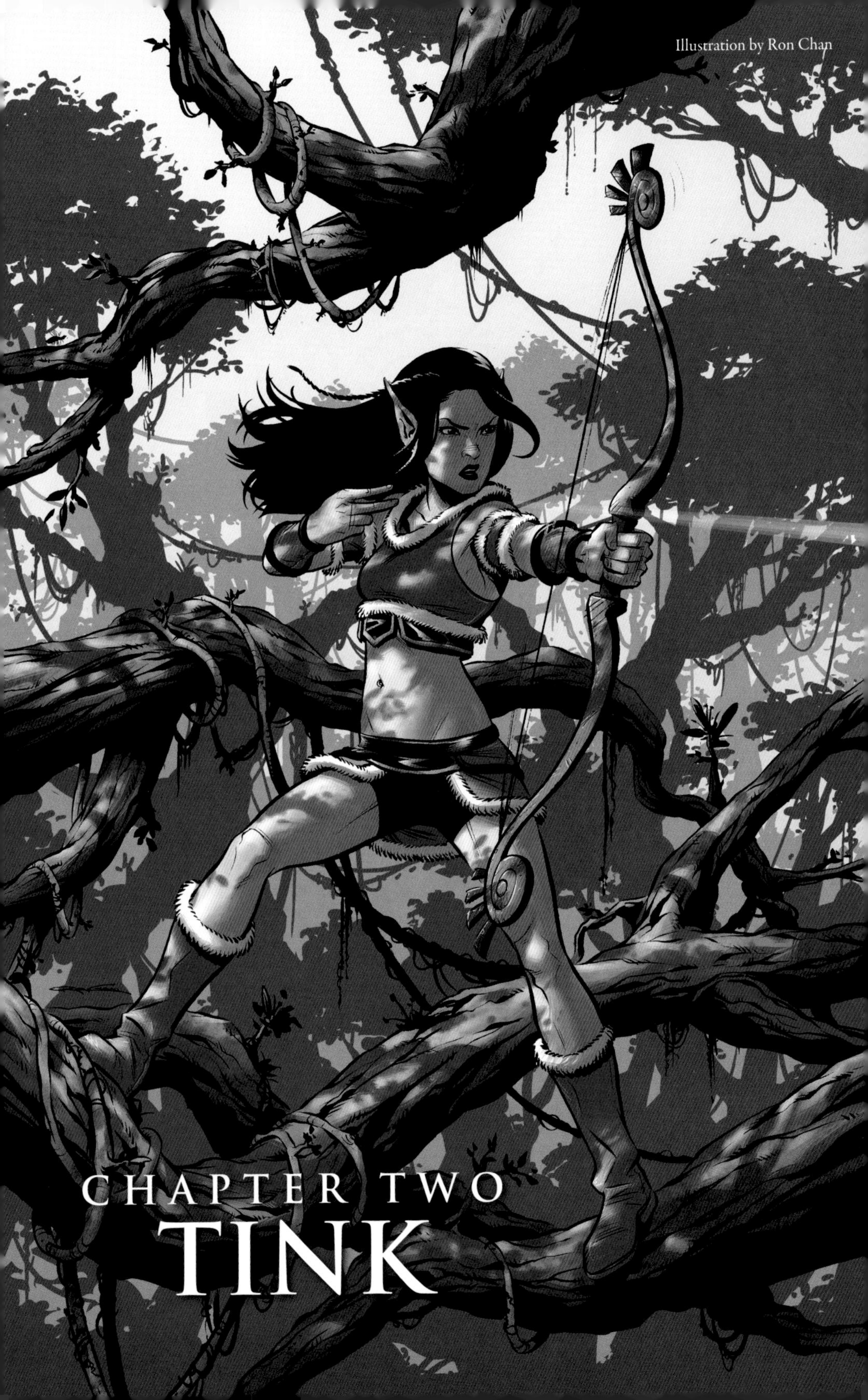

CHAPTER TWO
TINK

Illustration by Peter Bagge with Joanne Bagge

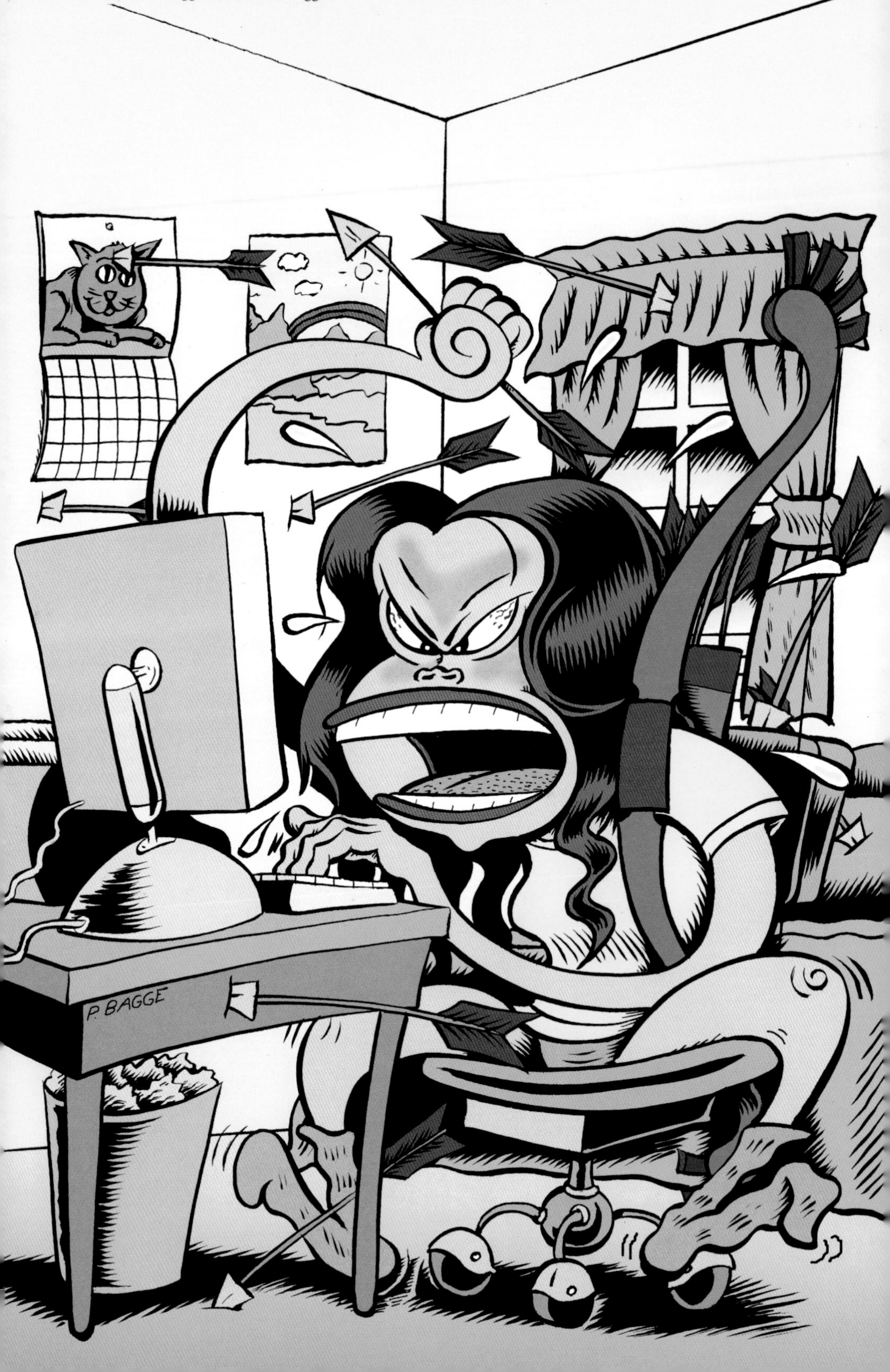
P. BAGGE

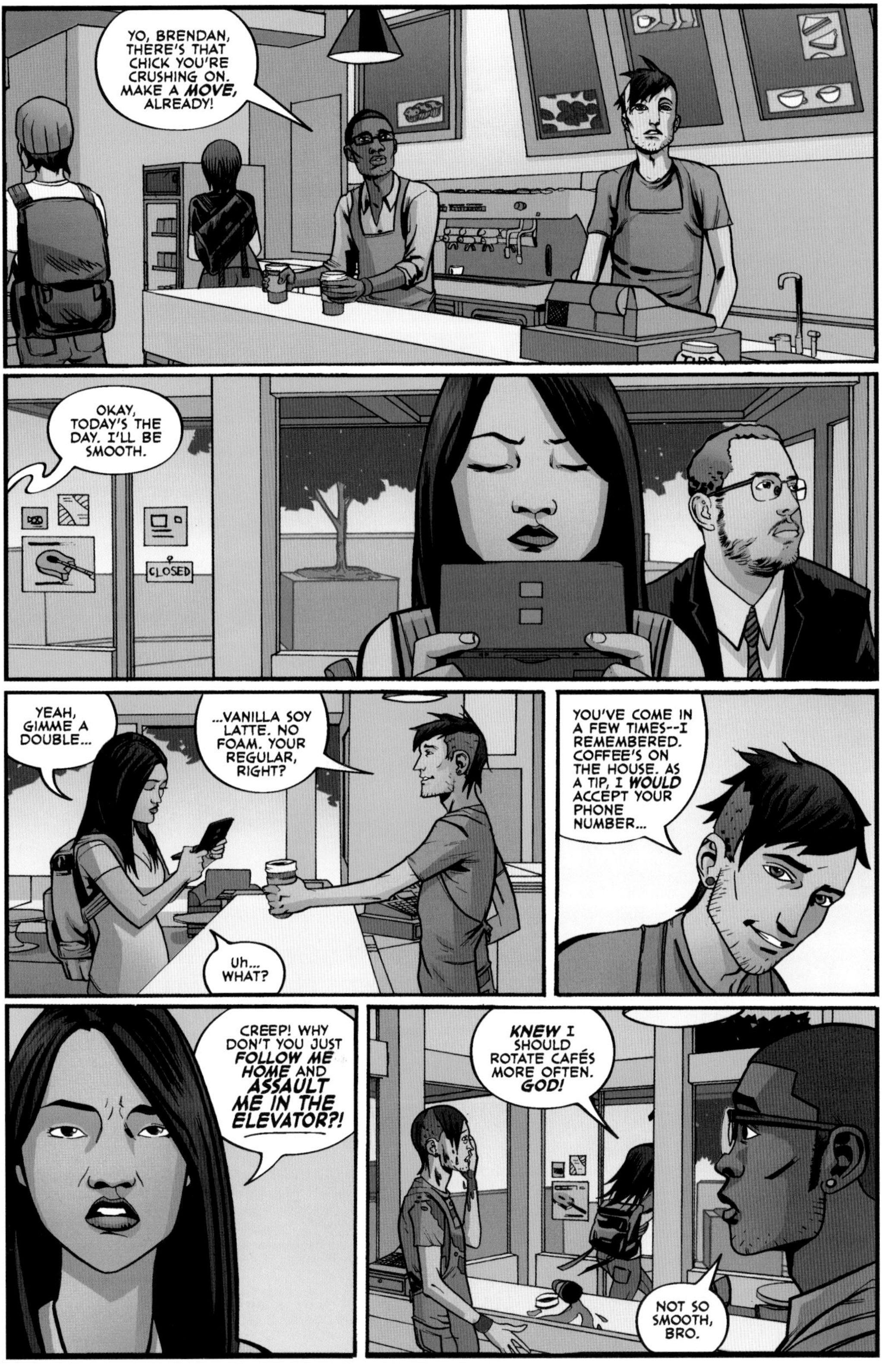
YO, BRENDAN, THERE'S THAT CHICK YOU'RE CRUSHING ON. MAKE A MOVE, ALREADY!
OKAY, TODAY'S THE DAY. I'LL BE SMOOTH.
CLOSED
YEAH, GIMME A DOUBLE...
...VANILLA SOY LATTE. NO FOAM. YOUR REGULAR, RIGHT?
Uh... WHAT?
YOU'VE COME IN A FEW TIMES--I REMEMBERED. COFFEE'S ON THE HOUSE. AS A TIP, I WOULD ACCEPT YOUR PHONE NUMBER...
CREEP! WHY DON'T YOU JUST FOLLOW ME HOME AND ASSAULT ME IN THE ELEVATOR?!
KNEW I SHOULD ROTATE CAFÉS MORE OFTEN. GOD!
NOT SO SMOOTH, BRO.

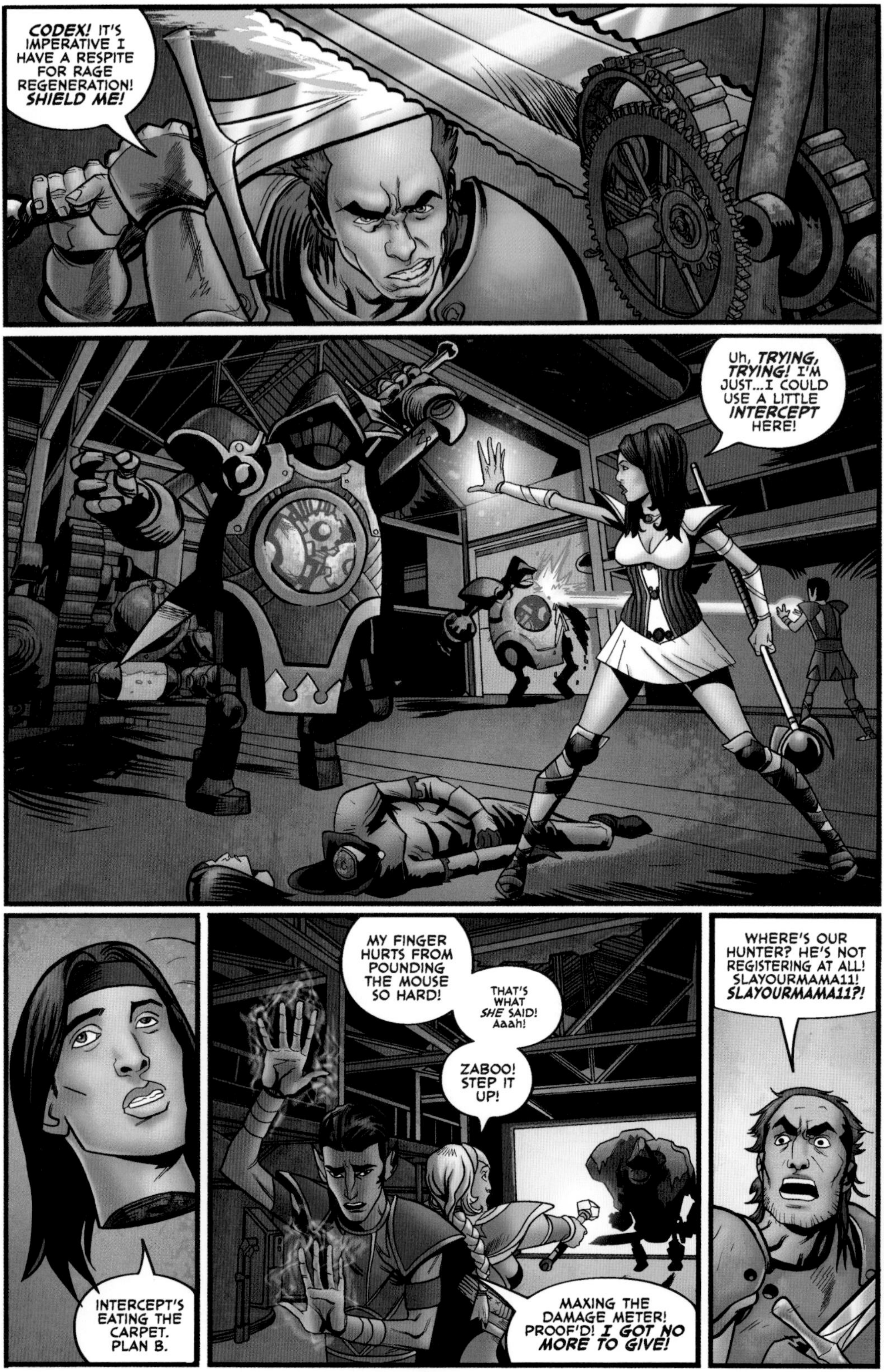
CODEX! IT'S IMPERATIVE I HAVE A RESPITE FOR RAGE REGENERATION! SHIELD ME!
Uh, TRYING, TRYING! I'M JUST...I COULD USE A LITTLE INTERCEPT HERE!
INTERCEPT'S EATING THE CARPET. PLAN B.
MY FINGER HURTS FROM POUNDING THE MOUSE SO HARD!
THAT'S WHAT SHE SAID! Aaah!
ZABOO! STEP IT UP!
MAXING THE DAMAGE METER! PROOF'D! I GOT NO MORE TO GIVE!
WHERE'S OUR HUNTER? HE'S NOT REGISTERING AT ALL! SLAYOURMAMA11! SLAYOURMAMA11?!

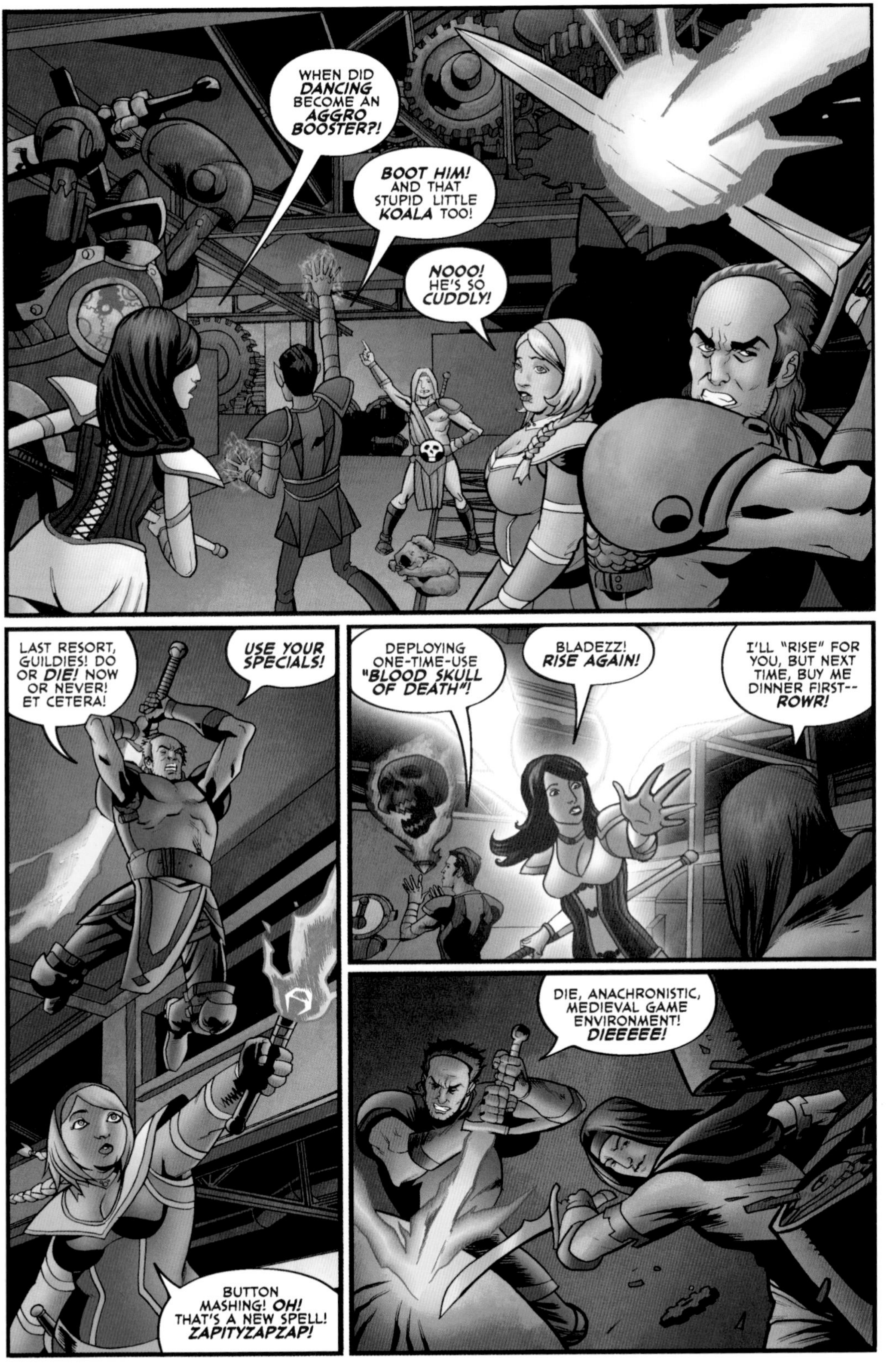
WHEN DID DANCING BECOME AN AGGRO BOOSTER?!
BOOT HIM! AND THAT STUPID LITTLE KOALA TOO!
NOOO! HE'S SO CUDDLY!
LAST RESORT, GUILDIES! DO OR DIE! NOW OR NEVER! ET CETERA!
USE YOUR SPECIALS!
BUTTON MASHING! OH! THAT'S A NEW SPELL! ZAPITYZAPZAP!
DEPLOYING ONE-TIME-USE "BLOOD SKULL OF DEATH"!
BLADEZZ! RISE AGAIN!
I'LL "RISE" FOR YOU, BUT NEXT TIME, BUY ME DINNER FIRST-- ROWR!
DIE, ANACHRONISTIC, MEDIEVAL GAME ENVIRONMENT! DIEEEEE!

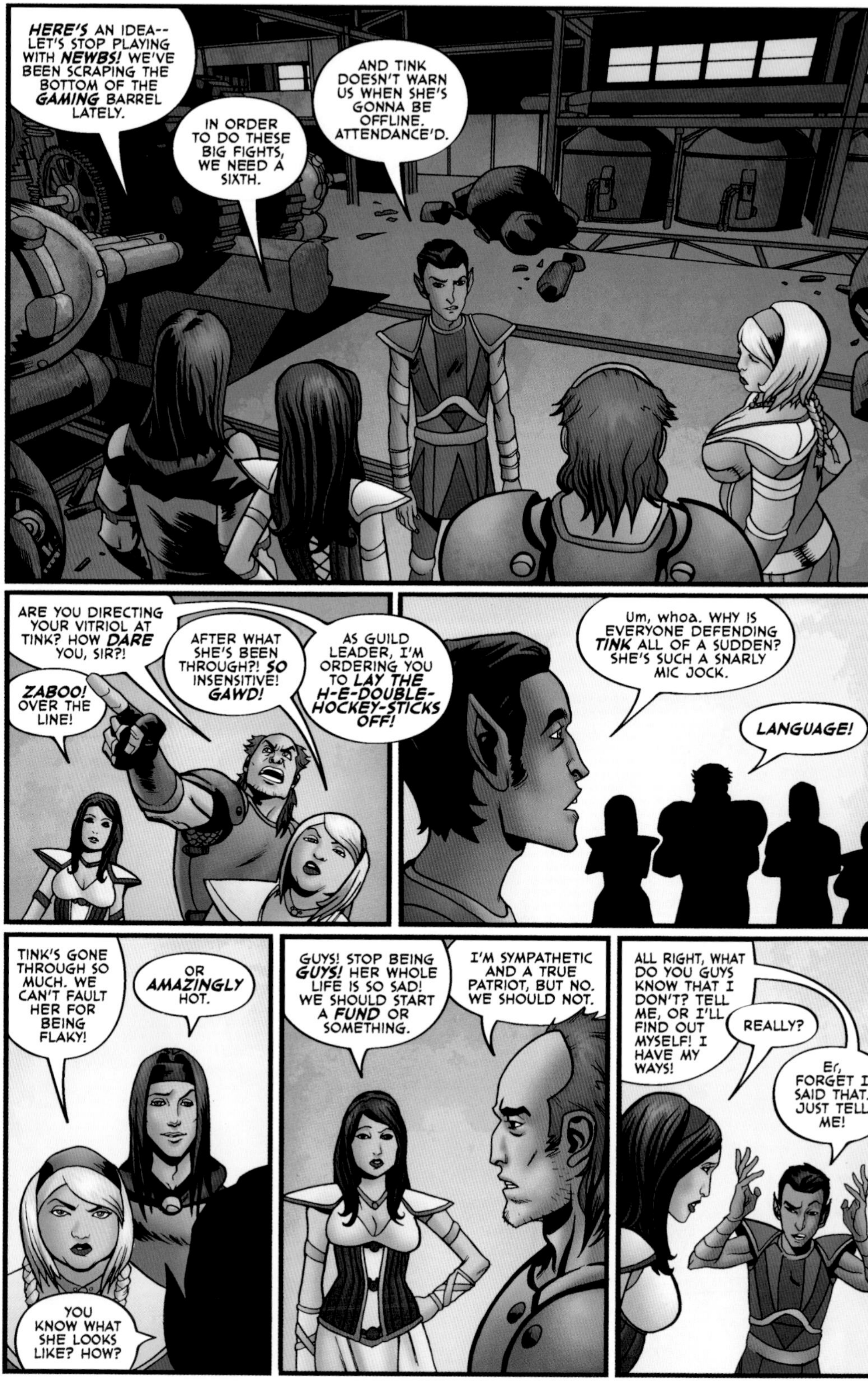
HERE'S AN IDEA-- LET'S STOP PLAYING WITH NEWBS! WE'VE BEEN SCRAPING THE BOTTOM OF THE GAMING BARREL LATELY.
IN ORDER TO DO THESE BIG FIGHTS, WE NEED A SIXTH.
AND TINK DOESN'T WARN US WHEN SHE'S GONNA BE OFFLINE. ATTENDANCE'D.
ARE YOU DIRECTING YOUR VITRIOL AT TINK? HOW DARE YOU, SIR?!
ZABOO! OVER THE LINE!
AFTER WHAT SHE'S BEEN THROUGH?! SO INSENSITIVE! GAWD!
AS GUILD LEADER, I'M ORDERING YOU TO LAY THE H-E-DOUBLE-HOCKEY-STICKS OFF!
Um, whoa. WHY IS EVERYONE DEFENDING TINK ALL OF A SUDDEN? SHE'S SUCH A SNARLY MIC JOCK.
LANGUAGE!
TINK'S GONE THROUGH SO MUCH. WE CAN'T FAULT HER FOR BEING FLAKY!
OR AMAZINGLY HOT.
YOU KNOW WHAT SHE LOOKS LIKE? HOW?
GUYS! STOP BEING GUYS! HER WHOLE LIFE IS SO SAD! WE SHOULD START A FUND OR SOMETHING.
I'M SYMPATHETIC AND A TRUE PATRIOT, BUT NO. WE SHOULD NOT.
ALL RIGHT, WHAT DO YOU GUYS KNOW THAT I DON'T? TELL ME, OR I'LL FIND OUT MYSELF! I HAVE MY WAYS!
REALLY?
Er, FORGET I SAID THAT. JUST TELL ME!

WHY? I GOT DIBS.

IT WAS KINDA PRIVATE...

I MADE NO PROMISES, BUT NO ONE MAKES ME TALK.

Uh...WELL, SHE *SWORE* ME TO SECRECY...

...BUT SOMEONE WILL SPILL SOON ENOUGH, SO WHATEVER!

FIRST'D.

"LAST WEEKEND TINK AND I WERE UP REALLY LATE FARMING CENTAUR, HAVING OUR FIRST GIRL-BONDING TIME TOGETHER ALONE. IT WAS GREAT!"

...AND WHEN I SEE THESE CENTAUR NIPPLES I GET SOOO HORNY! GOT A THING FOR MAN CHESTS. I SHARK MY HUBBY GEORGE WHEN HE WEARS SNAP SHIRTS. BEING MARRIED CAN BE BORING EXCEPT FOR THINGS LIKE THAT. YOU DO THAT TO YOUR BOYFRIEND?

Ugh...YOU ARE TALKING *SO MUCH! NO BOYFRIEND! THANKS!*

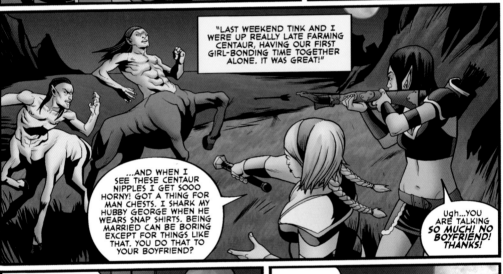

Oh! SO YOU'RE MARRIED?! WHAT'S HIS NAME? IS THE SPARK STILL THERE? NO WONDER YOU'RE SO BITTER! *TESTIFY!*

NOT MARRIED!

Aw, IT'S OKAY IF YOU'RE SINGLE. IS IT A "LOOKS" THING? HAVE YOU TRIED SKYPE SEX? YOU DON'T HAVE TO USE THE VIDEO CAMERA WITH THE OTHER PERSON. ALTHOUGH SOMETIMES IT TURNS ON ACCIDENTALLY. LEARNED THAT.

I AM *NOT* HIDEOUS! I'M PRETTY HOT, THANKS!

THEN WHY NO GUY?! THAT'S LIKE...SO *WEIRDVILLE.* Oh! ARE YOU A TRANS-LESB...

UGH! HERE'S A REASON! AND THEN WE HAVE TO PLAY. SILENTLY! GOT IT?!

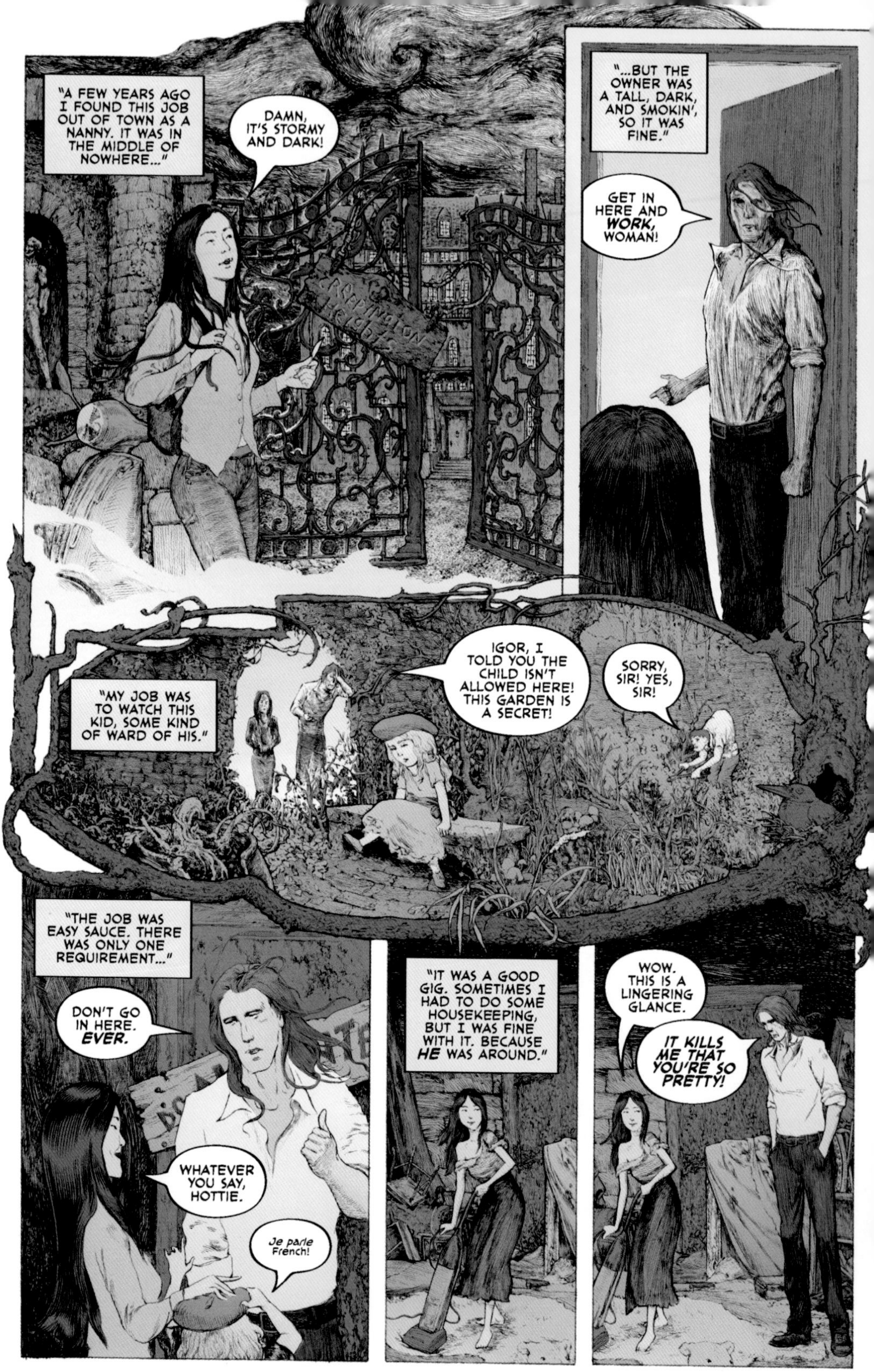
"A FEW YEARS AGO I FOUND THIS JOB OUT OF TOWN AS A NANNY. IT WAS IN THE MIDDLE OF NOWHERE..."
DAMN, IT'S STORMY AND DARK!
"...BUT THE OWNER WAS A TALL, DARK, AND SMOKIN', SO IT WAS FINE."
GET IN HERE AND WORK, WOMAN!
"MY JOB WAS TO WATCH THIS KID, SOME KIND OF WARD OF HIS."
IGOR, I TOLD YOU THE CHILD ISN'T ALLOWED HERE! THIS GARDEN IS A SECRET!
SORRY, SIR! YES, SIR!
"THE JOB WAS EASY SAUCE. THERE WAS ONLY ONE REQUIREMENT..."
DON'T GO IN HERE. EVER.
WHATEVER YOU SAY, HOTTIE.
Je parle French!
"IT WAS A GOOD GIG. SOMETIMES I HAD TO DO SOME HOUSEKEEPING, BUT I WAS FINE WITH IT. BECAUSE HE WAS AROUND."
WOW. THIS IS A LINGERING GLANCE.
IT KILLS ME THAT YOU'RE SO PRETTY!

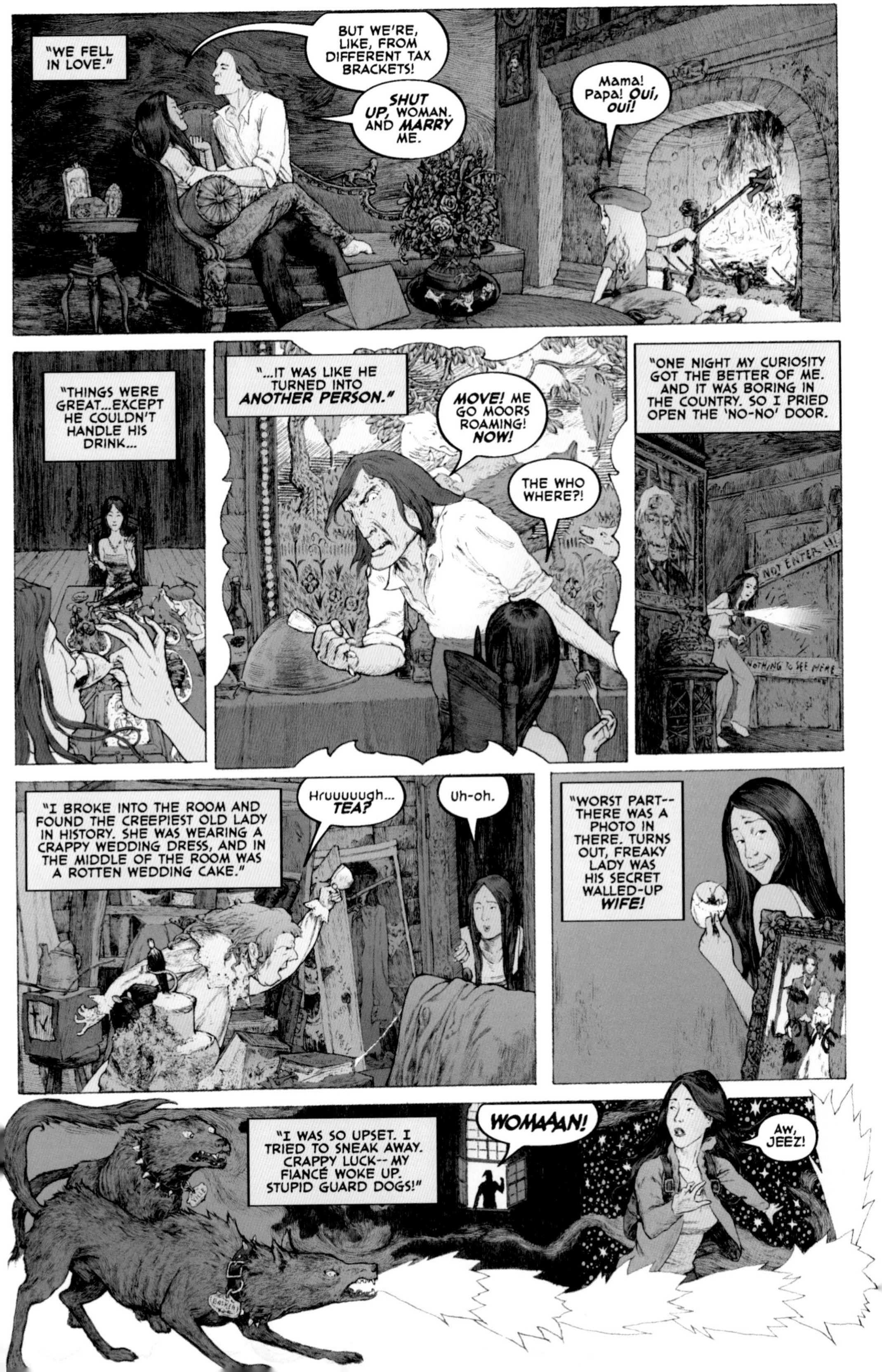

"WE FELL IN LOVE."
BUT WE'RE, LIKE, FROM DIFFERENT TAX BRACKETS!
SHUT UP, WOMAN. AND MARRY ME.
Mama! Papa! Oui, oui!
"THINGS WERE GREAT...EXCEPT HE COULDN'T HANDLE HIS DRINK...
"...IT WAS LIKE HE TURNED INTO ANOTHER PERSON."
MOVE! ME GO MOORS ROAMING! NOW!
THE WHO WHERE?!
"ONE NIGHT MY CURIOSITY GOT THE BETTER OF ME. AND IT WAS BORING IN THE COUNTRY. SO I PRIED OPEN THE 'NO-NO' DOOR.
NOT ENTER!!
NOTHING TO SEE HERE
"I BROKE INTO THE ROOM AND FOUND THE CREEPIEST OLD LADY IN HISTORY. SHE WAS WEARING A CRAPPY WEDDING DRESS, AND IN THE MIDDLE OF THE ROOM WAS A ROTTEN WEDDING CAKE."
Hruuuuugh... TEA?
Uh-oh.
"WORST PART-- THERE WAS A PHOTO IN THERE. TURNS OUT, FREAKY LADY WAS HIS SECRET WALLED-UP WIFE!
"I WAS SO UPSET. I TRIED TO SNEAK AWAY. CRAPPY LUCK-- MY FIANCÉ WOKE UP. STUPID GUARD DOGS!"
WOMAAAN!
AW, JEEZ!

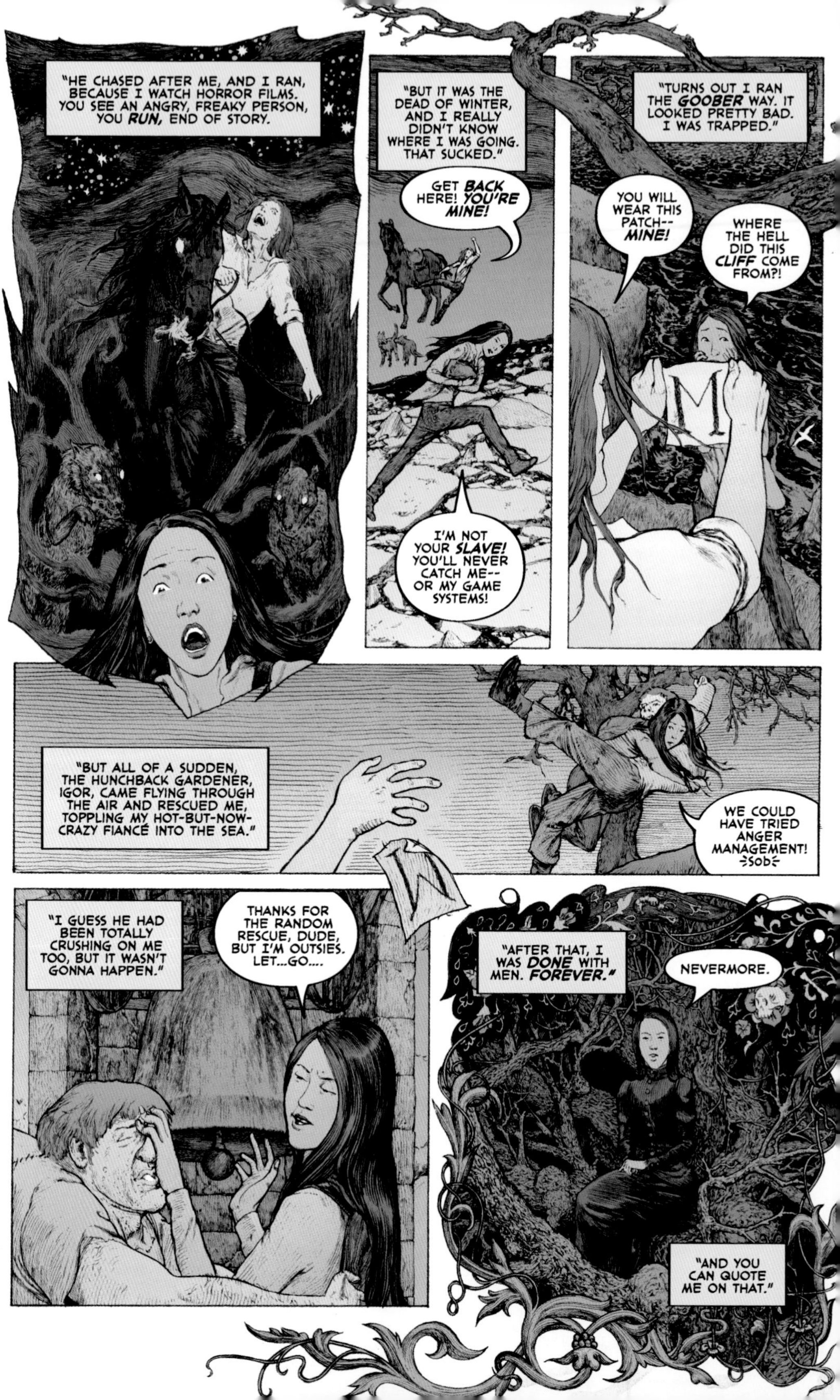
"HE CHASED AFTER ME, AND I RAN, BECAUSE I WATCH HORROR FILMS. YOU SEE AN ANGRY, FREAKY PERSON, YOU RUN, END OF STORY.
"BUT IT WAS THE DEAD OF WINTER, AND I REALLY DIDN'T KNOW WHERE I WAS GOING. THAT SUCKED."
GET BACK HERE! YOU'RE MINE!
I'M NOT YOUR SLAVE! YOU'LL NEVER CATCH ME-- OR MY GAME SYSTEMS!
"TURNS OUT I RAN THE GOOBER WAY. IT LOOKED PRETTY BAD. I WAS TRAPPED."
YOU WILL WEAR THIS PATCH-- MINE!
WHERE THE HELL DID THIS CLIFF COME FROM?!
M
"BUT ALL OF A SUDDEN, THE HUNCHBACK GARDENER, IGOR, CAME FLYING THROUGH THE AIR AND RESCUED ME, TOPPLING MY HOT-BUT-NOW-CRAZY FIANCÉ INTO THE SEA."
WE COULD HAVE TRIED ANGER MANAGEMENT! SOB
"I GUESS HE HAD BEEN TOTALLY CRUSHING ON ME TOO, BUT IT WASN'T GONNA HAPPEN."
THANKS FOR THE RANDOM RESCUE, DUDE, BUT I'M OUTSIES. LET...GO....
"AFTER THAT, I WAS DONE WITH MEN. FOREVER."
NEVERMORE.
"AND YOU CAN QUOTE ME ON THAT."

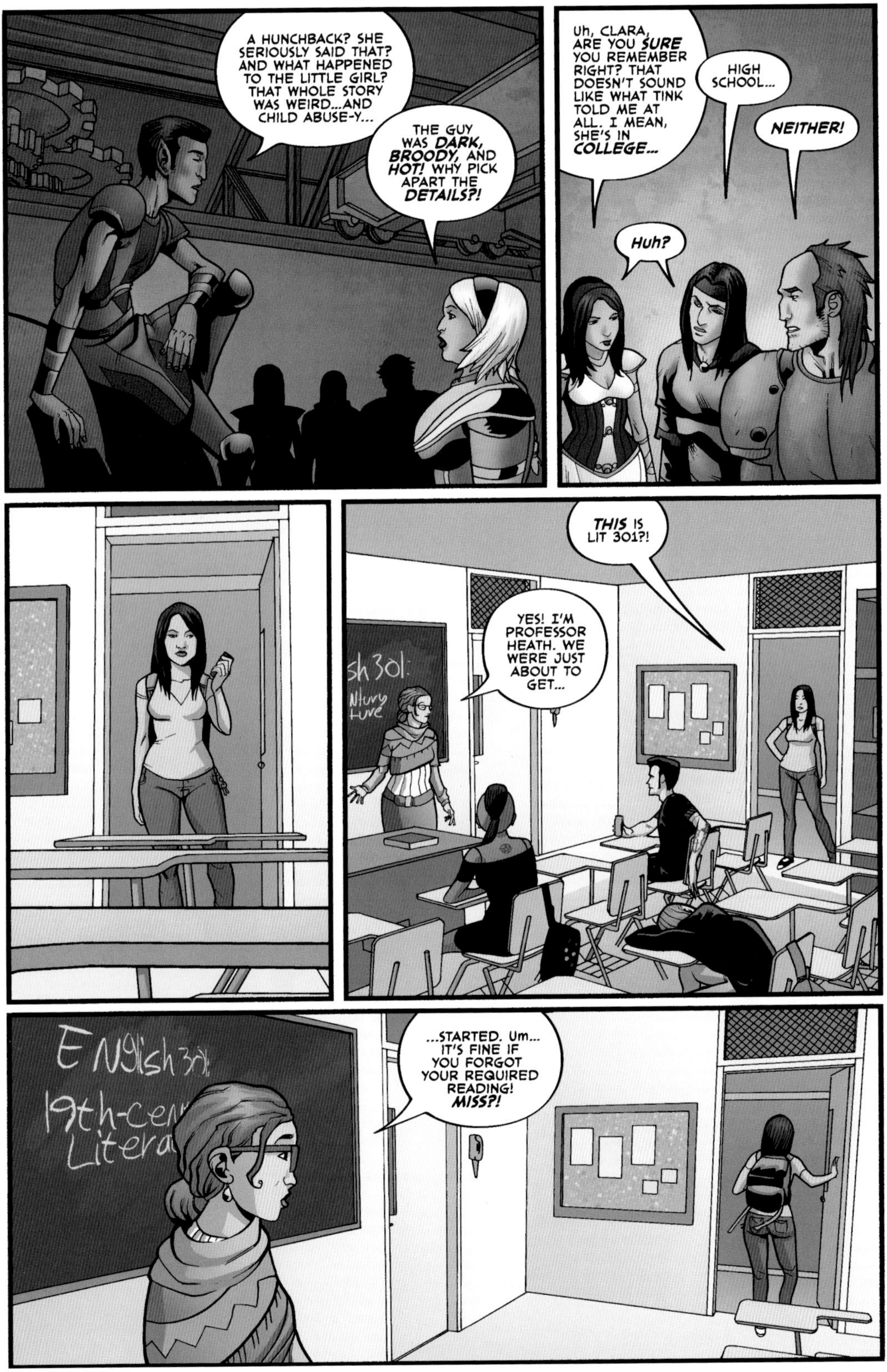

A HUNCHBACK? SHE SERIOUSLY SAID THAT? AND WHAT HAPPENED TO THE LITTLE GIRL? THAT WHOLE STORY WAS WEIRD...AND CHILD ABUSE-Y...
THE GUY WAS DARK, BROODY, AND HOT! WHY PICK APART THE DETAILS?!
Uh, CLARA, ARE YOU SURE YOU REMEMBER RIGHT? THAT DOESN'T SOUND LIKE WHAT TINK TOLD ME AT ALL. I MEAN, SHE'S IN COLLEGE...
HIGH SCHOOL...
NEITHER!
Huh?
THIS IS LIT 301?!
YES! I'M PROFESSOR HEATH. WE WERE JUST ABOUT TO GET...
...STARTED. Um... IT'S FINE IF YOU FORGOT YOUR REQUIRED READING! MISS?!
ENglish 301:
19th-cen
Litera

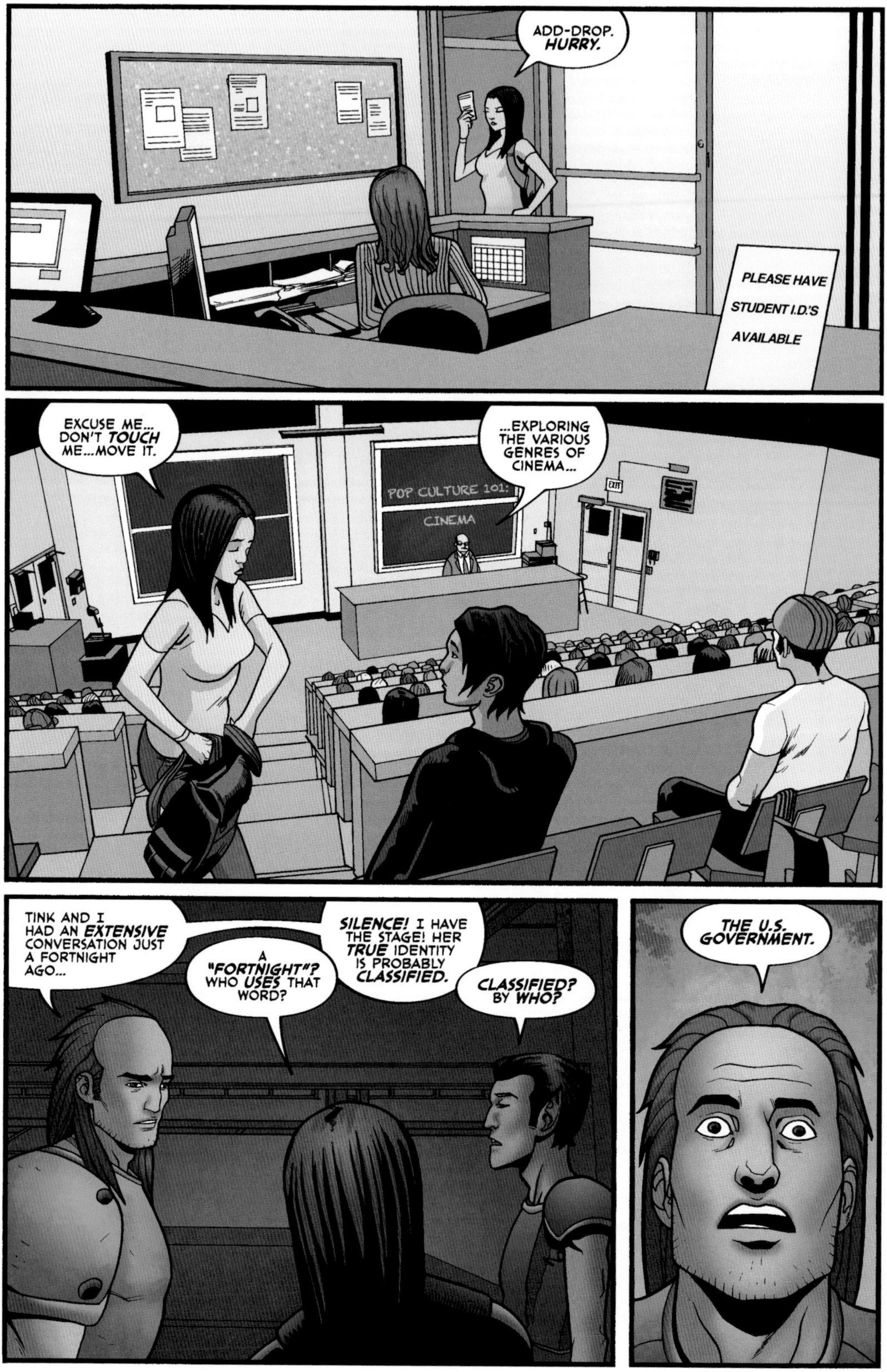
ADD-DROP. HURRY.
PLEASE HAVE STUDENT I.D.'S AVAILABLE
EXCUSE ME... DON'T TOUCH ME...MOVE IT.
...EXPLORING THE VARIOUS GENRES OF CINEMA...
POP CULTURE 101: CINEMA
EXIT
TINK AND I HAD AN EXTENSIVE CONVERSATION JUST A FORTNIGHT AGO...
A "FORTNIGHT"? WHO USES THAT WORD?
SILENCE! I HAVE THE STAGE! HER TRUE IDENTITY IS PROBABLY CLASSIFIED.
CLASSIFIED? BY WHO?
THE U.S. GOVERNMENT.

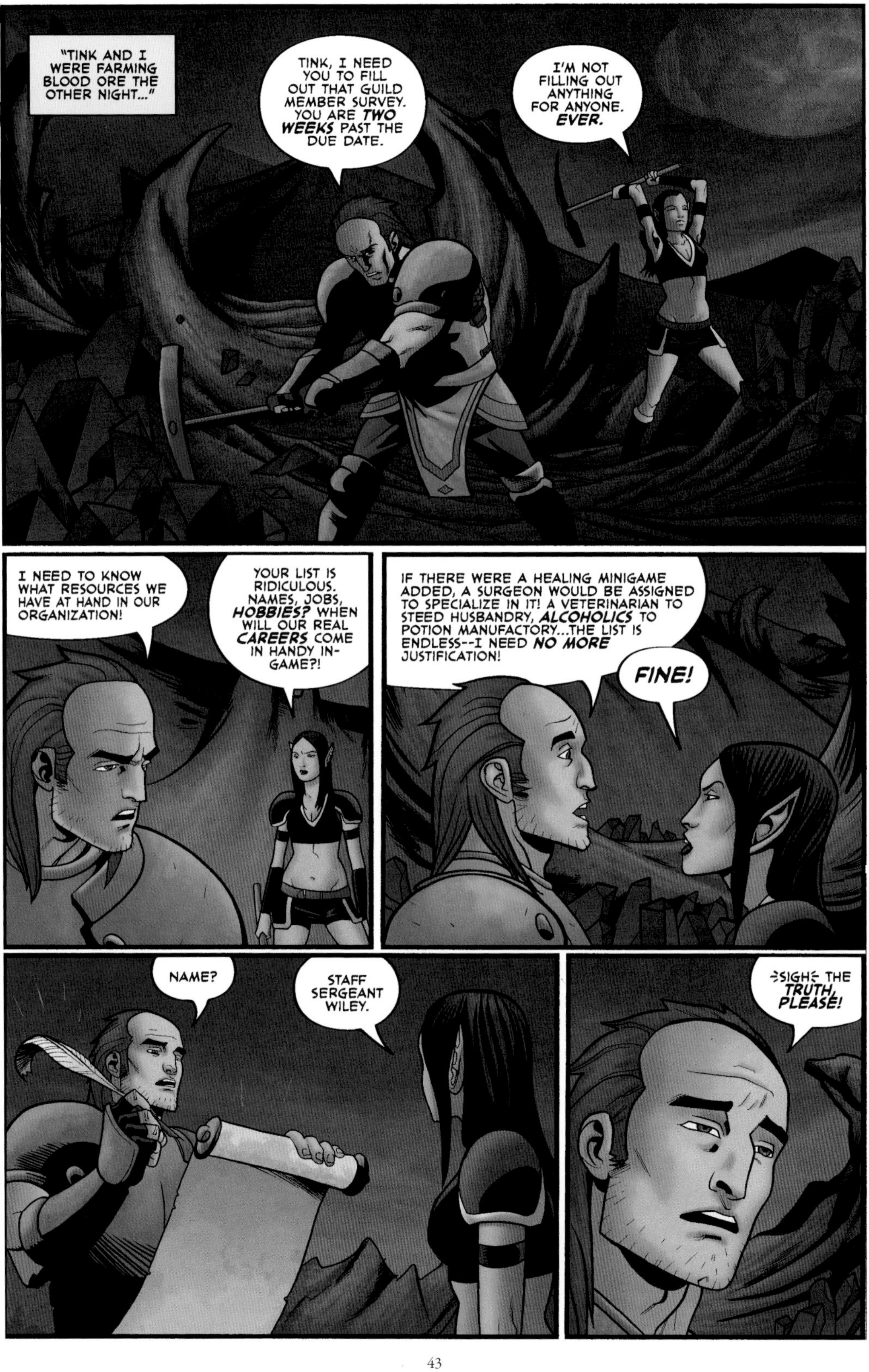
"TINK AND I WERE FARMING BLOOD ORE THE OTHER NIGHT..."
TINK, I NEED YOU TO FILL OUT THAT GUILD MEMBER SURVEY. YOU ARE TWO WEEKS PAST THE DUE DATE.
I'M NOT FILLING OUT ANYTHING FOR ANYONE. EVER.
I NEED TO KNOW WHAT RESOURCES WE HAVE AT HAND IN OUR ORGANIZATION!
YOUR LIST IS RIDICULOUS. NAMES, JOBS, HOBBIES? WHEN WILL OUR REAL CAREERS COME IN HANDY IN-GAME?!
IF THERE WERE A HEALING MINIGAME ADDED, A SURGEON WOULD BE ASSIGNED TO SPECIALIZE IN IT! A VETERINARIAN TO STEED HUSBANDRY, ALCOHOLICS TO POTION MANUFACTORY...THE LIST IS ENDLESS--I NEED NO MORE JUSTIFICATION!
FINE!
NAME?
STAFF SERGEANT WILEY.
SIGH THE TRUTH, PLEASE!

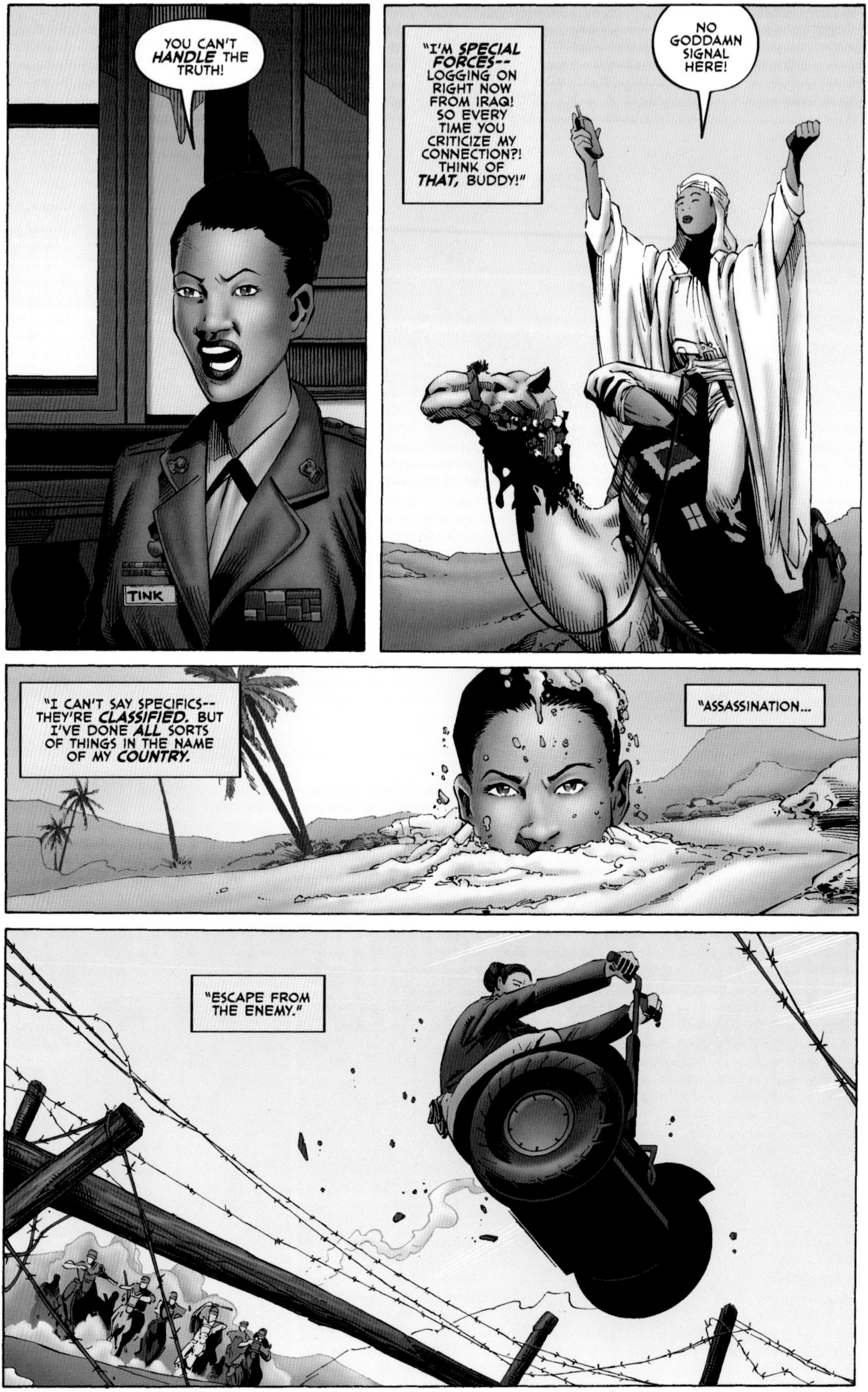
YOU CAN'T HANDLE THE TRUTH!
TINK
"I'M SPECIAL FORCES-- LOGGING ON RIGHT NOW FROM IRAQ! SO EVERY TIME YOU CRITICIZE MY CONNECTION?! THINK OF THAT, BUDDY!"
NO GODDAMN SIGNAL HERE!
"I CAN'T SAY SPECIFICS-- THEY'RE CLASSIFIED. BUT I'VE DONE ALL SORTS OF THINGS IN THE NAME OF MY COUNTRY.
"ASSASSINATION...
"ESCAPE FROM THE ENEMY."

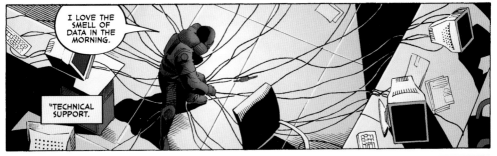

I LOVE THE SMELL OF DATA IN THE MORNING.

"TECHNICAL SUPPORT.

"I'VE ALWAYS BEEN A *MAVERICK.* ESPECIALLY AFTER I LOST MY *WINGMAN.*"

THIS IS FOR *YOU,* DUCKIE!

"WHEREVER THEY NEED ME, I'M *THERE.* A ONE-WOMAN ARMY FOR THE U.S. OF A."

"THEN HOW ARE YOU ONLINE *ALL THE TIME?!*"

"I'M ON *DISCIPLINARY LEAVE.* GOT INTO A *FIGHT* WITH MY C.O. FOR TRASH-TALKING."

"BECAUSE YOU'RE A *WOMAN?*"

"NO.

"BECAUSE I'M *BLACK.*"

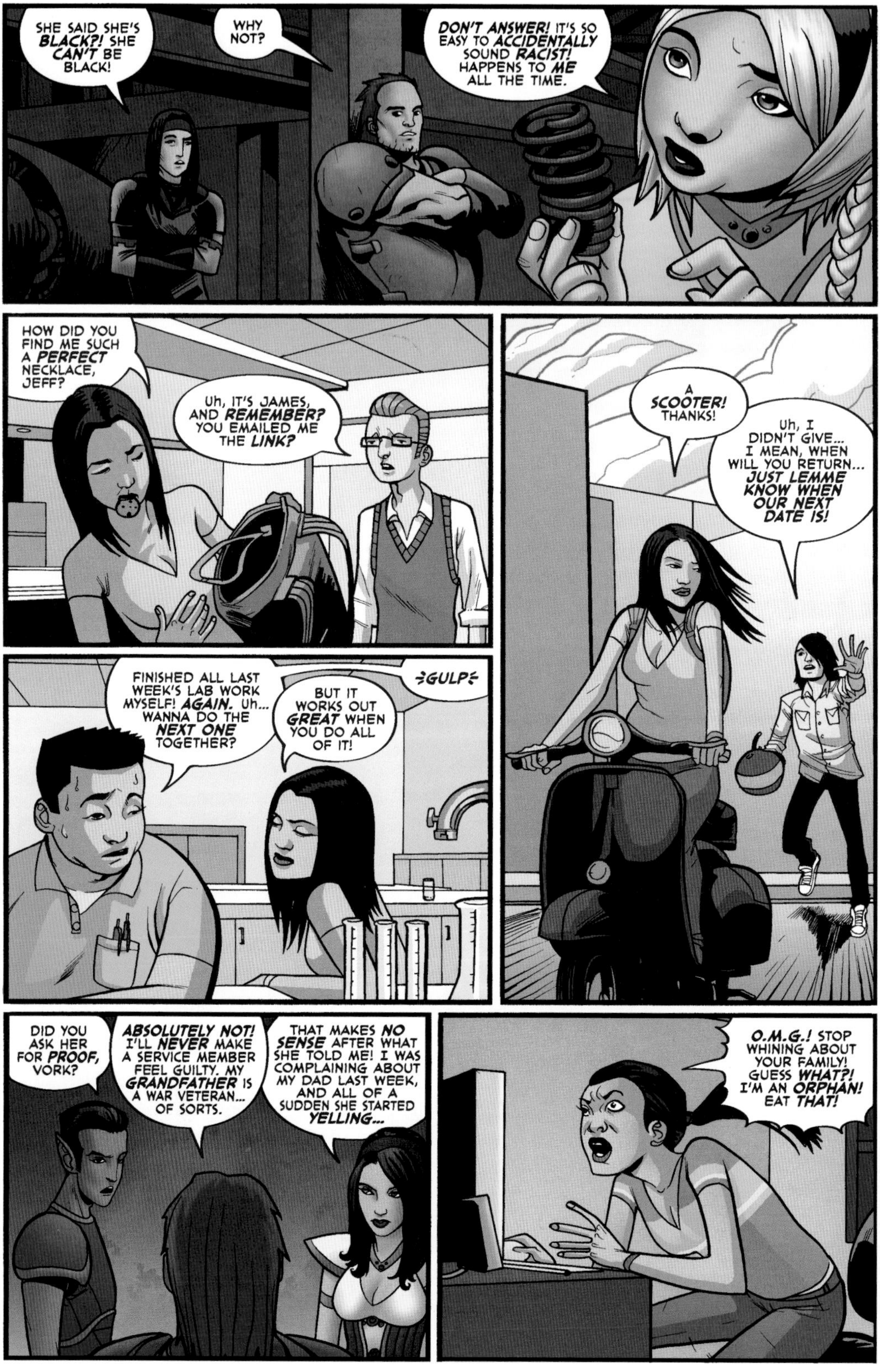
SHE SAID SHE'S BLACK?! SHE CAN'T BE BLACK!
WHY NOT?
DON'T ANSWER! IT'S SO EASY TO ACCIDENTALLY SOUND RACIST! HAPPENS TO ME ALL THE TIME.
HOW DID YOU FIND ME SUCH A PERFECT NECKLACE, JEFF?
Uh, IT'S JAMES, AND REMEMBER? YOU EMAILED ME THE LINK?
A SCOOTER! THANKS!
Uh, I DIDN'T GIVE... I MEAN, WHEN WILL YOU RETURN... JUST LEMME KNOW WHEN OUR NEXT DATE IS!
FINISHED ALL LAST WEEK'S LAB WORK MYSELF! AGAIN. Uh... WANNA DO THE NEXT ONE TOGETHER?
BUT IT WORKS OUT GREAT WHEN YOU DO ALL OF IT!
GULP
DID YOU ASK HER FOR PROOF, VORK?
ABSOLUTELY NOT! I'LL NEVER MAKE A SERVICE MEMBER FEEL GUILTY. MY GRANDFATHER IS A WAR VETERAN... OF SORTS.
THAT MAKES NO SENSE AFTER WHAT SHE TOLD ME! I WAS COMPLAINING ABOUT MY DAD LAST WEEK, AND ALL OF A SUDDEN SHE STARTED YELLING...
O.M.G.! STOP WHINING ABOUT YOUR FAMILY! GUESS WHAT?! I'M AN ORPHAN! EAT THAT!

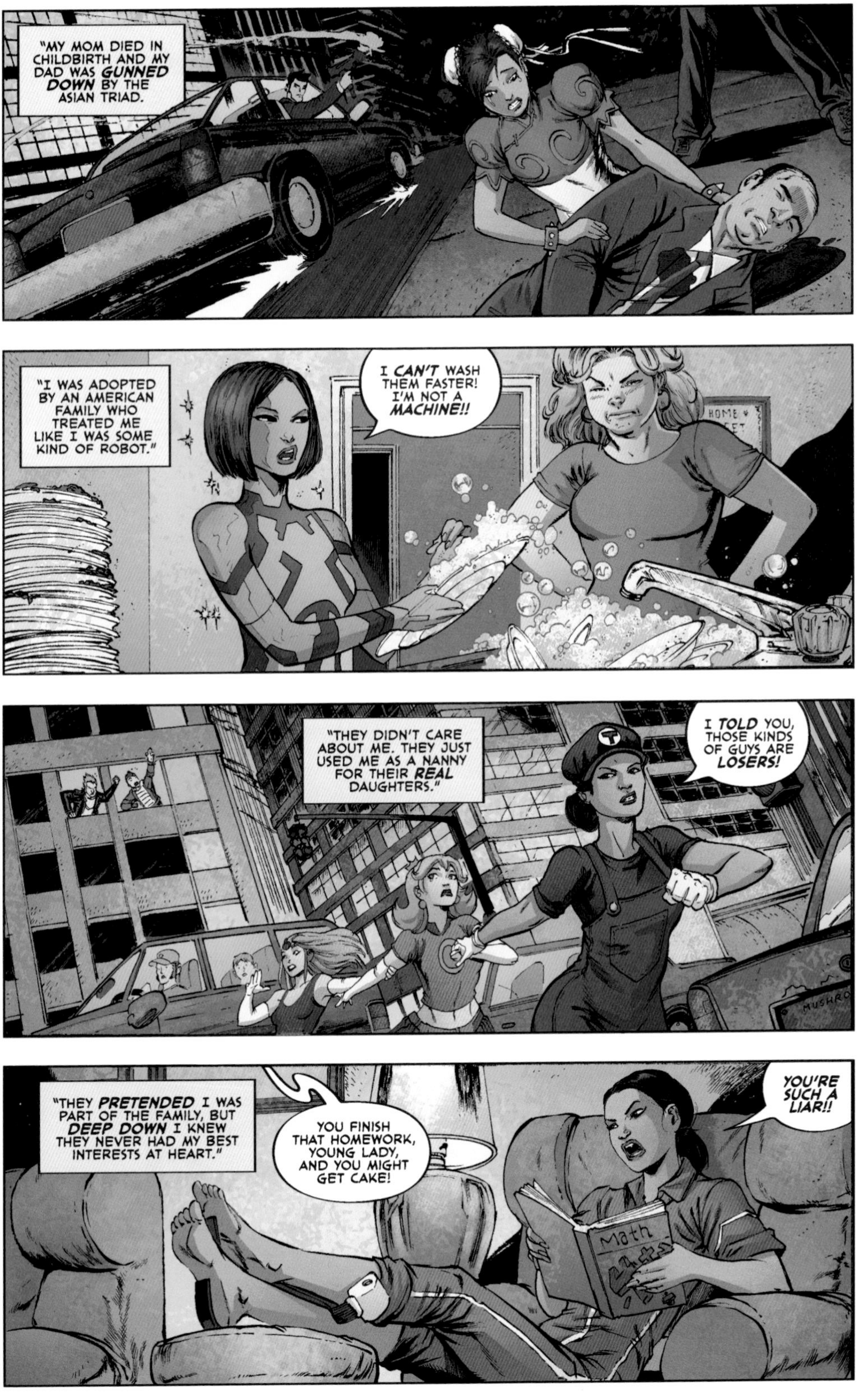
"MY MOM DIED IN CHILDBIRTH AND MY DAD WAS GUNNED DOWN BY THE ASIAN TRIAD.
"I WAS ADOPTED BY AN AMERICAN FAMILY WHO TREATED ME LIKE I WAS SOME KIND OF ROBOT."
I CAN'T WASH THEM FASTER! I'M NOT A MACHINE!!
"THEY DIDN'T CARE ABOUT ME. THEY JUST USED ME AS A NANNY FOR THEIR REAL DAUGHTERS."
I TOLD YOU, THOSE KINDS OF GUYS ARE LOSERS!
"THEY PRETENDED I WAS PART OF THE FAMILY, BUT DEEP DOWN I KNEW THEY NEVER HAD MY BEST INTERESTS AT HEART."
YOU FINISH THAT HOMEWORK, YOUNG LADY, AND YOU MIGHT GET CAKE!
YOU'RE SUCH A LIAR!!
Math

"SO ANY SMALL MEMORIES OF MY DEAD PARENTS, ANY ARTIFACT OF MY PAST, I GUARDED WITH MY LIFE."

GET AWAY FROM MY SCRAPBOOK!

"I WAS ISOLATED AND UNHAPPY. SO I BUILT A HELL AROUND MYSELF. NEVER LET ANYONE CLOSE."

YOU CAN'T TELL ME WHAT TO *DO!* YOU'RE NOT MY *REAL* FATHER!

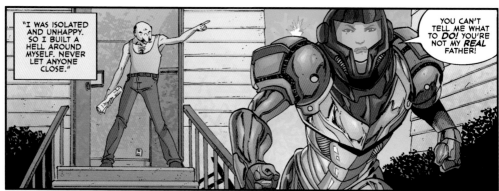

"IT WAS ONLY LAST YEAR, WHEN I GOT AWAY FROM THEM AND WENT TO COLLEGE, THAT I FELT LIKE I WAS FINALLY FREE.

"SO BE GRATEFUL YOU *HAVE* A FAMILY AT *ALL!* I'M *ALONE* NOW. I HAVE A FEELING THAT FATE WILL ALWAYS KEEP ME THAT WAY. WHO KNOWS--MAYBE IT WILL."

I'LL BE GOING NOW.

"SO... DUNGEON RUN?"

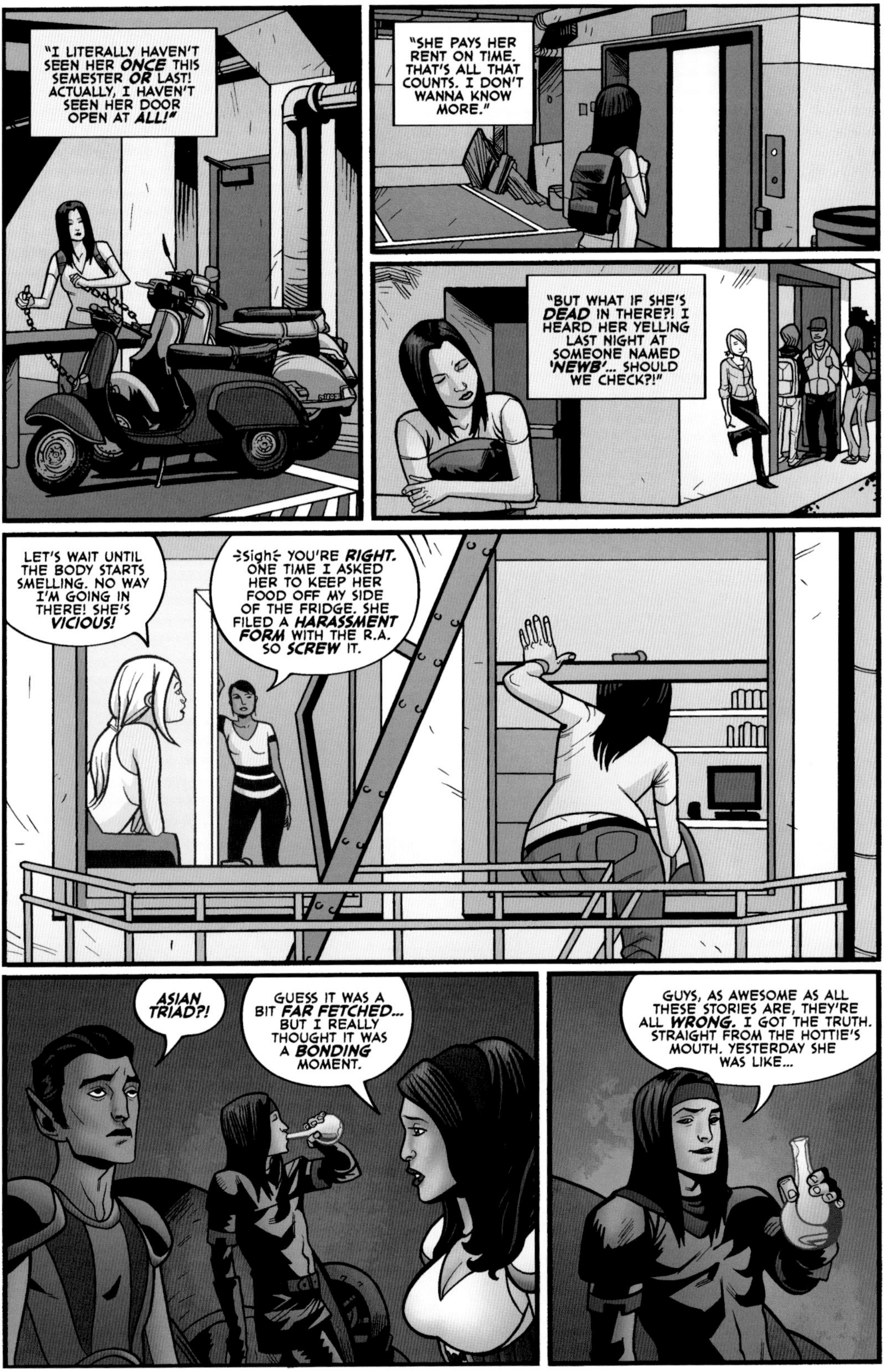
"I LITERALLY HAVEN'T SEEN HER ONCE THIS SEMESTER OR LAST! ACTUALLY, I HAVEN'T SEEN HER DOOR OPEN AT ALL!"
"SHE PAYS HER RENT ON TIME. THAT'S ALL THAT COUNTS. I DON'T WANNA KNOW MORE."
"BUT WHAT IF SHE'S DEAD IN THERE?! I HEARD HER YELLING LAST NIGHT AT SOMEONE NAMED 'NEWB'... SHOULD WE CHECK?!"
LET'S WAIT UNTIL THE BODY STARTS SMELLING. NO WAY I'M GOING IN THERE! SHE'S VICIOUS!
=SIGH= YOU'RE RIGHT. ONE TIME I ASKED HER TO KEEP HER FOOD OFF MY SIDE OF THE FRIDGE. SHE FILED A HARASSMENT FORM WITH THE R.A. SO SCREW IT.
ASIAN TRIAD?!
GUESS IT WAS A BIT FAR FETCHED... BUT I REALLY THOUGHT IT WAS A BONDING MOMENT.
GUYS, AS AWESOME AS ALL THESE STORIES ARE, THEY'RE ALL WRONG. I GOT THE TRUTH. STRAIGHT FROM THE HOTTIE'S MOUTH. YESTERDAY SHE WAS LIKE...

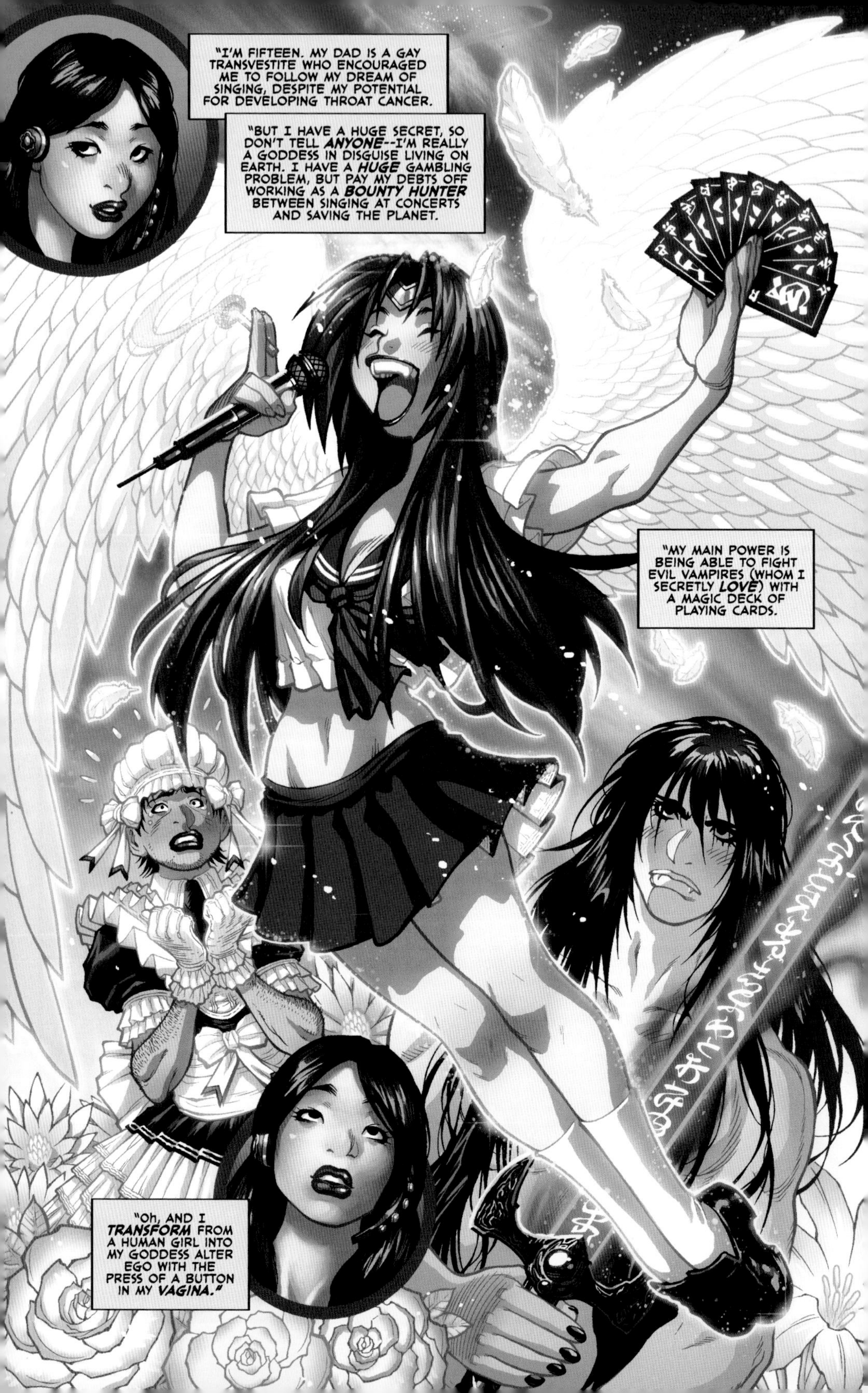
"I'M FIFTEEN. MY DAD IS A GAY TRANSVESTITE WHO ENCOURAGED ME TO FOLLOW MY DREAM OF SINGING, DESPITE MY POTENTIAL FOR DEVELOPING THROAT CANCER.
"BUT I HAVE A HUGE SECRET, SO DON'T TELL ANYONE--I'M REALLY A GODDESS IN DISGUISE LIVING ON EARTH. I HAVE A HUGE GAMBLING PROBLEM, BUT PAY MY DEBTS OFF WORKING AS A BOUNTY HUNTER BETWEEN SINGING AT CONCERTS AND SAVING THE PLANET.
"MY MAIN POWER IS BEING ABLE TO FIGHT EVIL VAMPIRES (WHOM I SECRETLY LOVE) WITH A MAGIC DECK OF PLAYING CARDS.
"Oh, AND I TRANSFORM FROM A HUMAN GIRL INTO MY GODDESS ALTER EGO WITH THE PRESS OF A BUTTON IN MY VAGINA."

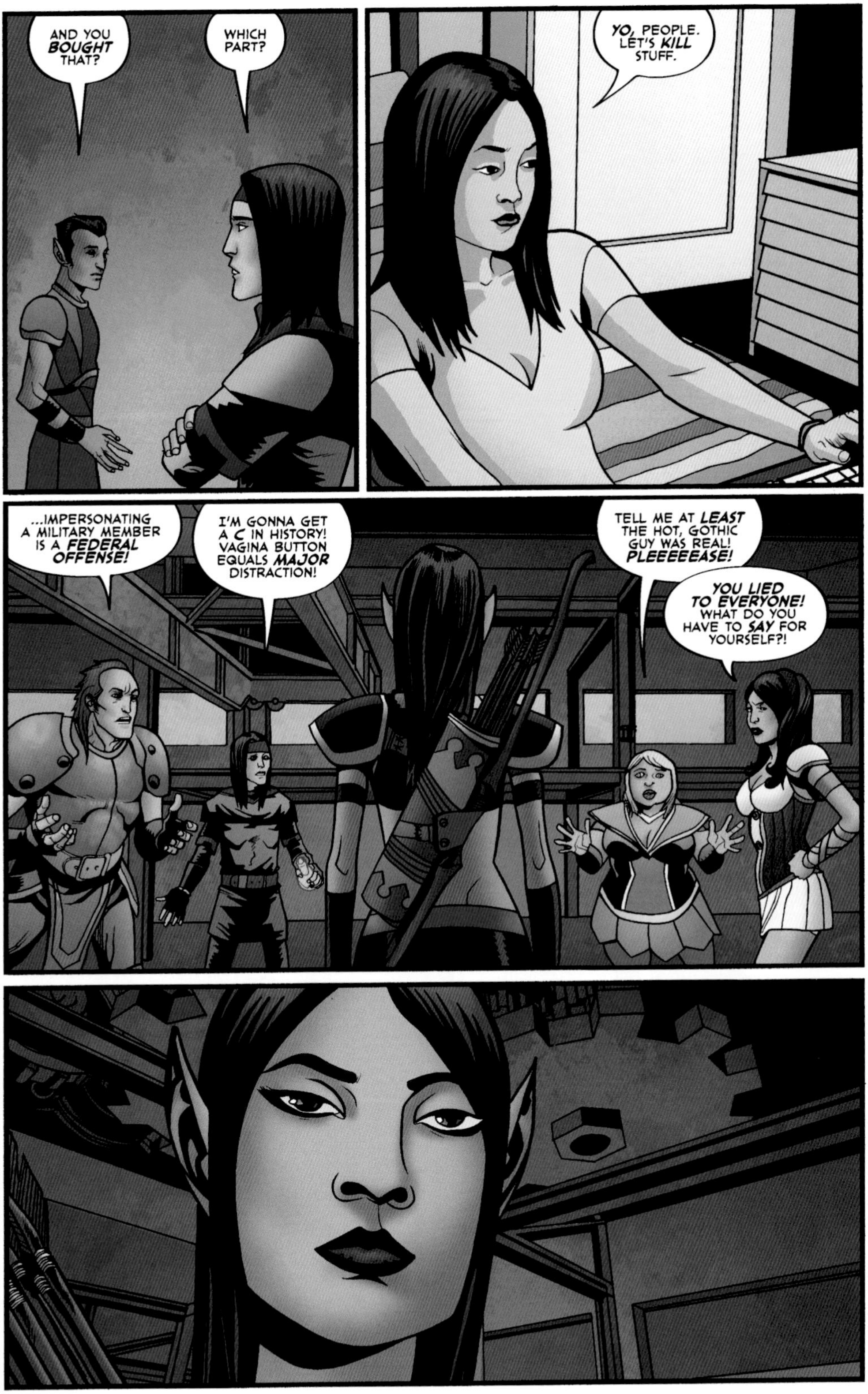
AND YOU BOUGHT THAT?
WHICH PART?
YO, PEOPLE. LET'S KILL STUFF.
...IMPERSONATING A MILITARY MEMBER IS A FEDERAL OFFENSE!
I'M GONNA GET A C IN HISTORY! VAGINA BUTTON EQUALS MAJOR DISTRACTION!
TELL ME AT LEAST THE HOT, GOTHIC GUY WAS REAL! PLEEEEEASE!
YOU LIED TO EVERYONE! WHAT DO YOU HAVE TO SAY FOR YOURSELF?!

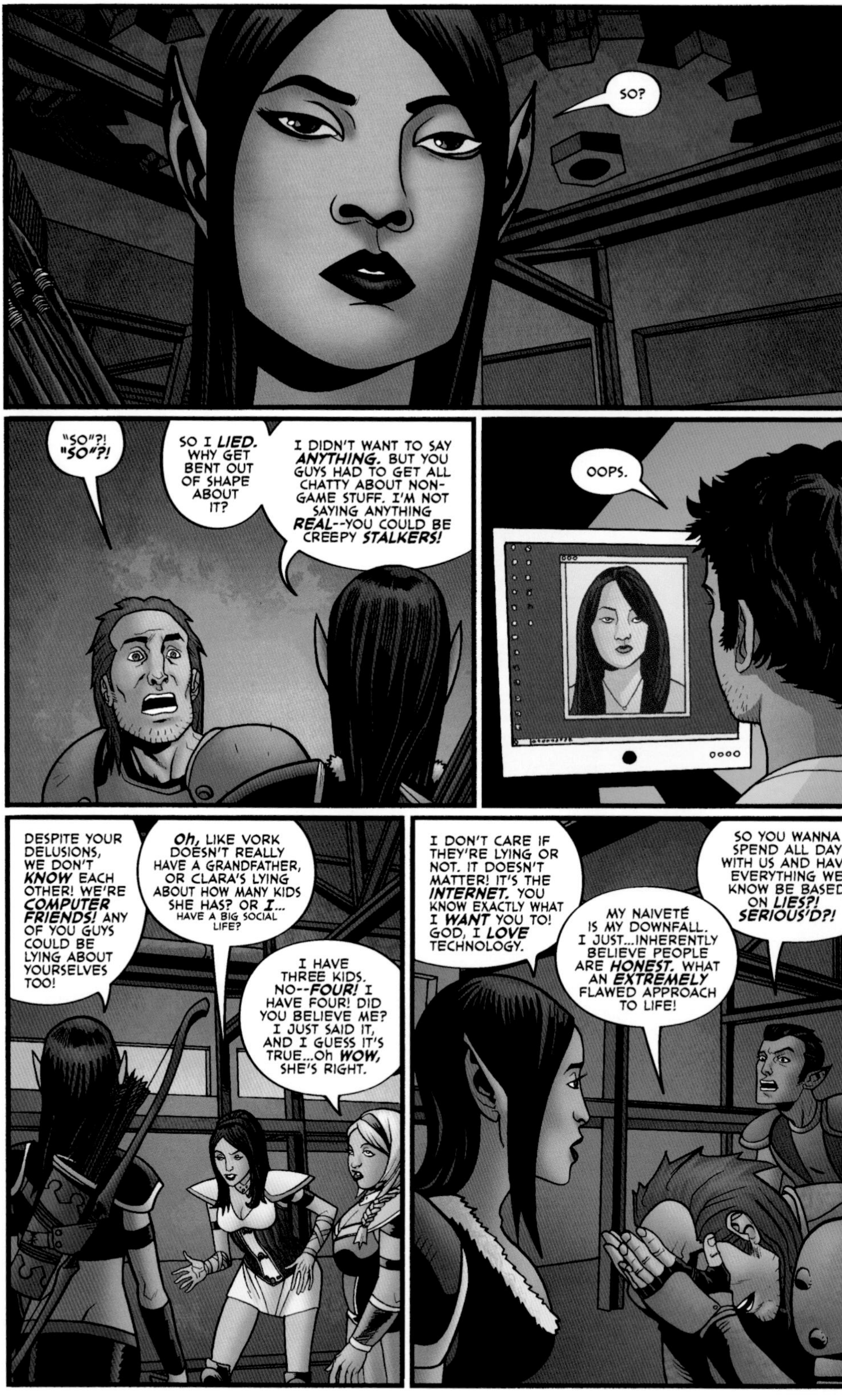
SO?
"SO"?! "SO"?!
SO I LIED. WHY GET BENT OUT OF SHAPE ABOUT IT?
I DIDN'T WANT TO SAY ANYTHING. BUT YOU GUYS HAD TO GET ALL CHATTY ABOUT NON-GAME STUFF. I'M NOT SAYING ANYTHING REAL--YOU COULD BE CREEPY STALKERS!
OOPS.
DESPITE YOUR DELUSIONS, WE DON'T KNOW EACH OTHER! WE'RE COMPUTER FRIENDS! ANY OF YOU GUYS COULD BE LYING ABOUT YOURSELVES TOO!
Oh, LIKE VORK DOESN'T REALLY HAVE A GRANDFATHER, OR CLARA'S LYING ABOUT HOW MANY KIDS SHE HAS? OR I... HAVE A BIG SOCIAL LIFE?
I HAVE THREE KIDS. NO--FOUR! I HAVE FOUR! DID YOU BELIEVE ME? I JUST SAID IT, AND I GUESS IT'S TRUE...Oh WOW, SHE'S RIGHT.
I DON'T CARE IF THEY'RE LYING OR NOT. IT DOESN'T MATTER! IT'S THE INTERNET. YOU KNOW EXACTLY WHAT I WANT YOU TO! GOD, I LOVE TECHNOLOGY.
MY NAIVETÉ IS MY DOWNFALL. I JUST...INHERENTLY BELIEVE PEOPLE ARE HONEST. WHAT AN EXTREMELY FLAWED APPROACH TO LIFE!
SO YOU WANNA SPEND ALL DAY WITH US AND HAVE EVERYTHING WE KNOW BE BASED ON LIES?! SERIOUS'D?!

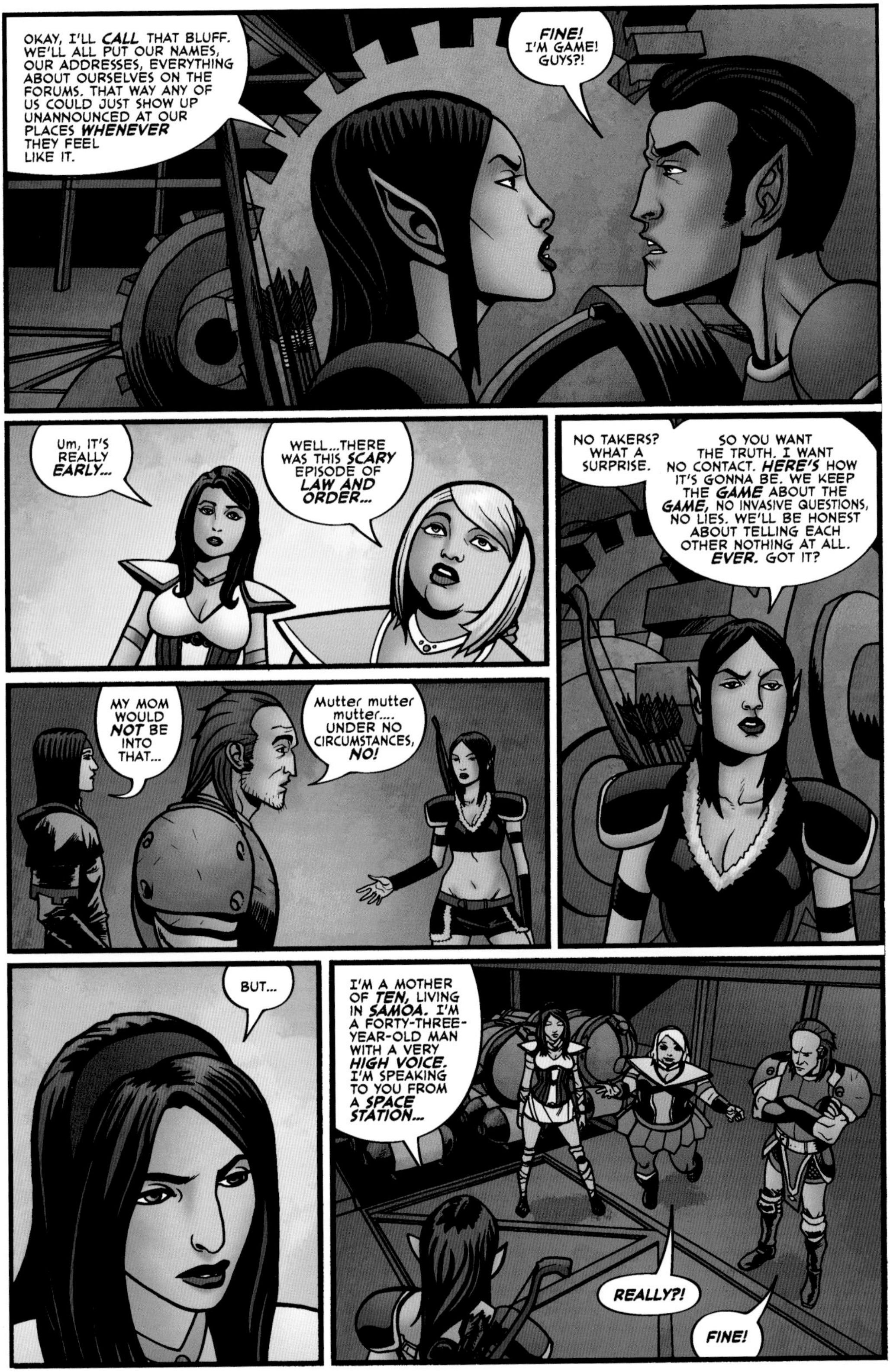
OKAY, I'LL CALL THAT BLUFF. WE'LL ALL PUT OUR NAMES, OUR ADDRESSES, EVERYTHING ABOUT OURSELVES ON THE FORUMS. THAT WAY ANY OF US COULD JUST SHOW UP UNANNOUNCED AT OUR PLACES WHENEVER THEY FEEL LIKE IT.
FINE! I'M GAME! GUYS?!
Um, IT'S REALLY EARLY...
WELL...THERE WAS THIS SCARY EPISODE OF LAW AND ORDER...
MY MOM WOULD NOT BE INTO THAT...
Mutter mutter mutter.... UNDER NO CIRCUMSTANCES, NO!
NO TAKERS? WHAT A SURPRISE.
SO YOU WANT THE TRUTH. I WANT NO CONTACT. HERE'S HOW IT'S GONNA BE. WE KEEP THE GAME ABOUT THE GAME, NO INVASIVE QUESTIONS, NO LIES. WE'LL BE HONEST ABOUT TELLING EACH OTHER NOTHING AT ALL. EVER. GOT IT?
BUT...
I'M A MOTHER OF TEN, LIVING IN SAMOA. I'M A FORTY-THREE-YEAR-OLD MAN WITH A VERY HIGH VOICE. I'M SPEAKING TO YOU FROM A SPACE STATION...
REALLY?!
FINE!

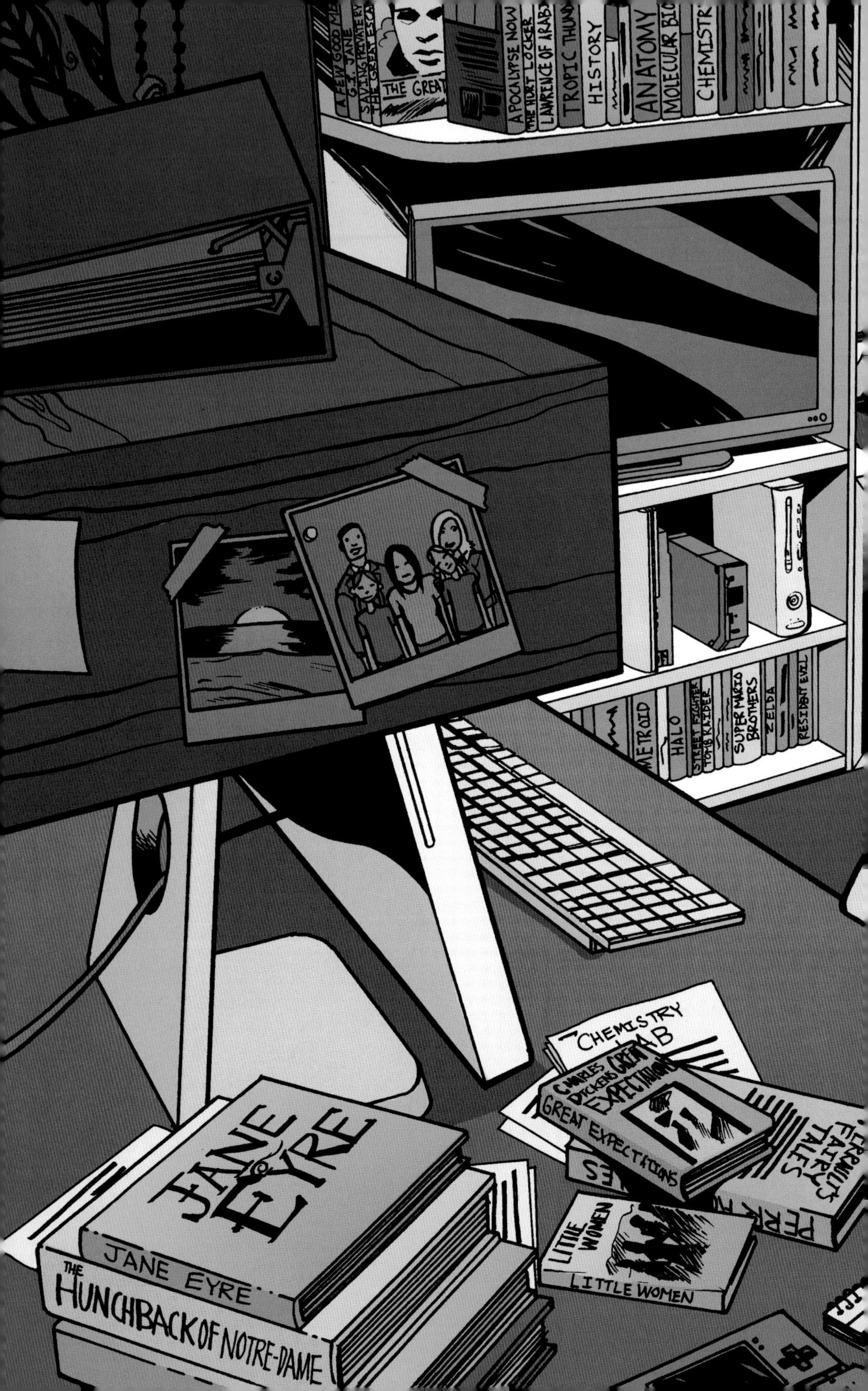
A FEW GOOD ME
G.I. JANE
SAVING PRIVATE RY
THE GREAT ESCA
THE GREAT
APOCALYPSE NOW
THE HURT LOCKER
LAWRENCE OF ARAB
TROPIC THUND
HISTORY
ANATOMY
MOLECULAR BIO
CHEMISTR
METROID
HALO
STREET FIGHTER
TOMB RAIDER
SUPER MARIO BROTHERS
ZELDA
RESIDENT EVIL
CHEMISTRY LAB
CHARLES DICKENS GREAT EXPECTATIONS
GREAT EXPECTATIONS
PERRAULT'S FAIRY TALES
LITTLE WOMEN
LITTLE WOMEN
JANE EYRE
JANE EYRE
THE HUNCHBACK OF NOTRE-DAME

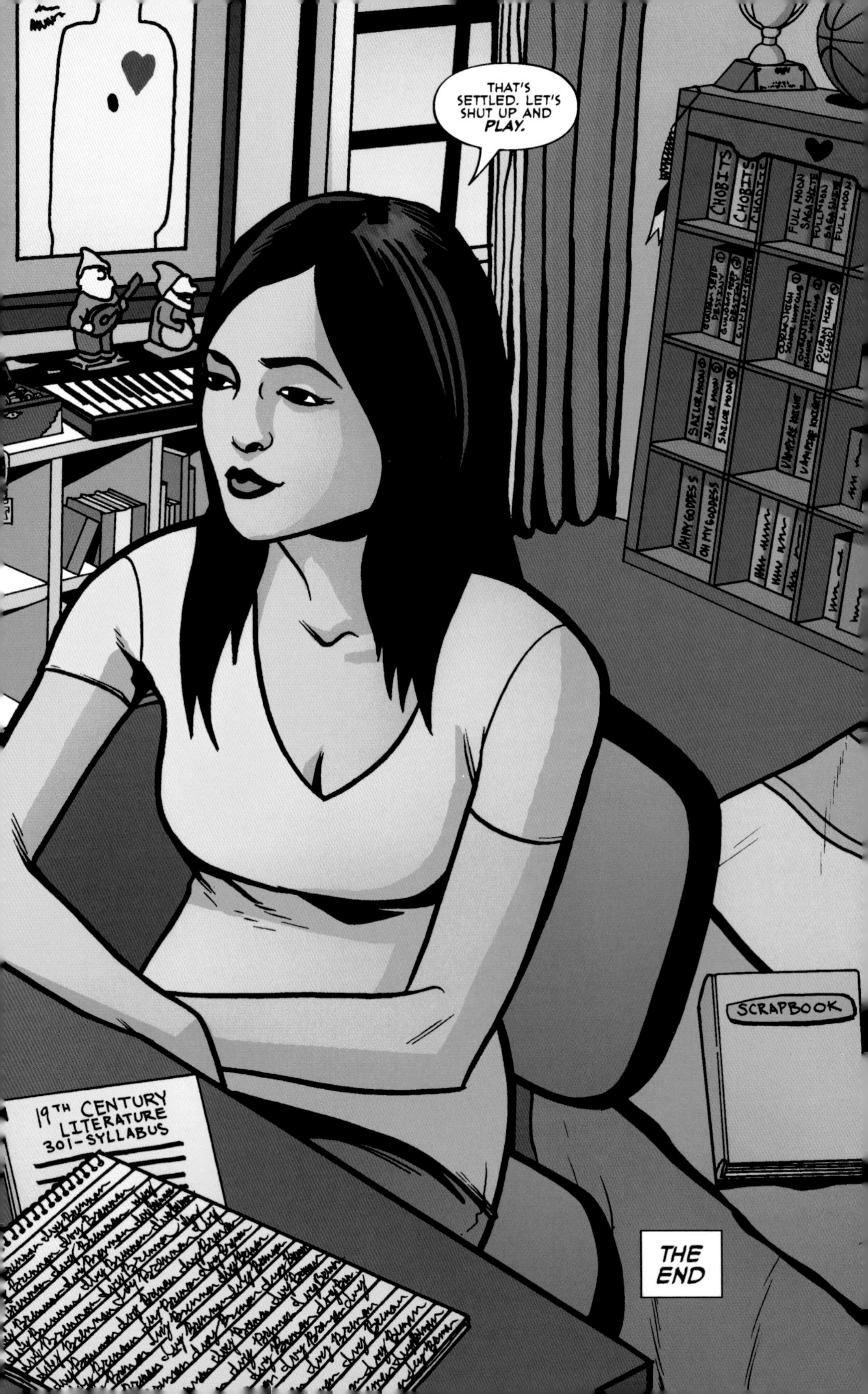
THAT'S SETTLED. LET'S SHUT UP AND *PLAY.*
CHOBITS
FULL MOON
SAILOR MOON
VAMPIRE KNIGHT
OH MY GODDESS
SCRAPBOOK
19TH CENTURY LITERATURE 301-SYLLABUS
THE END

CHAPTER THREE
BLADEZZ

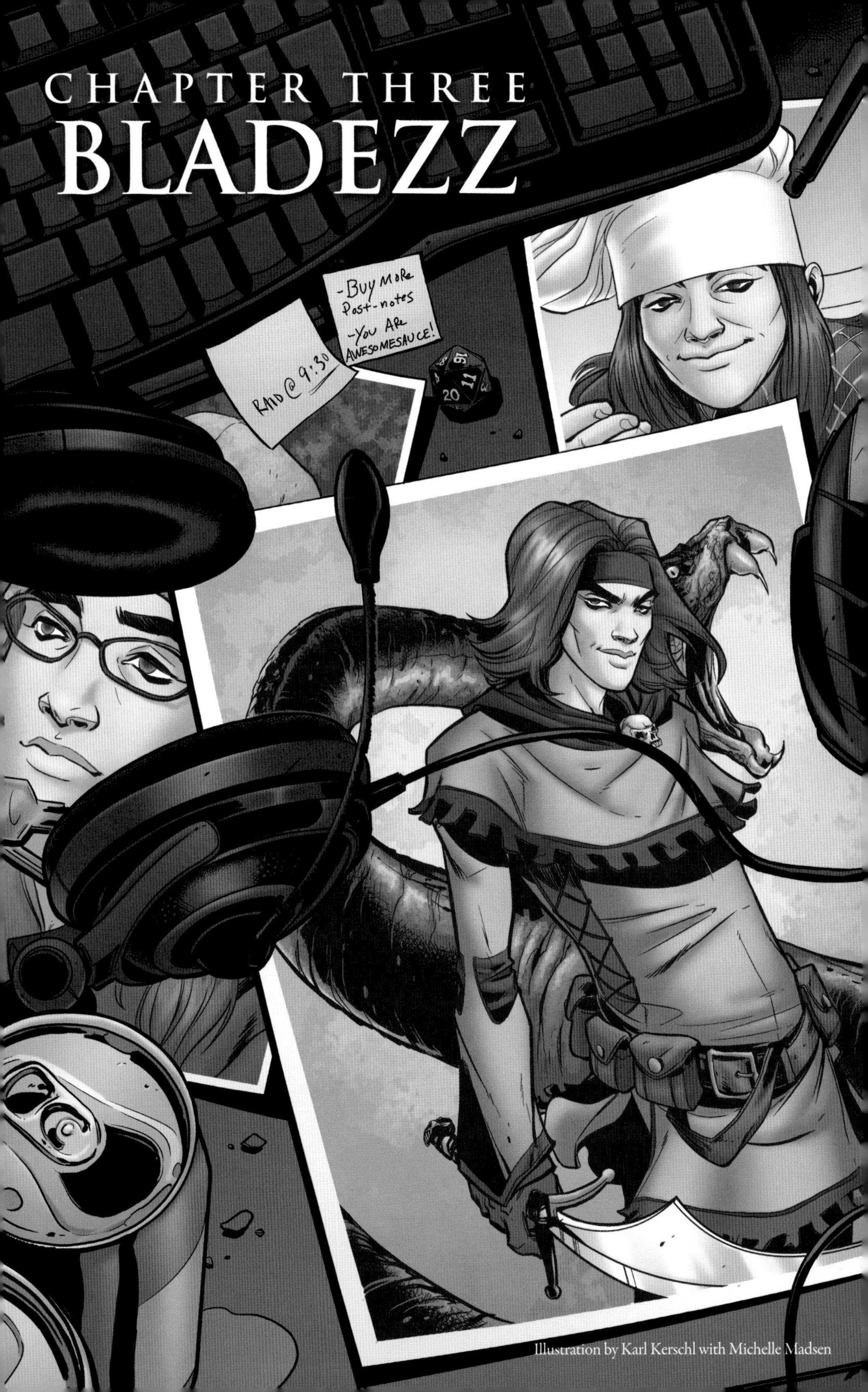
-Buy More
Post-notes
-You Are
AWESOMESAUCE!
RAID @ 9:30

Illustration by Karl Kerschl with Michelle Madsen

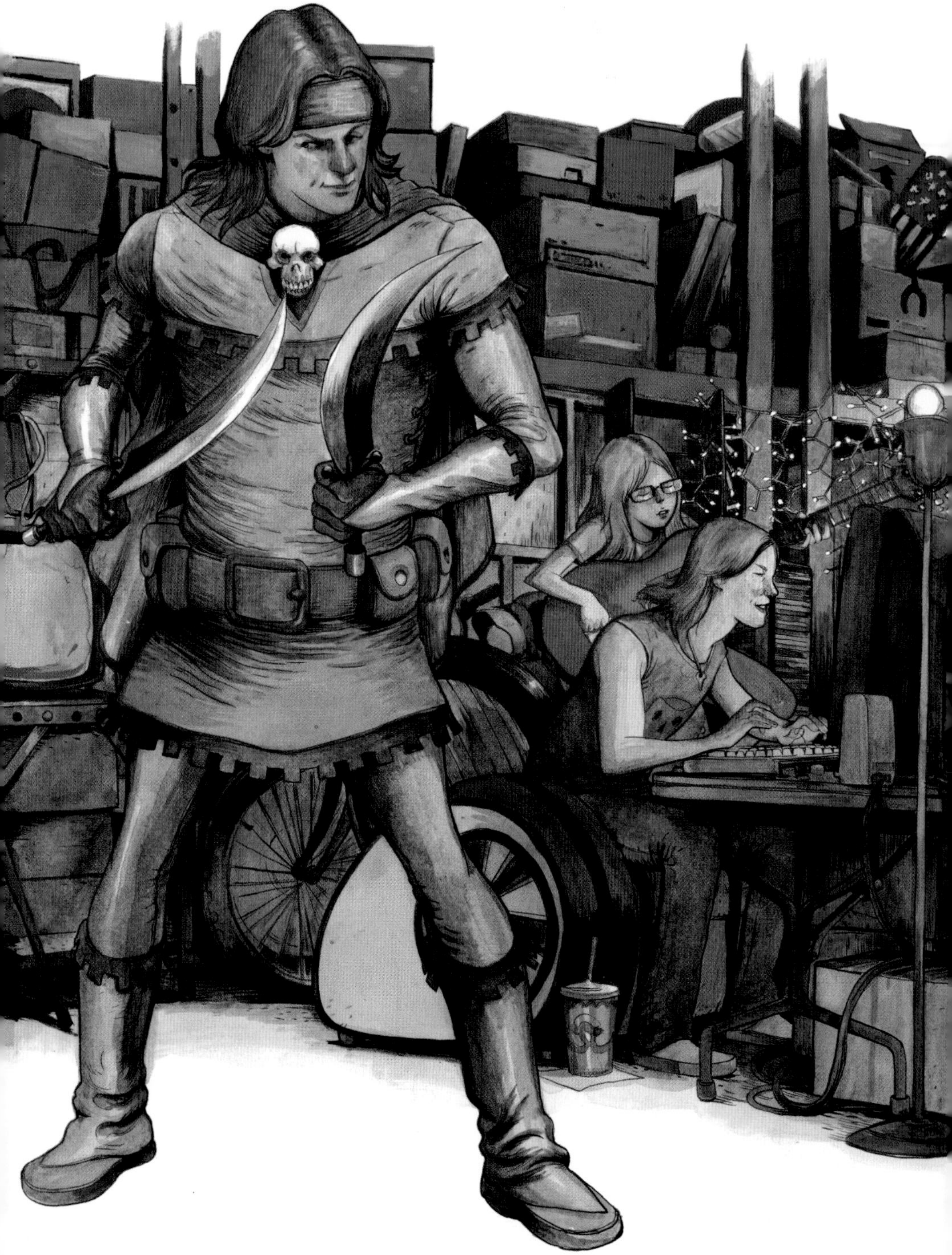

Illustration by Farel Dalrymple

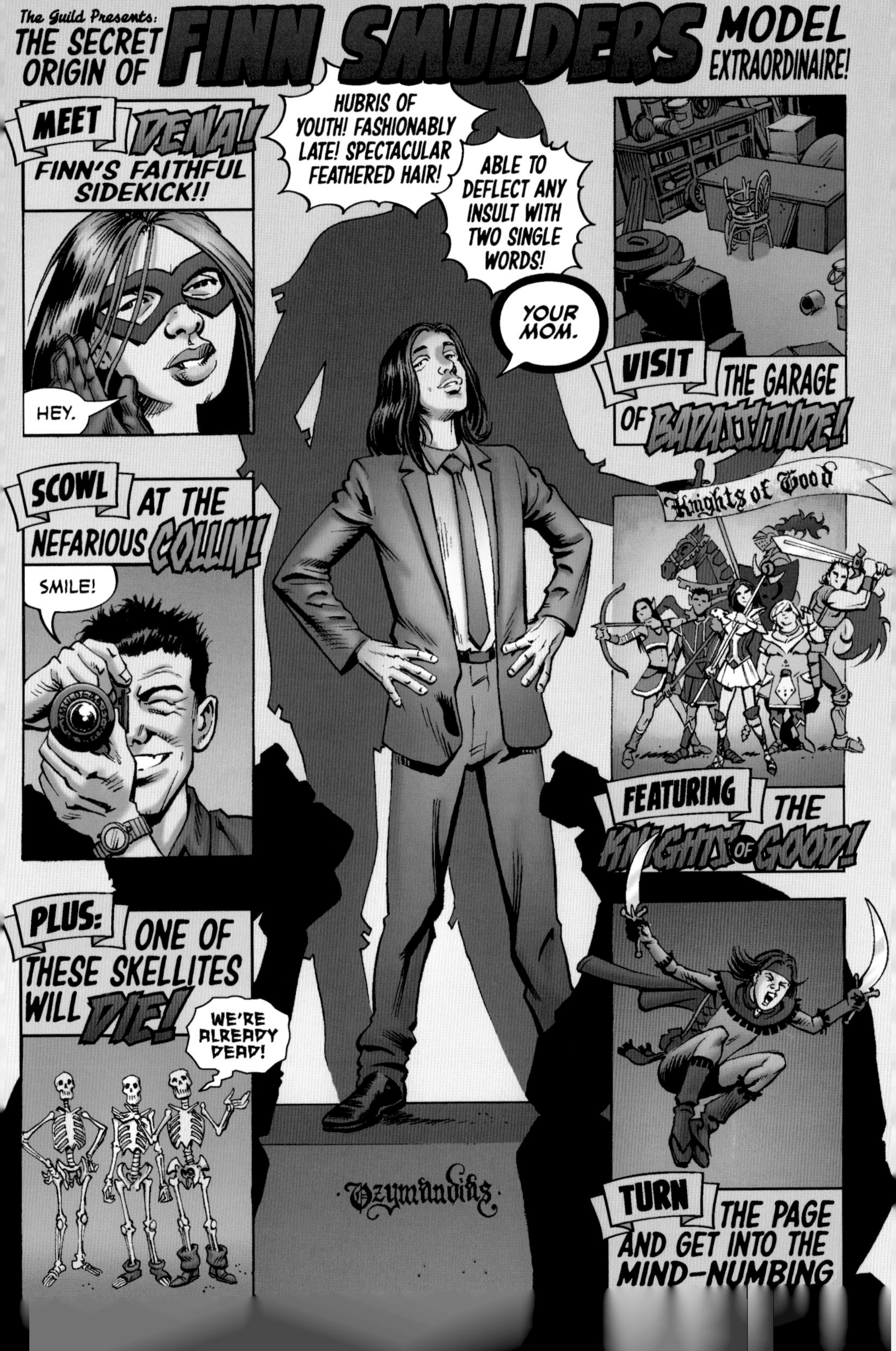
The Guild Presents:
THE SECRET ORIGIN OF FINN SMULDERS MODEL EXTRAORDINAIRE!
MEET DENA! FINN'S FAITHFUL SIDEKICK!!
HEY.
HUBRIS OF YOUTH! FASHIONABLY LATE! SPECTACULAR FEATHERED HAIR!
ABLE TO DEFLECT ANY INSULT WITH TWO SINGLE WORDS!
YOUR MOM.
VISIT THE GARAGE OF BADASSITUDE!
SCOWL AT THE NEFARIOUS COLLIN!
SMILE!
Knights of Good
FEATURING THE KNIGHTS OF GOOD!
PLUS: ONE OF THESE SKELLITES WILL DIE!
WE'RE ALREADY DEAD!
Ozymandias
TURN THE PAGE AND GET INTO THE MIND-NUMBING

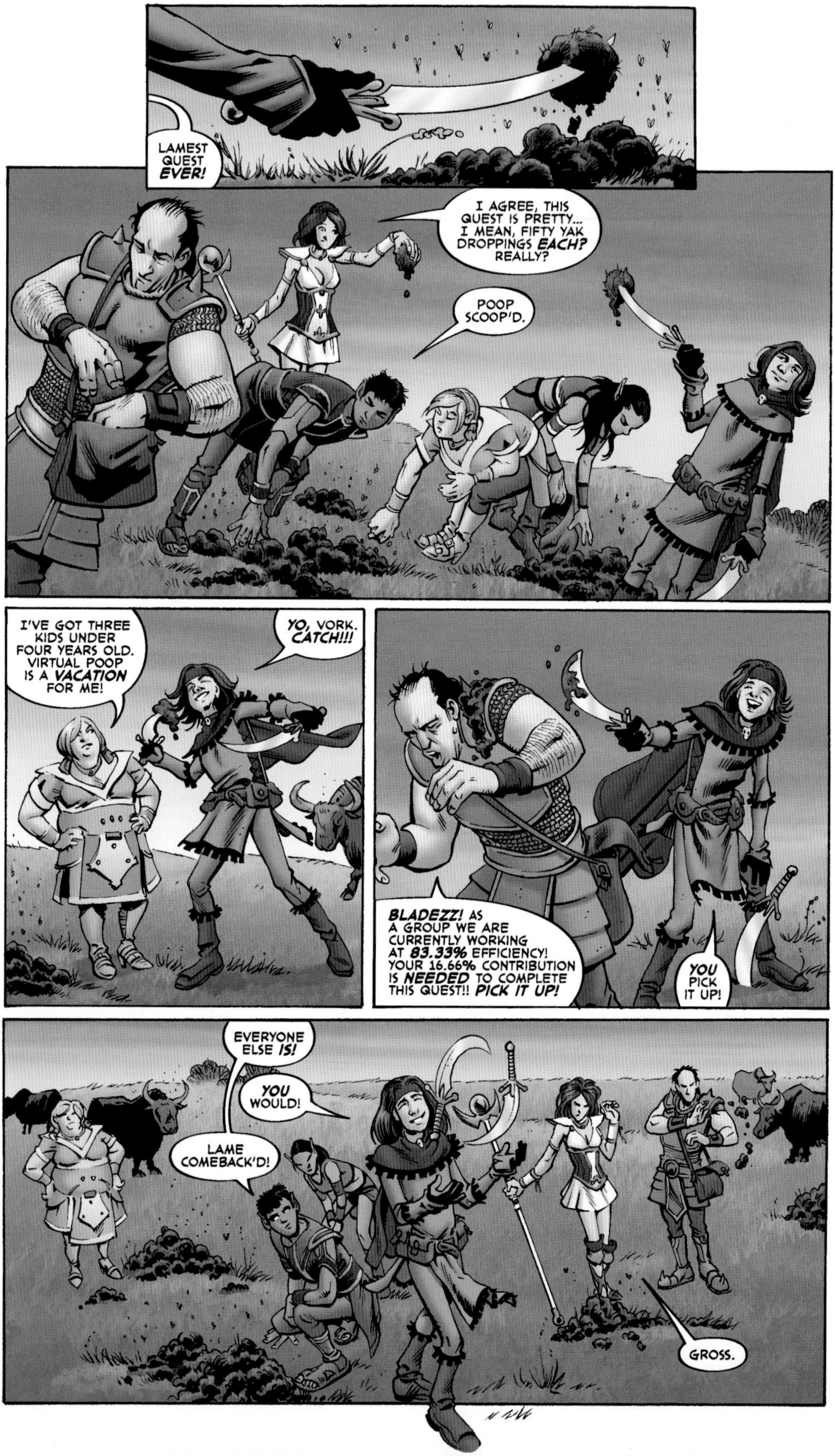
LAMEST QUEST EVER!
I AGREE, THIS QUEST IS PRETTY... I MEAN, FIFTY YAK DROPPINGS EACH? REALLY?
POOP SCOOP'D.
I'VE GOT THREE KIDS UNDER FOUR YEARS OLD. VIRTUAL POOP IS A VACATION FOR ME!
YO, VORK. CATCH!!!
BLADEZZ! AS A GROUP WE ARE CURRENTLY WORKING AT 83.33% EFFICIENCY! YOUR 16.66% CONTRIBUTION IS NEEDED TO COMPLETE THIS QUEST!! PICK IT UP!
YOU PICK IT UP!
EVERYONE ELSE IS!
YOU WOULD!
LAME COMEBACK'D!
GROSS.

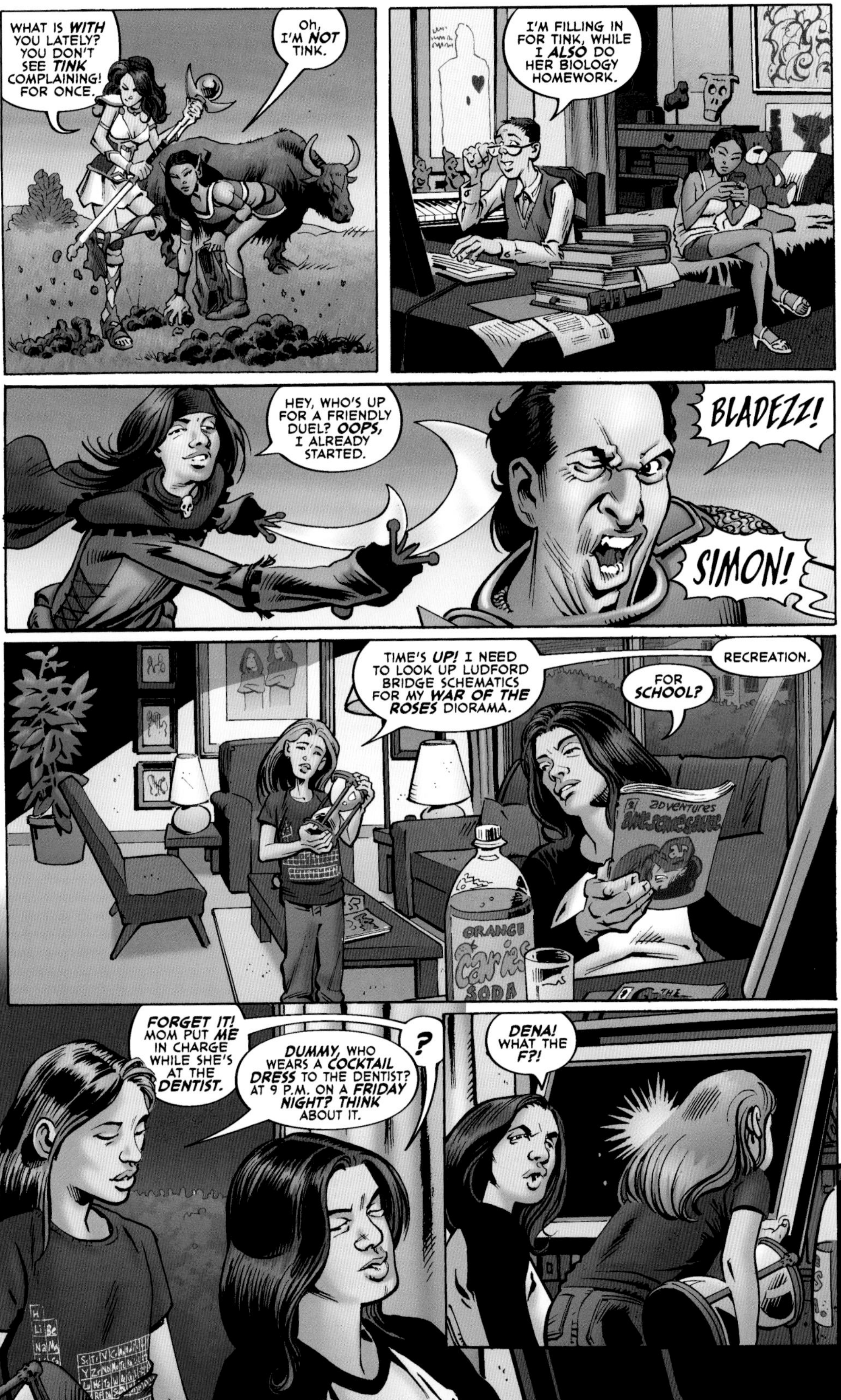

WHAT IS WITH YOU LATELY? YOU DON'T SEE TINK COMPLAINING! FOR ONCE.
Oh, I'M NOT TINK.
I'M FILLING IN FOR TINK, WHILE I ALSO DO HER BIOLOGY HOMEWORK.
HEY, WHO'S UP FOR A FRIENDLY DUEL? OOPS, I ALREADY STARTED.
BLADEZZ!
SIMON!
TIME'S UP! I NEED TO LOOK UP LUDFORD BRIDGE SCHEMATICS FOR MY WAR OF THE ROSES DIORAMA.
FOR SCHOOL?
RECREATION.
ADVENTURES
ORANGE
SODA
FORGET IT! MOM PUT ME IN CHARGE WHILE SHE'S AT THE DENTIST.
?
DUMMY, WHO WEARS A COCKTAIL DRESS TO THE DENTIST? AT 9 P.M. ON A FRIDAY NIGHT? THINK ABOUT IT.
DENA! WHAT THE F?!

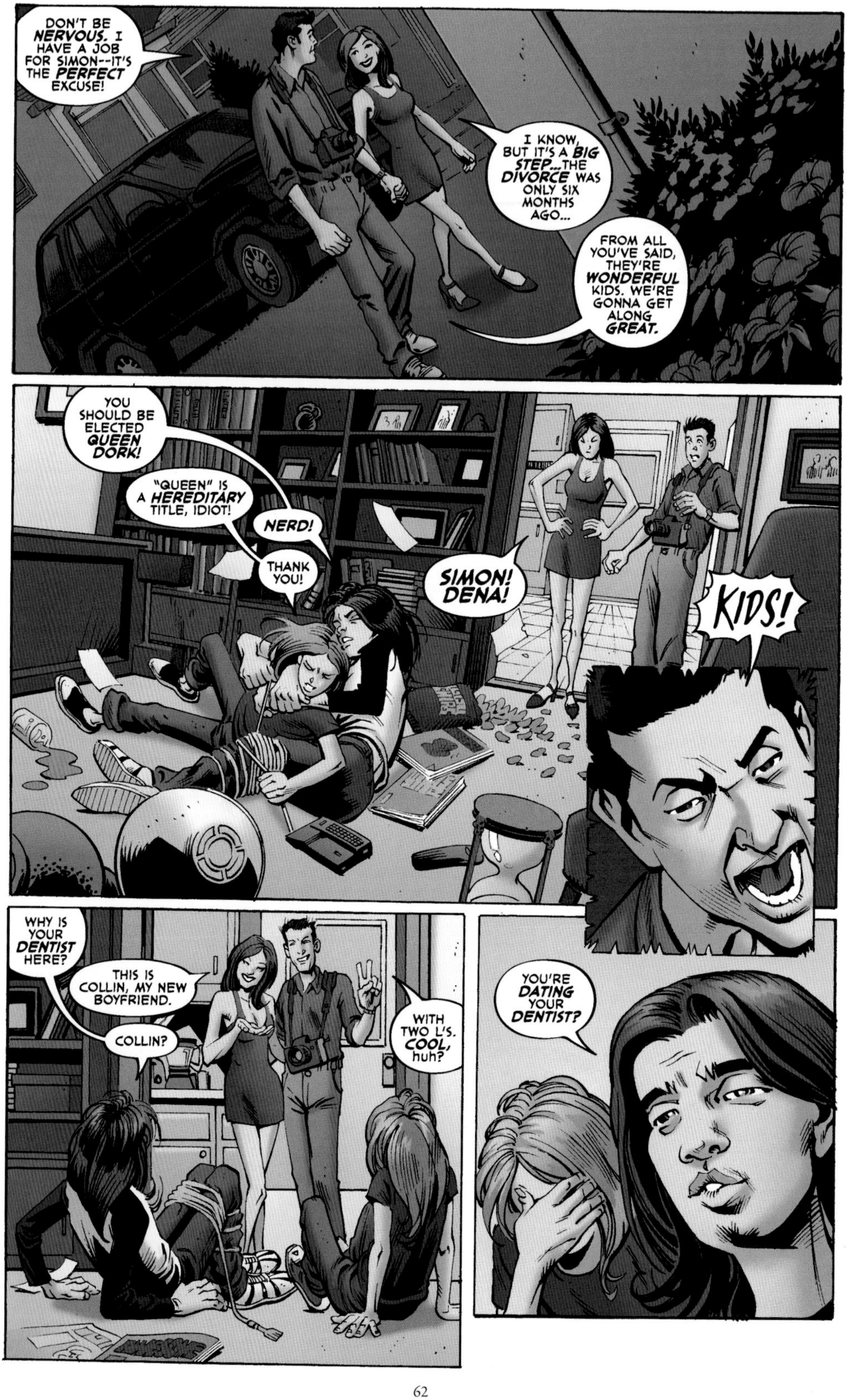
DON'T BE NERVOUS. I HAVE A JOB FOR SIMON--IT'S THE PERFECT EXCUSE!
I KNOW, BUT IT'S A BIG STEP... THE DIVORCE WAS ONLY SIX MONTHS AGO...
FROM ALL YOU'VE SAID, THEY'RE WONDERFUL KIDS. WE'RE GONNA GET ALONG GREAT.
YOU SHOULD BE ELECTED QUEEN DORK!
"QUEEN" IS A HEREDITARY TITLE, IDIOT!
NERD!
THANK YOU!
SIMON! DENA!
KIDS!
WHY IS YOUR DENTIST HERE?
THIS IS COLLIN, MY NEW BOYFRIEND.
COLLIN?
WITH TWO L'S. COOL, huh?
YOU'RE DATING YOUR DENTIST?

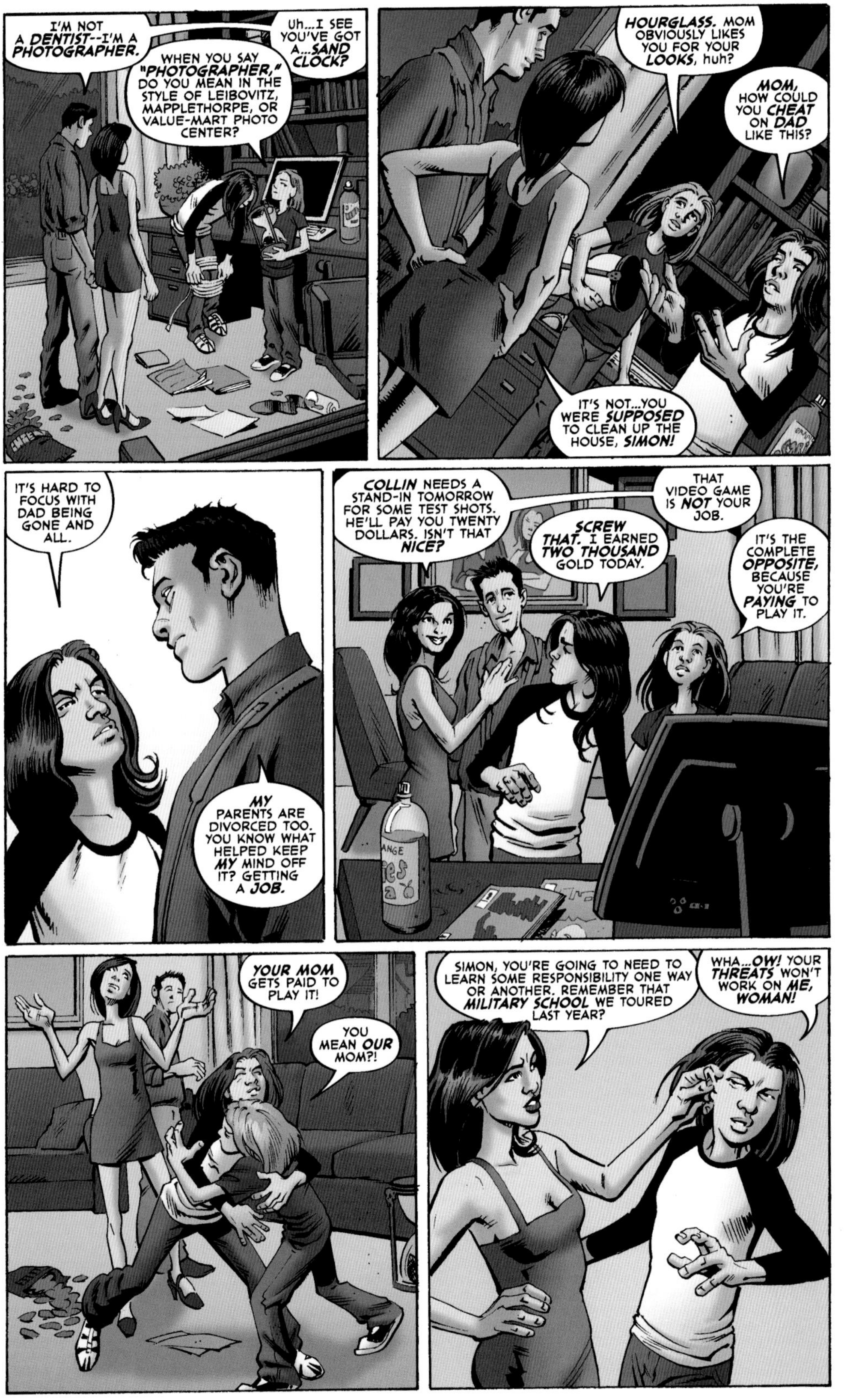

I'M NOT A DENTIST--I'M A PHOTOGRAPHER.
Uh...I SEE YOU'VE GOT A...SAND CLOCK?
WHEN YOU SAY "PHOTOGRAPHER," DO YOU MEAN IN THE STYLE OF LEIBOVITZ, MAPPLETHORPE, OR VALUE-MART PHOTO CENTER?
HOURGLASS. MOM OBVIOUSLY LIKES YOU FOR YOUR LOOKS, huh?
MOM, HOW COULD YOU CHEAT ON DAD LIKE THIS?
IT'S NOT...YOU WERE SUPPOSED TO CLEAN UP THE HOUSE, SIMON!
IT'S HARD TO FOCUS WITH DAD BEING GONE AND ALL.
MY PARENTS ARE DIVORCED TOO. YOU KNOW WHAT HELPED KEEP MY MIND OFF IT? GETTING A JOB.
COLLIN NEEDS A STAND-IN TOMORROW FOR SOME TEST SHOTS. HE'LL PAY YOU TWENTY DOLLARS. ISN'T THAT NICE?
THAT VIDEO GAME IS NOT YOUR JOB.
SCREW THAT. I EARNED TWO THOUSAND GOLD TODAY.
IT'S THE COMPLETE OPPOSITE, BECAUSE YOU'RE PAYING TO PLAY IT.
YOUR MOM GETS PAID TO PLAY IT!
YOU MEAN OUR MOM?!
SIMON, YOU'RE GOING TO NEED TO LEARN SOME RESPONSIBILITY ONE WAY OR ANOTHER. REMEMBER THAT MILITARY SCHOOL WE TOURED LAST YEAR?
WHA...OW! YOUR THREATS WON'T WORK ON ME, WOMAN!

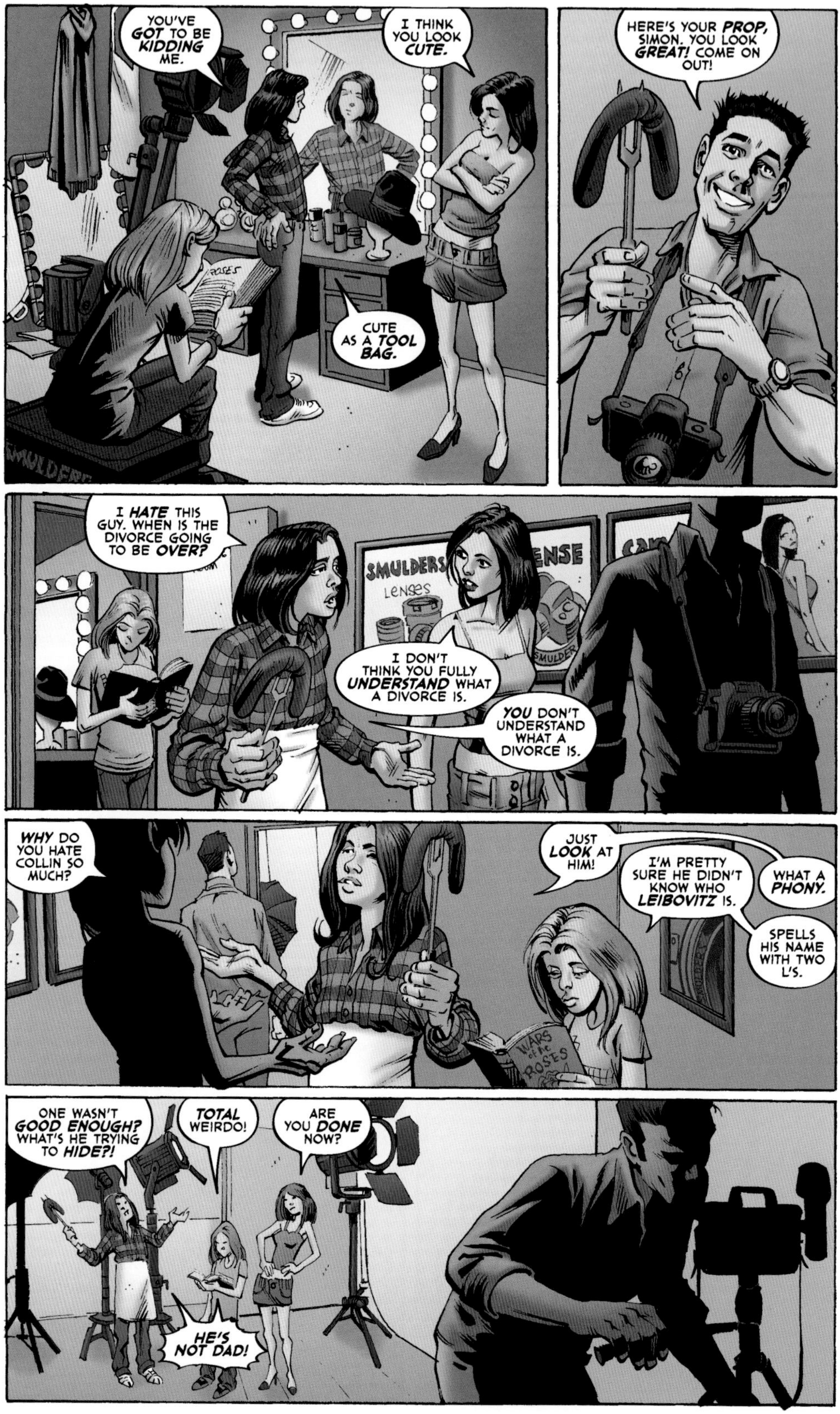
YOU'VE GOT TO BE KIDDING ME.
I THINK YOU LOOK CUTE.
CUTE AS A TOOL BAG.
ROSES
SMULDERS
HERE'S YOUR PROP, SIMON. YOU LOOK GREAT! COME ON OUT!
I HATE THIS GUY. WHEN IS THE DIVORCE GOING TO BE OVER?
SMULDERS
LENSES
ENSE
I DON'T THINK YOU FULLY UNDERSTAND WHAT A DIVORCE IS.
YOU DON'T UNDERSTAND WHAT A DIVORCE IS.
SMULDER
WHY DO YOU HATE COLLIN SO MUCH?
JUST LOOK AT HIM!
WHAT A PHONY.
I'M PRETTY SURE HE DIDN'T KNOW WHO LEIBOVITZ IS.
SPELLS HIS NAME WITH TWO L'S.
WARS of the ROSES
ONE WASN'T GOOD ENOUGH? WHAT'S HE TRYING TO HIDE?!
TOTAL WEIRDO!
ARE YOU DONE NOW?
HE'S NOT DAD!

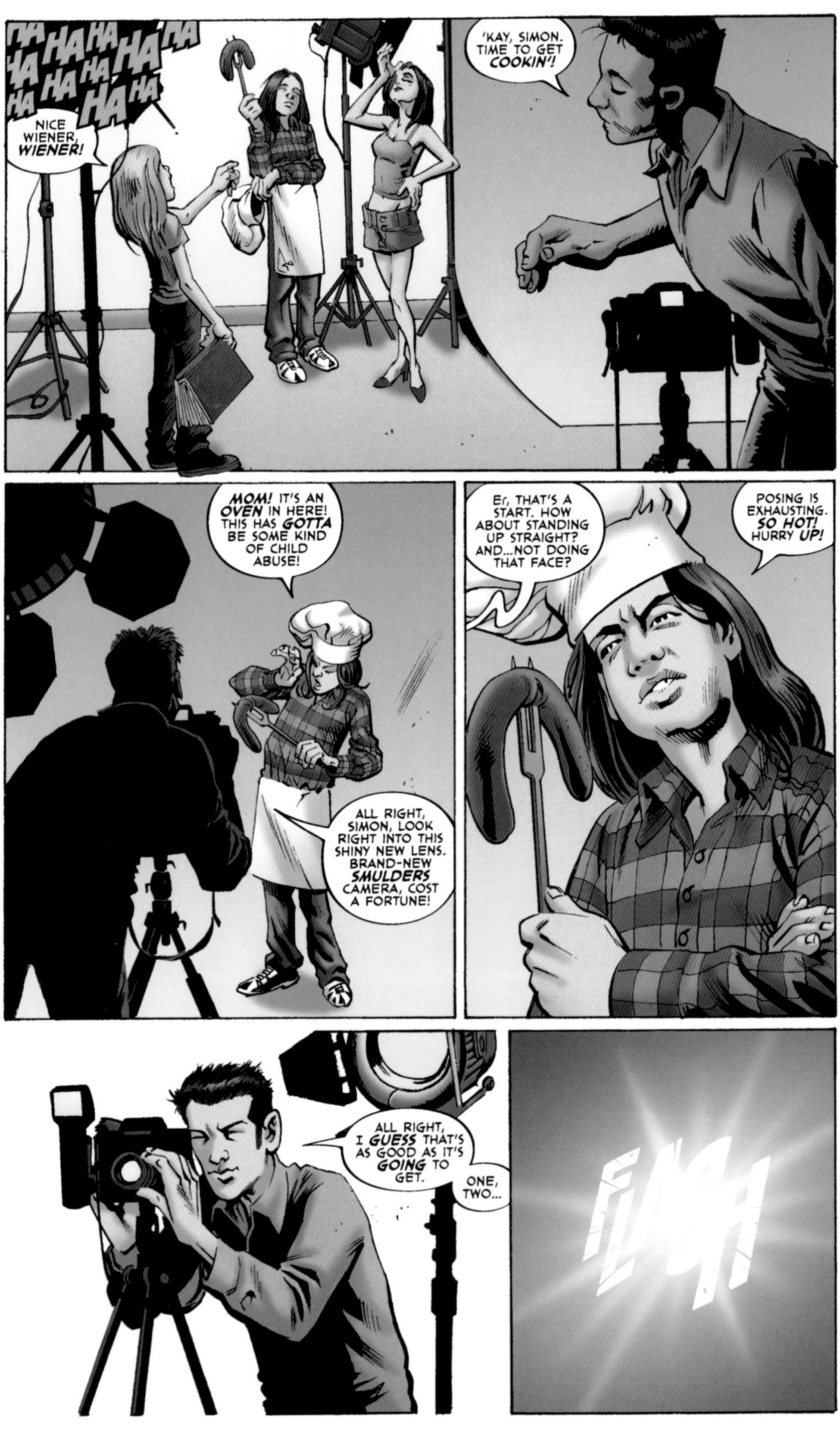
HA HA HA HA HA HA HA HA HA HA HA HA
NICE WIENER, WIENER!
'KAY, SIMON. TIME TO GET COOKIN'!
MOM! IT'S AN OVEN IN HERE! THIS HAS GOTTA BE SOME KIND OF CHILD ABUSE!
ALL RIGHT, SIMON, LOOK RIGHT INTO THIS SHINY NEW LENS. BRAND-NEW SMULDERS CAMERA, COST A FORTUNE!
Er, THAT'S A START. HOW ABOUT STANDING UP STRAIGHT? AND...NOT DOING THAT FACE?
POSING IS EXHAUSTING. SO HOT! HURRY UP!
ALL RIGHT, I GUESS THAT'S AS GOOD AS IT'S GOING TO GET.
ONE, TWO...
FLASH

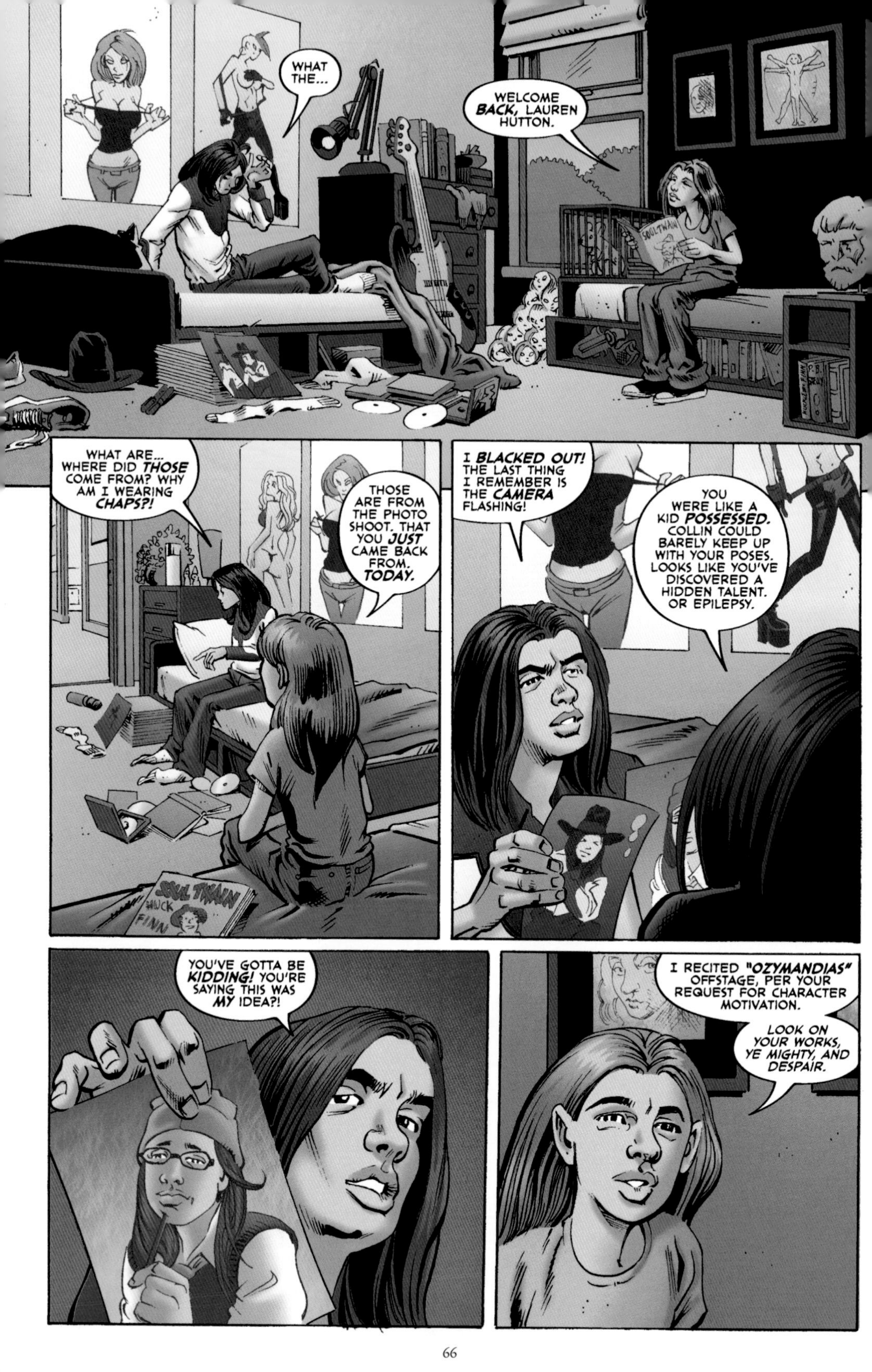
WHAT THE...
WELCOME BACK, LAUREN HUTTON.
WHAT ARE... WHERE DID THOSE COME FROM? WHY AM I WEARING CHAPS?!
THOSE ARE FROM THE PHOTO SHOOT. THAT YOU JUST CAME BACK FROM. TODAY.
I BLACKED OUT! THE LAST THING I REMEMBER IS THE CAMERA FLASHING!
YOU WERE LIKE A KID POSSESSED. COLLIN COULD BARELY KEEP UP WITH YOUR POSES. LOOKS LIKE YOU'VE DISCOVERED A HIDDEN TALENT. OR EPILEPSY.
YOU'VE GOTTA BE KIDDING! YOU'RE SAYING THIS WAS MY IDEA?!
I RECITED "OZYMANDIAS" OFFSTAGE, PER YOUR REQUEST FOR CHARACTER MOTIVATION.
LOOK ON YOUR WORKS, YE MIGHTY, AND DESPAIR.

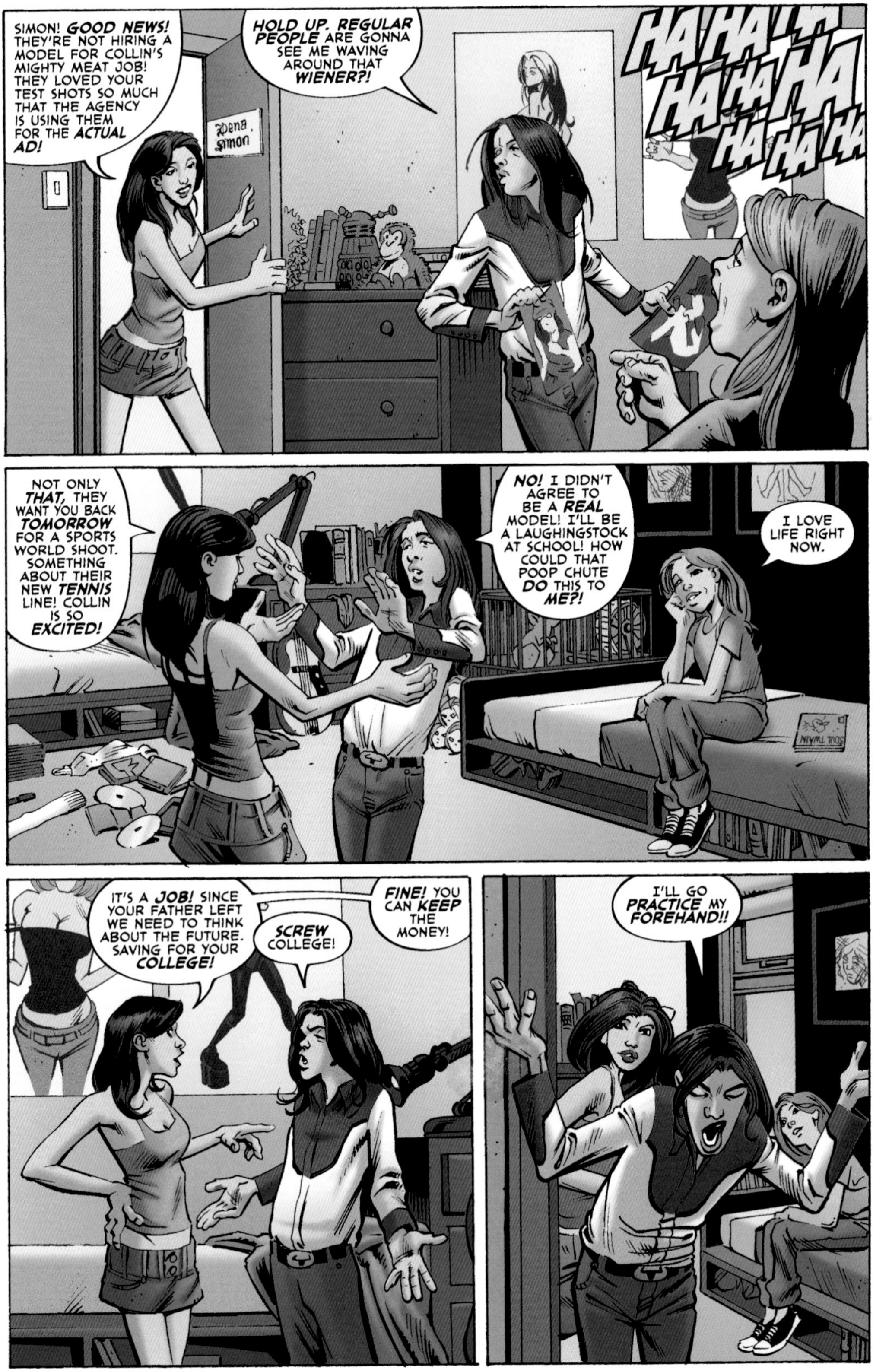
SIMON! GOOD NEWS! THEY'RE NOT HIRING A MODEL FOR COLLIN'S MIGHTY MEAT JOB! THEY LOVED YOUR TEST SHOTS SO MUCH THAT THE AGENCY IS USING THEM FOR THE ACTUAL AD!
Dena Simon
HOLD UP. REGULAR PEOPLE ARE GONNA SEE ME WAVING AROUND THAT WIENER?!
HA HA HA HA HA HA HA HA HA HA
NOT ONLY THAT, THEY WANT YOU BACK TOMORROW FOR A SPORTS WORLD SHOOT. SOMETHING ABOUT THEIR NEW TENNIS LINE! COLLIN IS SO EXCITED!
NO! I DIDN'T AGREE TO BE A REAL MODEL! I'LL BE A LAUGHINGSTOCK AT SCHOOL! HOW COULD THAT POOP CHUTE DO THIS TO ME?!
I LOVE LIFE RIGHT NOW.
IT'S A JOB! SINCE YOUR FATHER LEFT WE NEED TO THINK ABOUT THE FUTURE. SAVING FOR YOUR COLLEGE!
SCREW COLLEGE!
FINE! YOU CAN KEEP THE MONEY!
I'LL GO PRACTICE MY FOREHAND!!

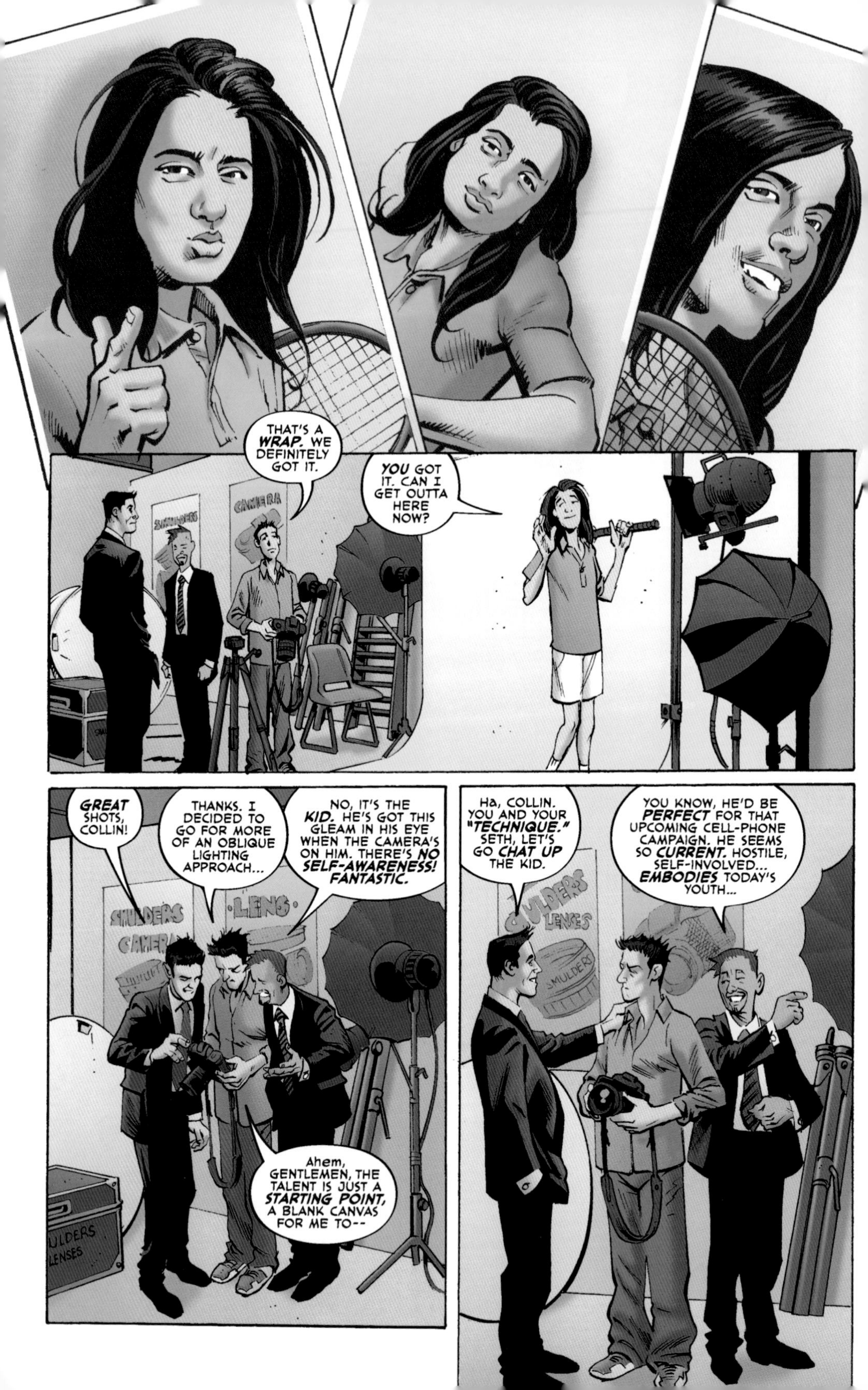

CAMERA
SMULDERS
THAT'S A WRAP. WE DEFINITELY GOT IT.
YOU GOT IT. CAN I GET OUTTA HERE NOW?
GREAT SHOTS, COLLIN!
THANKS. I DECIDED TO GO FOR MORE OF AN OBLIQUE LIGHTING APPROACH...
NO, IT'S THE KID. HE'S GOT THIS GLEAM IN HIS EYE WHEN THE CAMERA'S ON HIM. THERE'S NO SELF-AWARENESS! FANTASTIC.
SMULDERS CAMERA
LENS
Ahem, GENTLEMEN, THE TALENT IS JUST A STARTING POINT, A BLANK CANVAS FOR ME TO--
ULDERS LENSES
Ha, COLLIN. YOU AND YOUR "TECHNIQUE." SETH, LET'S GO CHAT UP THE KID.
YOU KNOW, HE'D BE PERFECT FOR THAT UPCOMING CELL-PHONE CAMPAIGN. HE SEEMS SO CURRENT. HOSTILE, SELF-INVOLVED... EMBODIES TODAY'S YOUTH...
ULDERS LENSES
SMULDERS

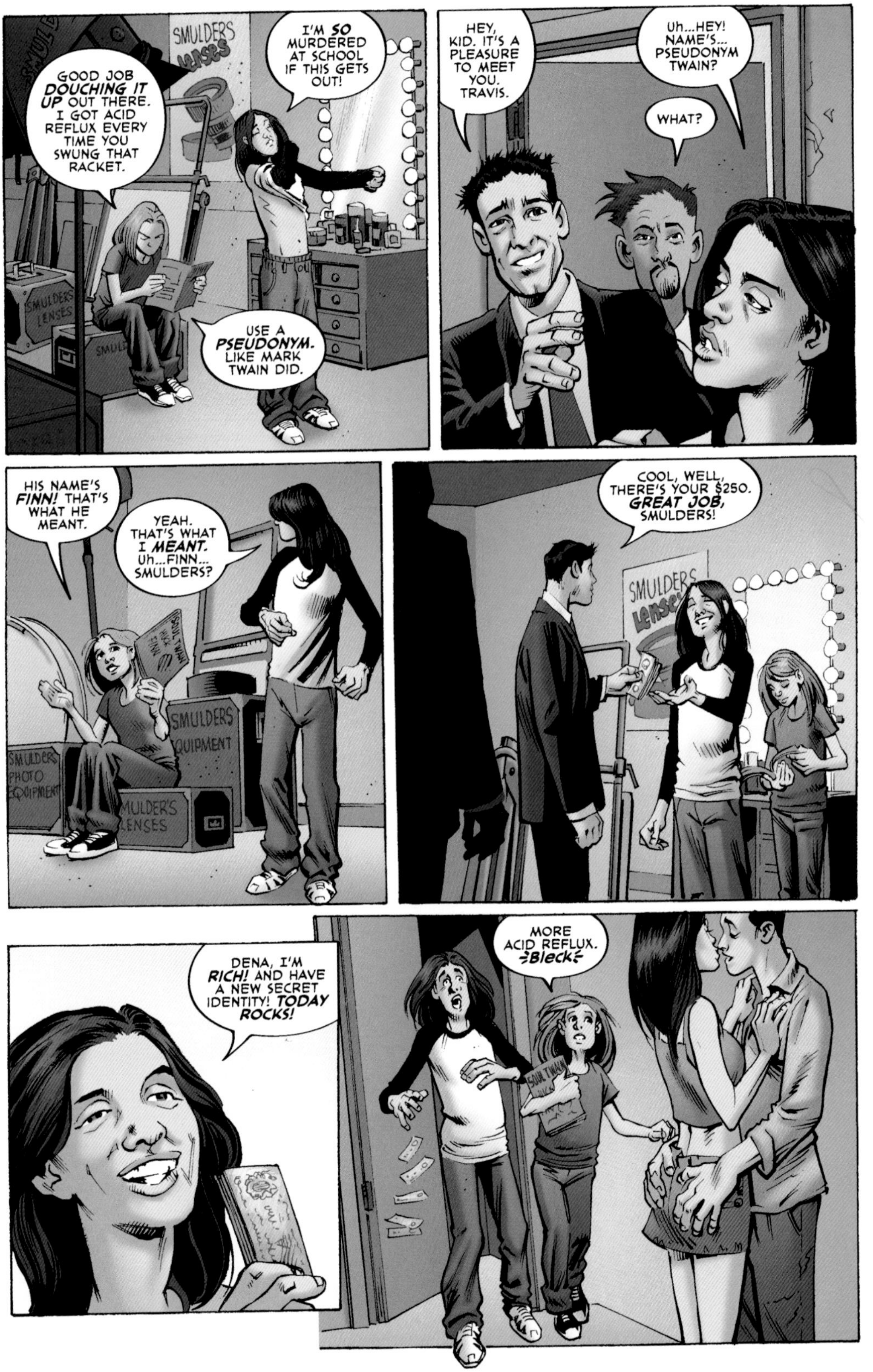
GOOD JOB DOUCHING IT UP OUT THERE. I GOT ACID REFLUX EVERY TIME YOU SWUNG THAT RACKET.
I'M SO MURDERED AT SCHOOL IF THIS GETS OUT!
USE A PSEUDONYM. LIKE MARK TWAIN DID.
SMULDERS LENSES
HEY, KID. IT'S A PLEASURE TO MEET YOU. TRAVIS.
Uh...HEY! NAME'S... PSEUDONYM TWAIN?
WHAT?
HIS NAME'S FINN! THAT'S WHAT HE MEANT.
YEAH. THAT'S WHAT I MEANT. Uh...FINN... SMULDERS?
SMULDERS EQUIPMENT
SMULDERS PHOTO EQUIPMENT
SMULDER'S LENSES
COOL, WELL, THERE'S YOUR $250. GREAT JOB, SMULDERS!
DENA, I'M RICH! AND HAVE A NEW SECRET IDENTITY! TODAY ROCKS!
MORE ACID REFLUX. Bleck

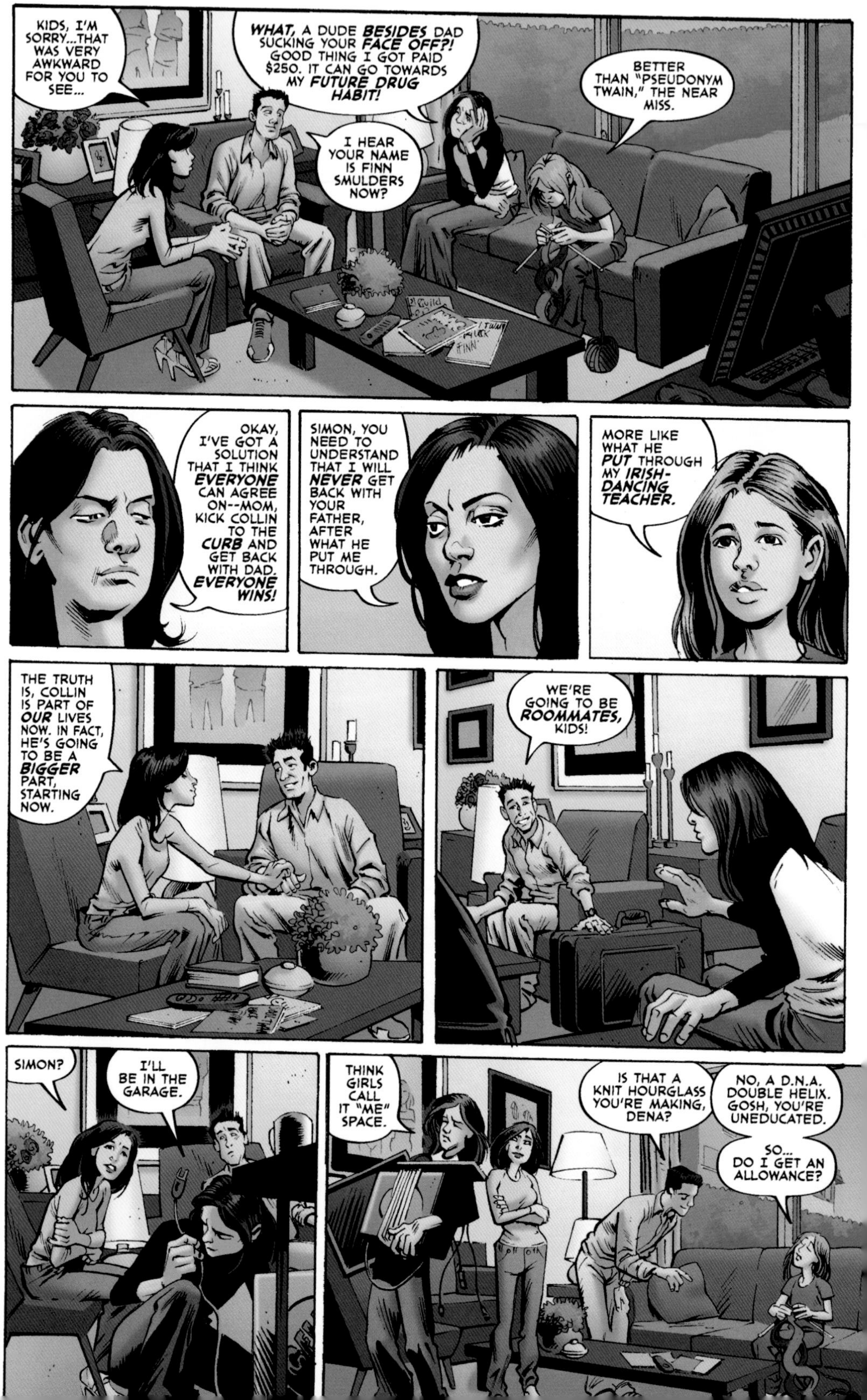
KIDS, I'M SORRY...THAT WAS VERY AWKWARD FOR YOU TO SEE...
WHAT, A DUDE BESIDES DAD SUCKING YOUR FACE OFF?! GOOD THING I GOT PAID $250. IT CAN GO TOWARDS MY FUTURE DRUG HABIT!
I HEAR YOUR NAME IS FINN SMULDERS NOW?
BETTER THAN "PSEUDONYM TWAIN," THE NEAR MISS.
OKAY, I'VE GOT A SOLUTION THAT I THINK EVERYONE CAN AGREE ON--MOM, KICK COLLIN TO THE CURB AND GET BACK WITH DAD. EVERYONE WINS!
SIMON, YOU NEED TO UNDERSTAND THAT I WILL NEVER GET BACK WITH YOUR FATHER, AFTER WHAT HE PUT ME THROUGH.
MORE LIKE WHAT HE PUT THROUGH MY IRISH-DANCING TEACHER.
THE TRUTH IS, COLLIN IS PART OF OUR LIVES NOW. IN FACT, HE'S GOING TO BE A BIGGER PART, STARTING NOW.
WE'RE GOING TO BE ROOMMATES, KIDS!
SIMON?
I'LL BE IN THE GARAGE.
THINK GIRLS CALL IT "ME" SPACE.
IS THAT A KNIT HOURGLASS YOU'RE MAKING, DENA?
NO, A D.N.A. DOUBLE HELIX. GOSH, YOU'RE UNEDUCATED.
SO... DO I GET AN ALLOWANCE?

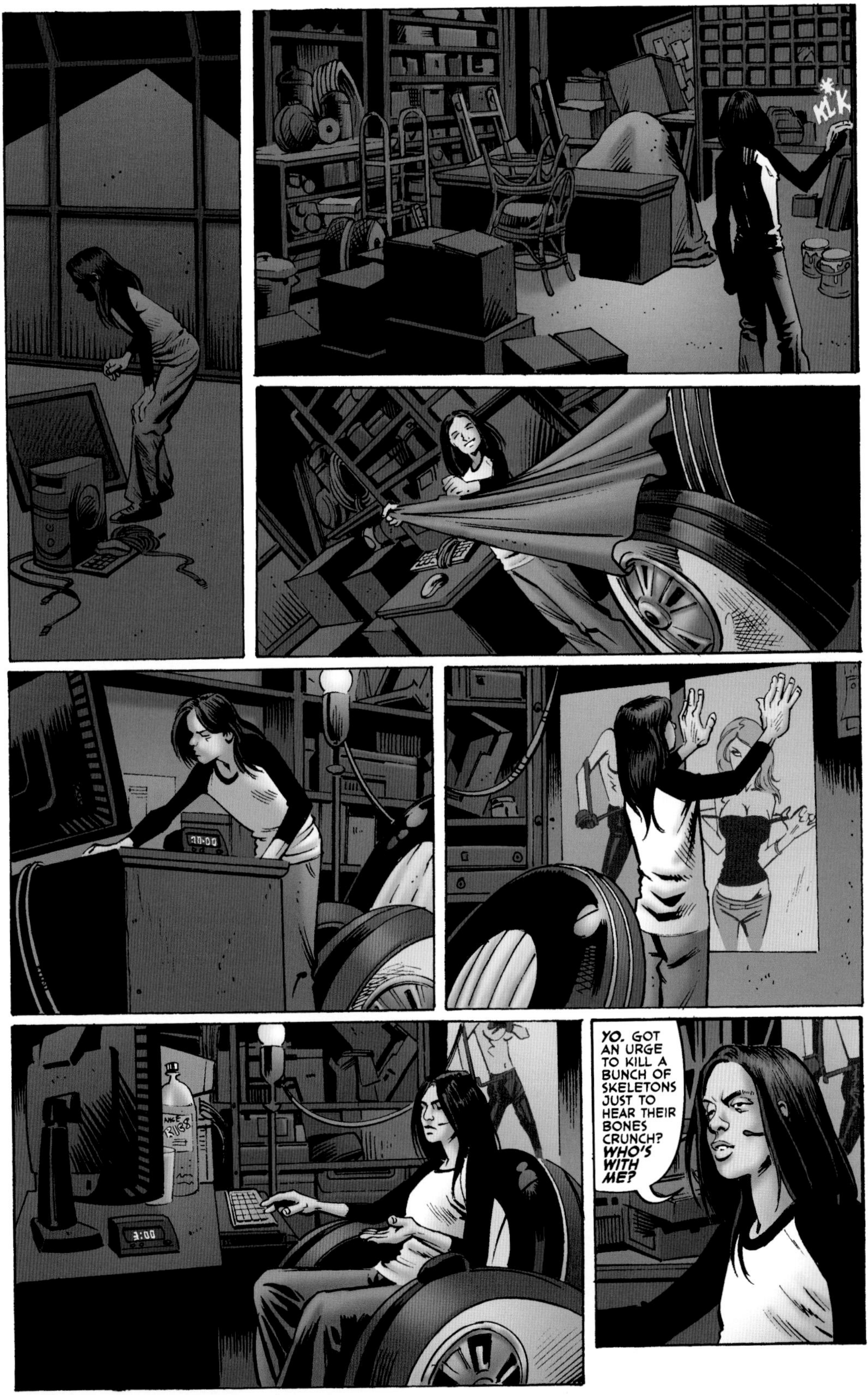
KLIK
YO. GOT AN URGE TO KILL A BUNCH OF SKELETONS JUST TO HEAR THEIR BONES CRUNCH? WHO'S WITH ME?

OVERTIME IS OVERRATED

3.00

WE'RE THE ONLY ONES ONLINE. BUT *I'LL* JOIN YOU. GLADLY.

WHOA, WHERE'S THE USUAL *RULES BOOB?* USUALLY YOU GOTTA CHECK YOUR *SPREADSHEET AGENDA* BEFORE YOU AGREE TO *ANYTHING.*

DAMN! I'VE HAD THE WORST DAY *EVER*, DUDE! DON'T RUB IT IN!

TODAY, RULES CAN BE BROKEN. I'VE JUST CLEARED THREE DUNGEONS SOLO, MADE FIVE THOUSAND GOLD IN FOUR HOURS. VORK IS DOING *FANTASTIC.*

PARDON. MY *SEMANTICS* ARE OFF. *VORK* IS DOING GREAT. *ME*, ON THE OTHER HAND...

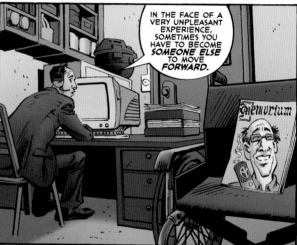

IN THE FACE OF A VERY UNPLEASANT EXPERIENCE, SOMETIMES YOU HAVE TO BECOME *SOMEONE ELSE* TO MOVE *FORWARD.*

Huh. THAT'S SOME *DEEP* WORDS, DUDE.

WHATEVER. LET'S *DOUBLE-TEAM* THE SKELLIES SO WE GET REVERB SKULL CRUNCHING, 'KAY?

I KNOW. NORMALLY I WOULDN'T WASTE THEM ON YOU, BUT MY *EMOTIONAL SHIELDS* ARE DOWN. YOU SEE, TODAY MY *GRANDFA*--

AGREED.

BLADEZZ AND VORK *HO!*

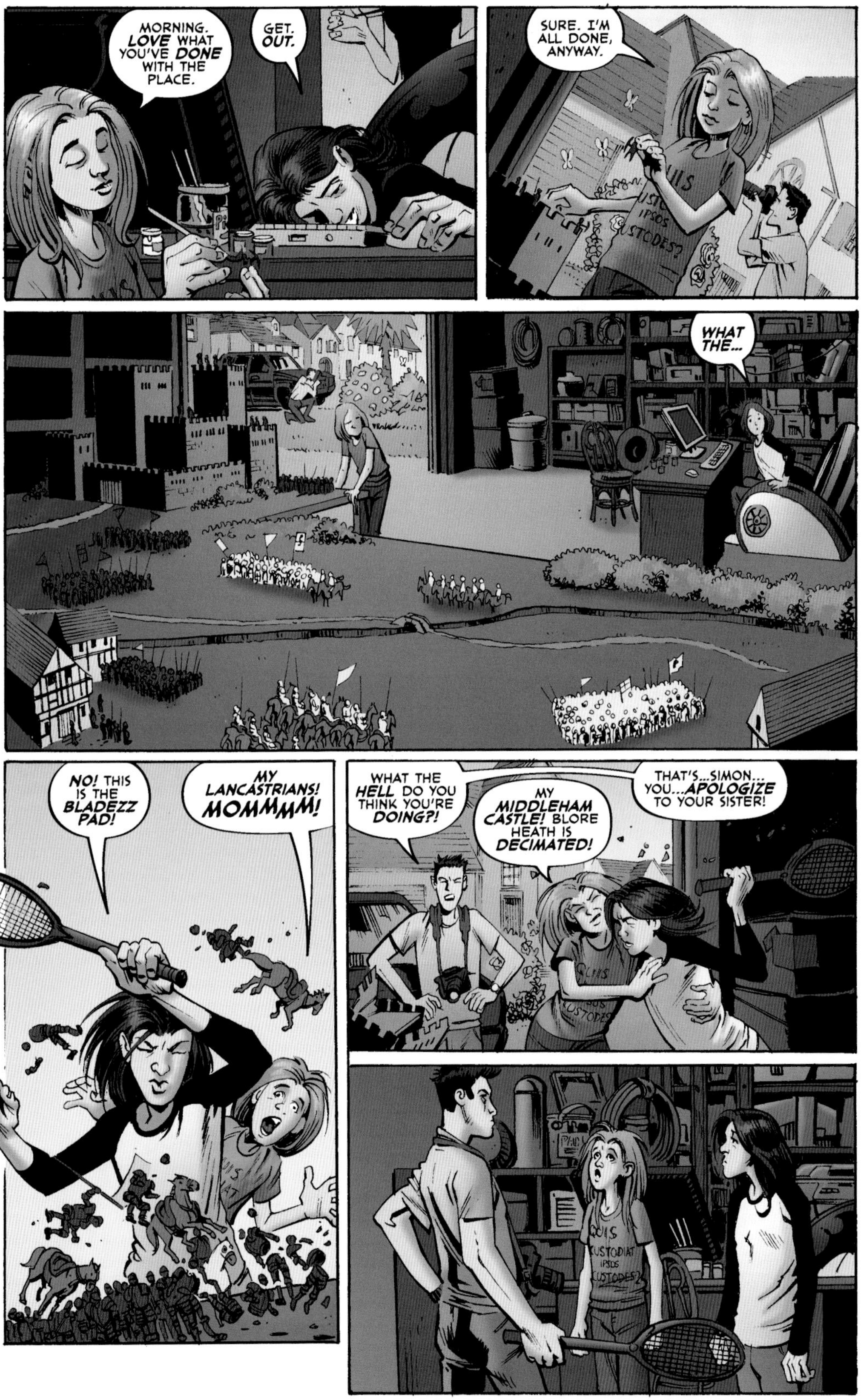

MORNING. LOVE WHAT YOU'VE DONE WITH THE PLACE.
GET. OUT.
SURE. I'M ALL DONE, ANYWAY.
QUIS CUSTODIAT IPSOS CUSTODES?
WHAT THE...
NO! THIS IS THE BLADEZZ PAD!
MY LANCASTRIANS! MOMMMM!
WHAT THE HELL DO YOU THINK YOU'RE DOING?!
MY MIDDLEHAM CASTLE! BLORE HEATH IS DECIMATED!
THAT'S...SIMON... YOU...APOLOGIZE TO YOUR SISTER!
QUIS CUSTODIAT IPSOS CUSTODES?

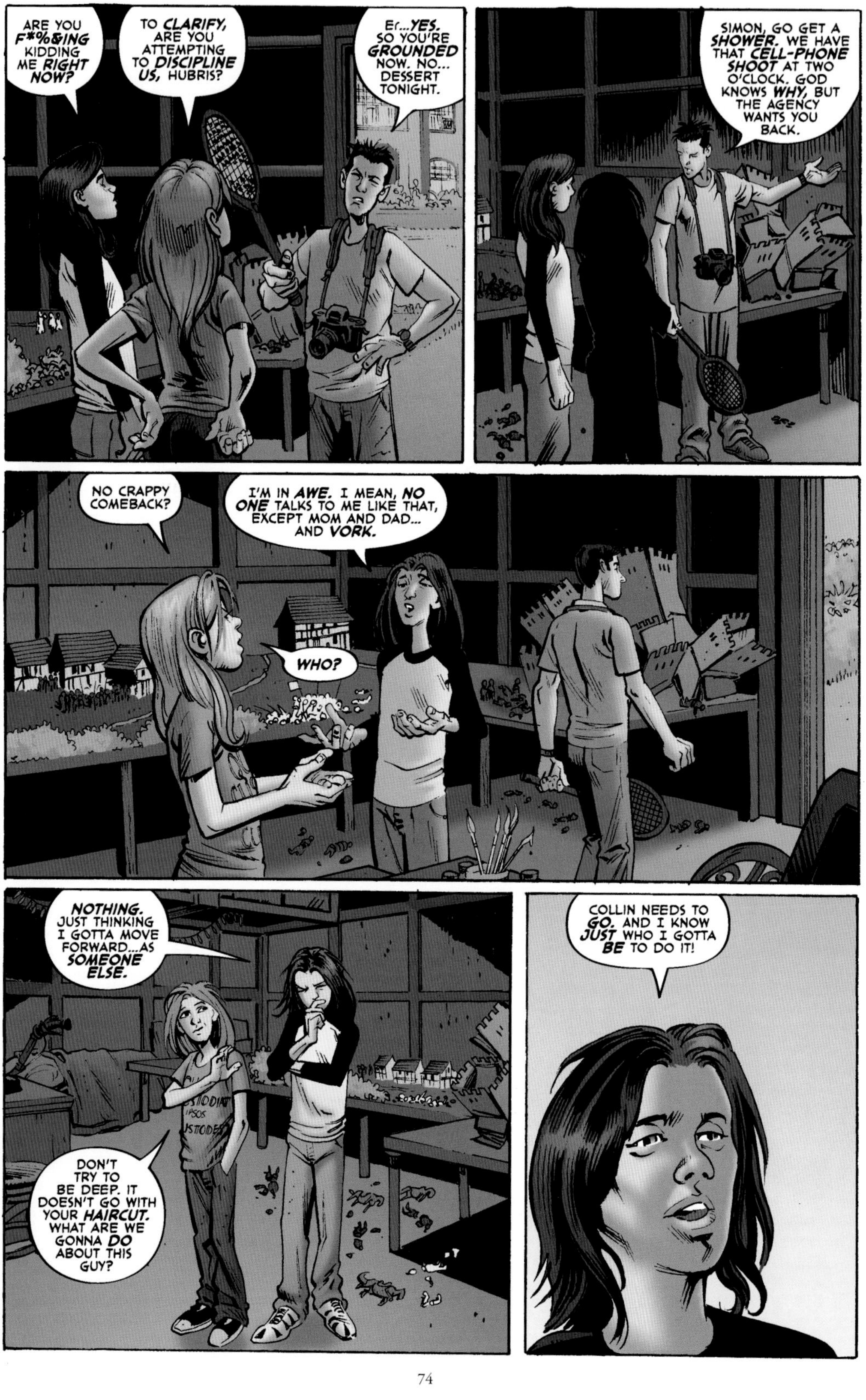
ARE YOU F*%&ING KIDDING ME RIGHT NOW?
TO CLARIFY, ARE YOU ATTEMPTING TO DISCIPLINE US, HUBRIS?
Er...YES. SO YOU'RE GROUNDED NOW. NO... DESSERT TONIGHT.
SIMON, GO GET A SHOWER. WE HAVE THAT CELL-PHONE SHOOT AT TWO O'CLOCK. GOD KNOWS WHY, BUT THE AGENCY WANTS YOU BACK.
NO CRAPPY COMEBACK?
I'M IN AWE. I MEAN, NO ONE TALKS TO ME LIKE THAT, EXCEPT MOM AND DAD... AND VORK.
WHO?
NOTHING. JUST THINKING I GOTTA MOVE FORWARD...AS SOMEONE ELSE.
DON'T TRY TO BE DEEP. IT DOESN'T GO WITH YOUR HAIRCUT. WHAT ARE WE GONNA DO ABOUT THIS GUY?
COLLIN NEEDS TO GO. AND I KNOW JUST WHO I GOTTA BE TO DO IT!

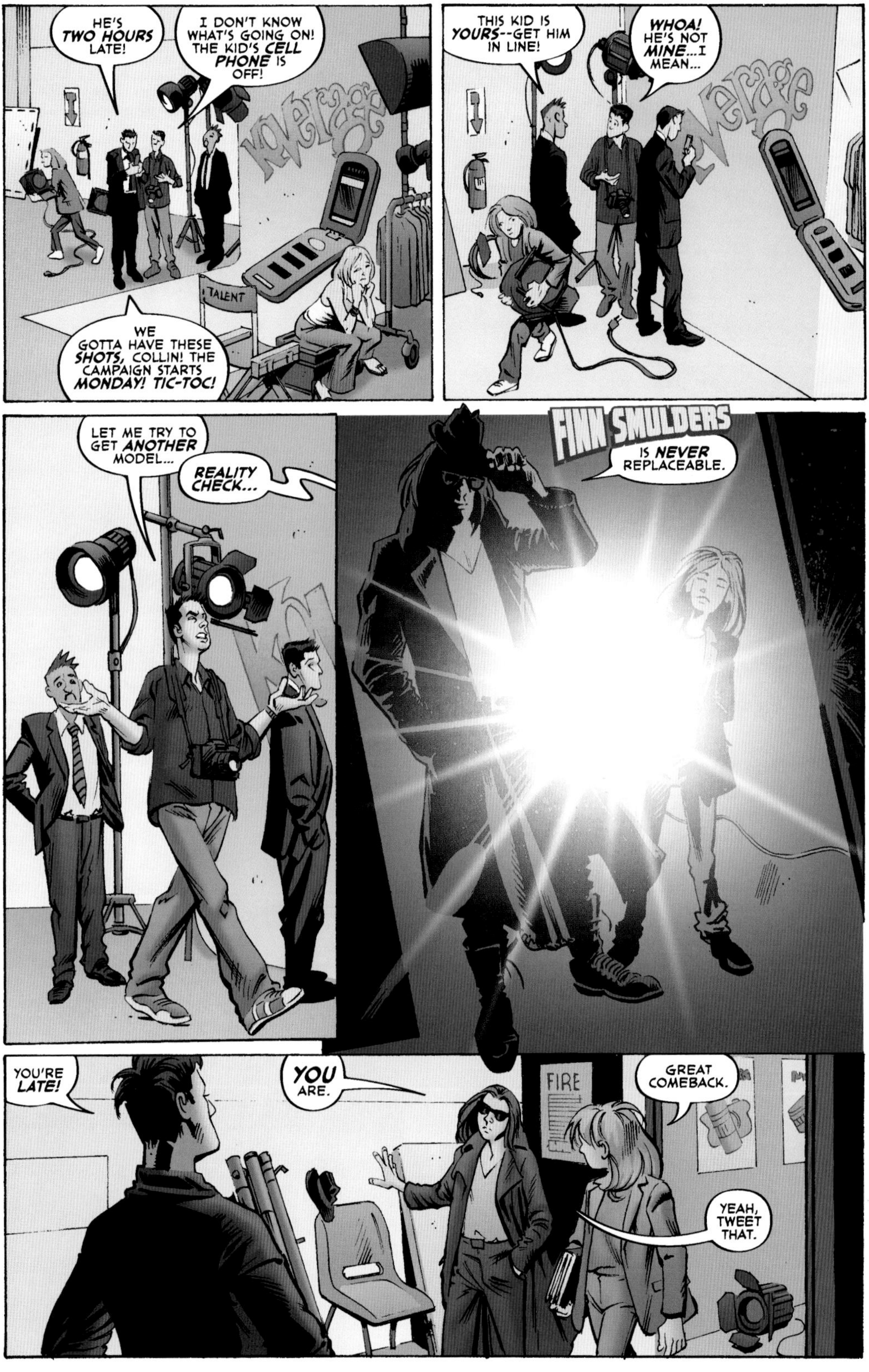
HE'S TWO HOURS LATE!
I DON'T KNOW WHAT'S GOING ON! THE KID'S CELL PHONE IS OFF!
WE GOTTA HAVE THESE SHOTS, COLLIN! THE CAMPAIGN STARTS MONDAY! TIC-TOC!
TALENT
THIS KID IS YOURS--GET HIM IN LINE!
WHOA! HE'S NOT MINE...I MEAN...
LET ME TRY TO GET ANOTHER MODEL...
REALITY CHECK...
FINN SMULDERS IS NEVER REPLACEABLE.
YOU'RE LATE!
YOU ARE.
FIRE
GREAT COMEBACK.
YEAH, TWEET THAT.

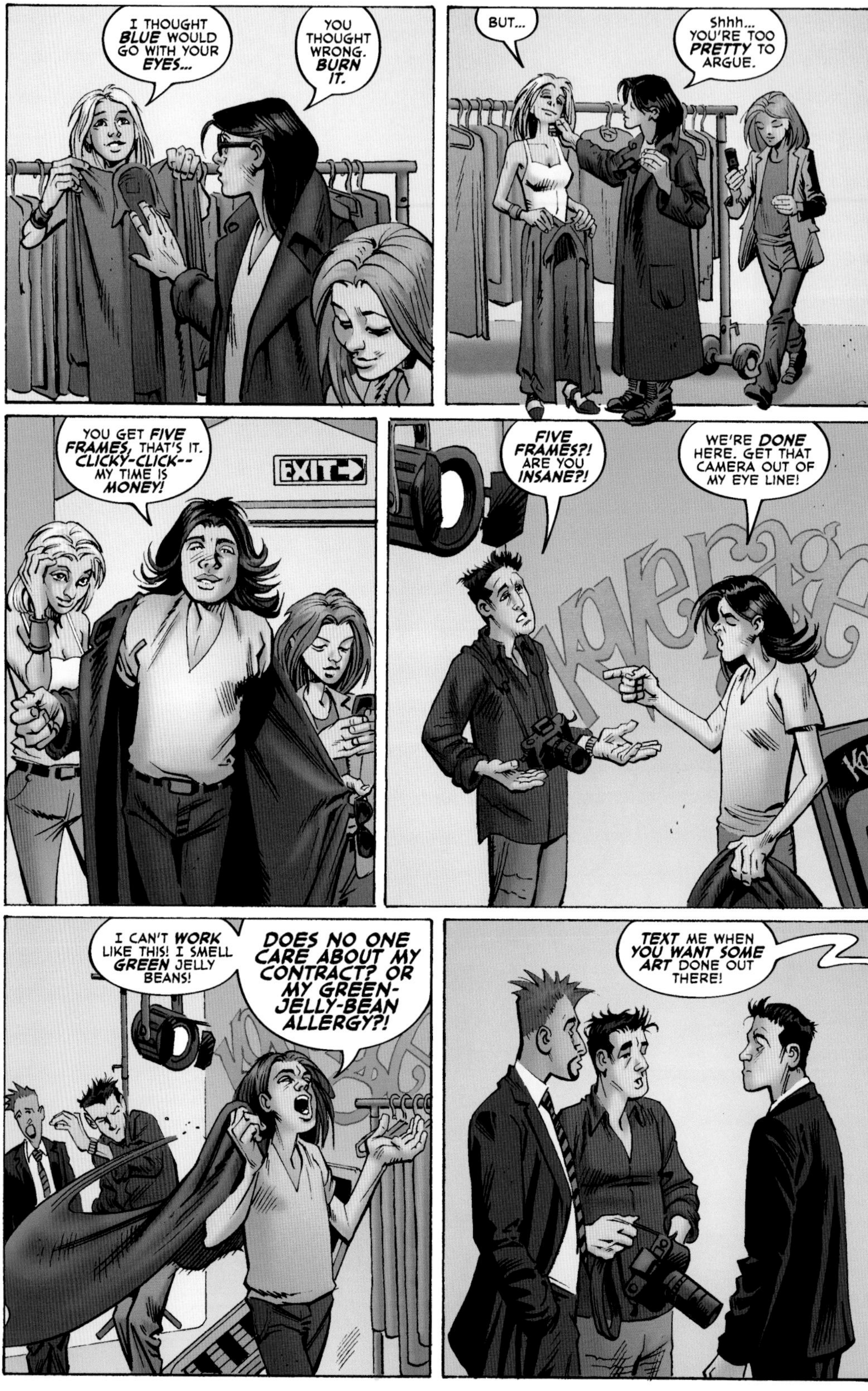
I THOUGHT BLUE WOULD GO WITH YOUR EYES...
YOU THOUGHT WRONG. BURN IT.
BUT...
Shhh... YOU'RE TOO PRETTY TO ARGUE.
YOU GET FIVE FRAMES, THAT'S IT. CLICKY-CLICK-- MY TIME IS MONEY!
EXIT
FIVE FRAMES?! ARE YOU INSANE?!
WE'RE DONE HERE. GET THAT CAMERA OUT OF MY EYE LINE!
I CAN'T WORK LIKE THIS! I SMELL GREEN JELLY BEANS!
DOES NO ONE CARE ABOUT MY CONTRACT? OR MY GREEN-JELLY-BEAN ALLERGY?!
TEXT ME WHEN YOU WANT SOME ART DONE OUT THERE!

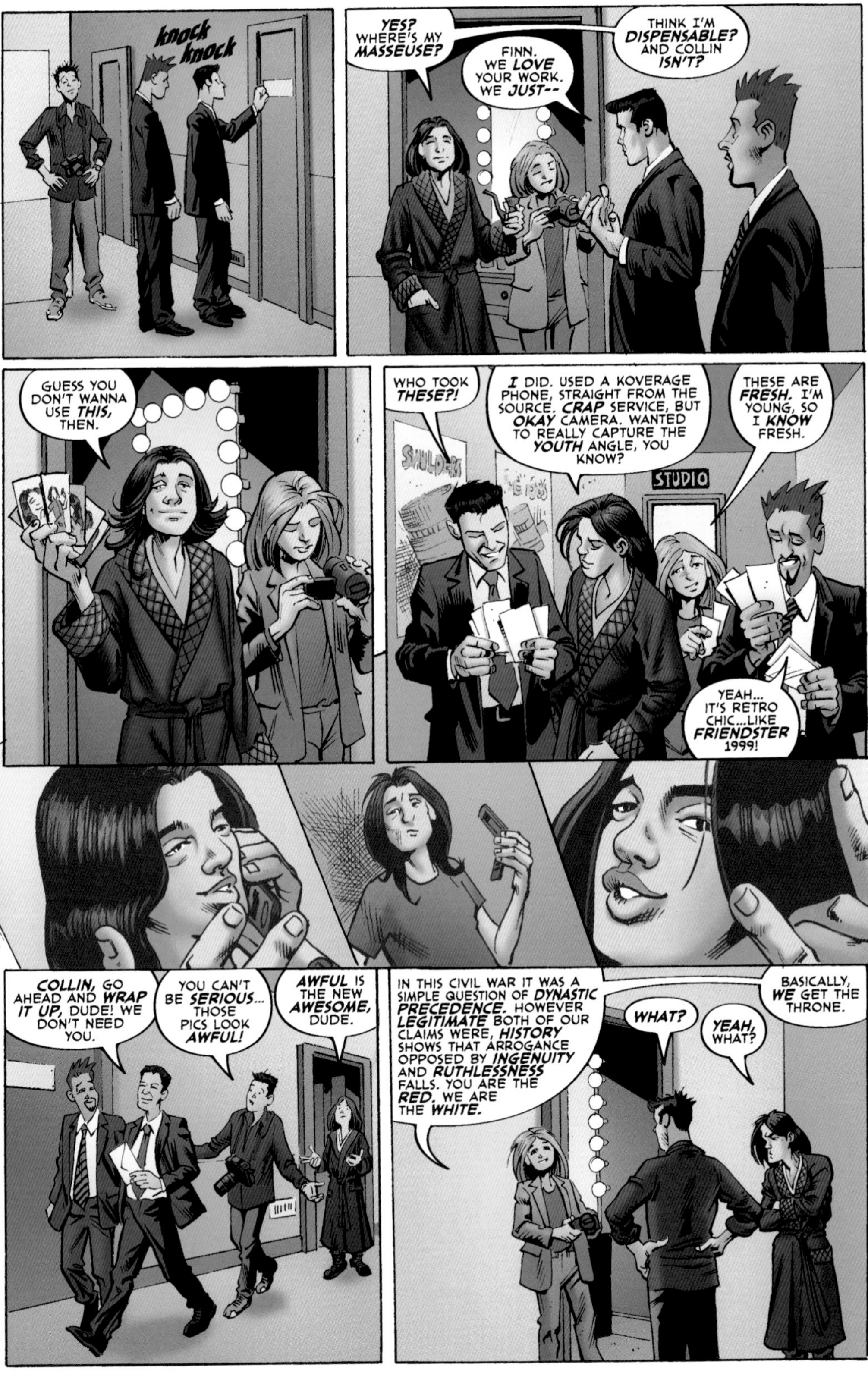
knock knock
YES? WHERE'S MY MASSEUSE?
FINN. WE LOVE YOUR WORK. WE JUST--
THINK I'M DISPENSABLE? AND COLLIN ISN'T?
GUESS YOU DON'T WANNA USE THIS, THEN.
WHO TOOK THESE?!
I DID. USED A KOVERAGE PHONE, STRAIGHT FROM THE SOURCE. CRAP SERVICE, BUT OKAY CAMERA. WANTED TO REALLY CAPTURE THE YOUTH ANGLE, YOU KNOW?
THESE ARE FRESH. I'M YOUNG, SO I KNOW FRESH.
STUDIO
YEAH... IT'S RETRO CHIC...LIKE FRIENDSTER 1999!
COLLIN, GO AHEAD AND WRAP IT UP, DUDE! WE DON'T NEED YOU.
YOU CAN'T BE SERIOUS... THOSE PICS LOOK AWFUL!
AWFUL IS THE NEW AWESOME, DUDE.
IN THIS CIVIL WAR IT WAS A SIMPLE QUESTION OF DYNASTIC PRECEDENCE. HOWEVER LEGITIMATE BOTH OF OUR CLAIMS WERE, HISTORY SHOWS THAT ARROGANCE OPPOSED BY INGENUITY AND RUTHLESSNESS FALLS. YOU ARE THE RED. WE ARE THE WHITE.
WHAT?
YEAH, WHAT?
BASICALLY, WE GET THE THRONE.

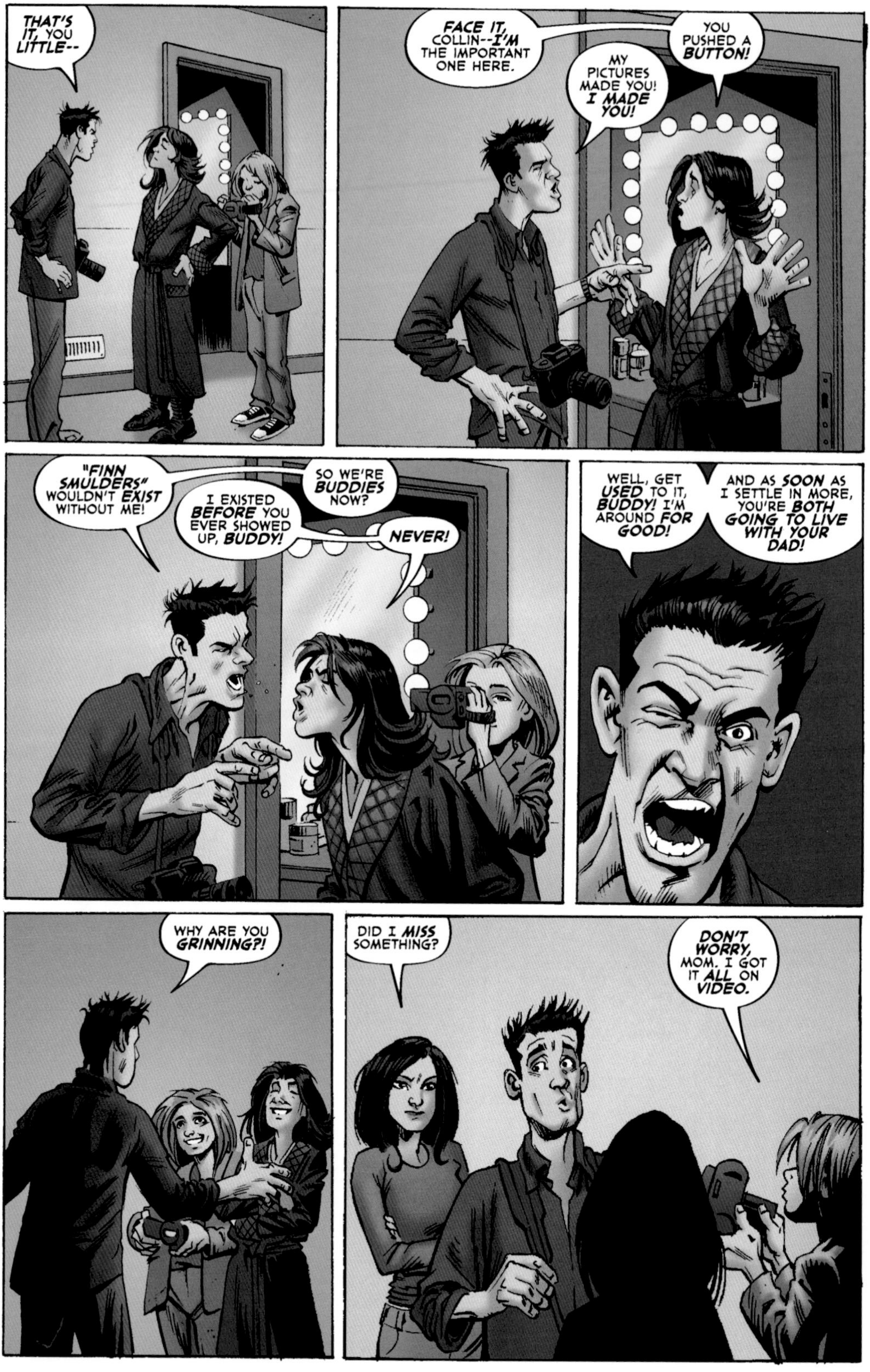
THAT'S IT, YOU LITTLE--
FACE IT, COLLIN--I'M THE IMPORTANT ONE HERE.
MY PICTURES MADE YOU! I MADE YOU!
YOU PUSHED A BUTTON!
"FINN SMULDERS" WOULDN'T EXIST WITHOUT ME!
I EXISTED BEFORE YOU EVER SHOWED UP, BUDDY!
SO WE'RE BUDDIES NOW?
NEVER!
WELL, GET USED TO IT, BUDDY! I'M AROUND FOR GOOD!
AND AS SOON AS I SETTLE IN MORE, YOU'RE BOTH GOING TO LIVE WITH YOUR DAD!
WHY ARE YOU GRINNING?!
DID I MISS SOMETHING?
DON'T WORRY, MOM. I GOT IT ALL ON VIDEO.

...YOU CAN CHALK IT UP TO ARTISTIC TEMPERAMENT? PLEASE...

COLLIN, IT'S JUST TOO SOON. WE JUST... NEED TO PUT THE BRAKES ON. UH... FOREVER.

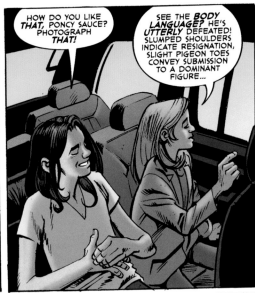

HOW DO YOU LIKE THAT, PONCY SAUCE? PHOTOGRAPH THAT!

SEE THE BODY LANGUAGE? HE'S UTTERLY DEFEATED! SLUMPED SHOULDERS INDICATE RESIGNATION, SLIGHT PIGEON TOES CONVEY SUBMISSION TO A DOMINANT FIGURE...

IS THIS A NEW WEIRD HOBBY? READING PEOPLE?

THE PROPER TERMINOLOGY IS "KINESICS." WAR OF THE ROSES HAS BEEN PLAYED.

OKAY, KIDS. UH, I'M SORRY COLLIN YELLED AT YOU. HE WON'T BE AROUND ANYMORE.

I JUST WANT TO LET YOU KNOW, WHATEVER HAPPENS, YOU GUYS COME FIRST, OKAY?

COOL. CAN WE GET SOME BURGERS?

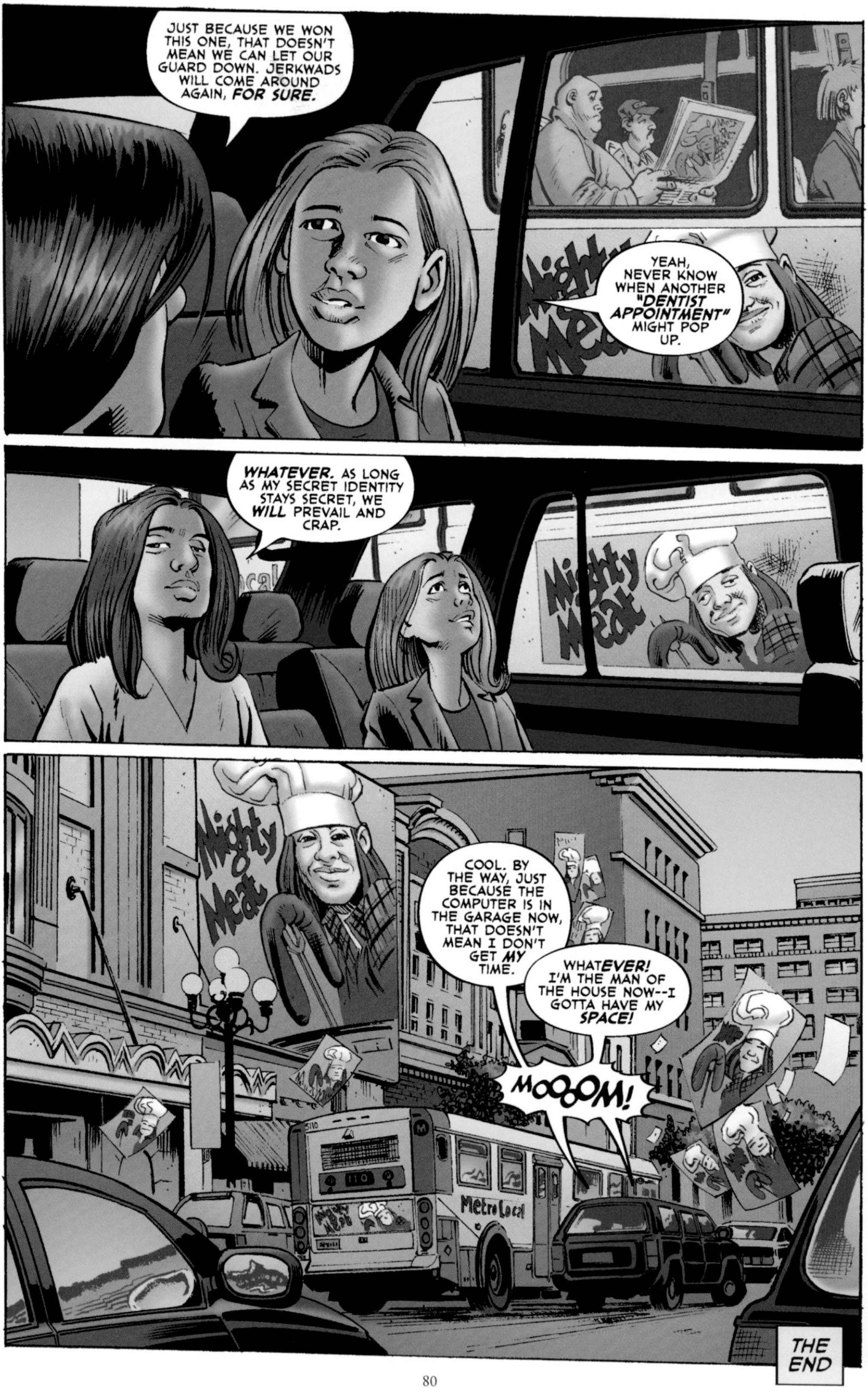
JUST BECAUSE WE WON THIS ONE, THAT DOESN'T MEAN WE CAN LET OUR GUARD DOWN. JERKWADS WILL COME AROUND AGAIN, FOR SURE.
YEAH, NEVER KNOW WHEN ANOTHER "DENTIST APPOINTMENT" MIGHT POP UP.
Mighty Meat
WHATEVER. AS LONG AS MY SECRET IDENTITY STAYS SECRET, WE WILL PREVAIL AND CRAP.
Mighty Meat
Mighty Meat
COOL. BY THE WAY, JUST BECAUSE THE COMPUTER IS IN THE GARAGE NOW, THAT DOESN'T MEAN I DON'T GET MY TIME.
WHATEVER! I'M THE MAN OF THE HOUSE NOW--I GOTTA HAVE MY SPACE!
MOOOOM!
Metro Local
THE END

CHAPTER FOUR
CLARA

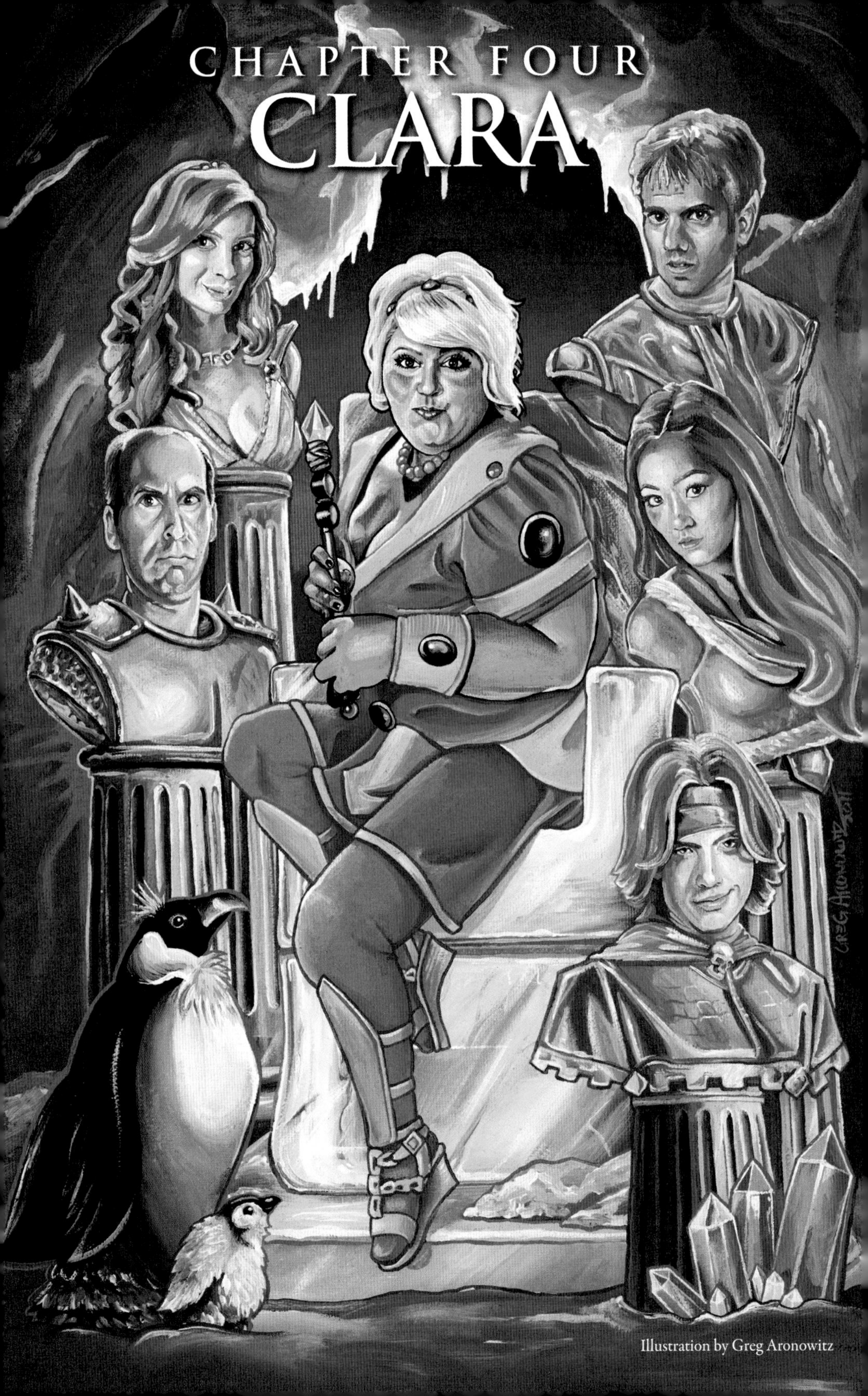

Illustration by Greg Aronowitz

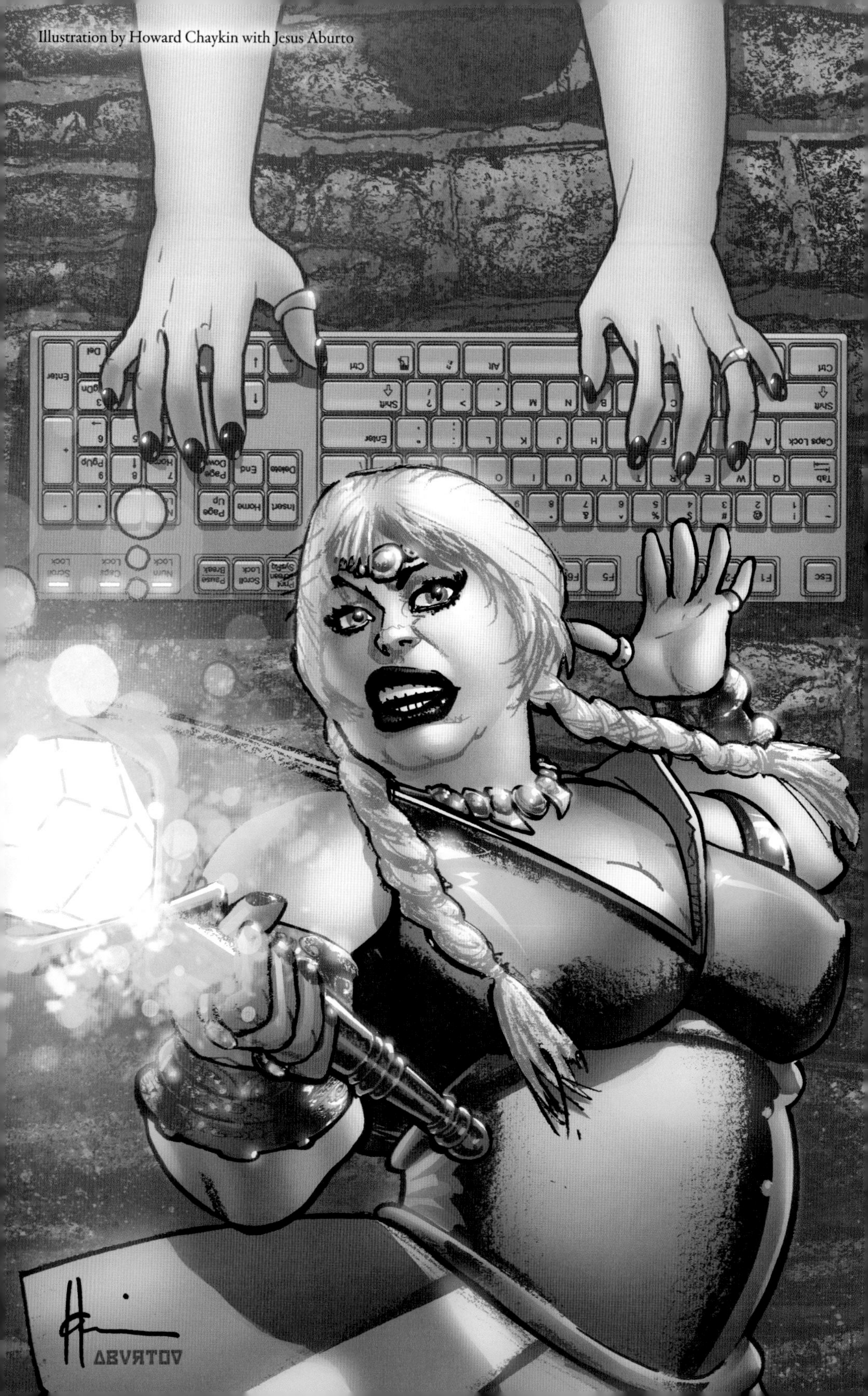
Illustration by Howard Chaykin with Jesus Aburto

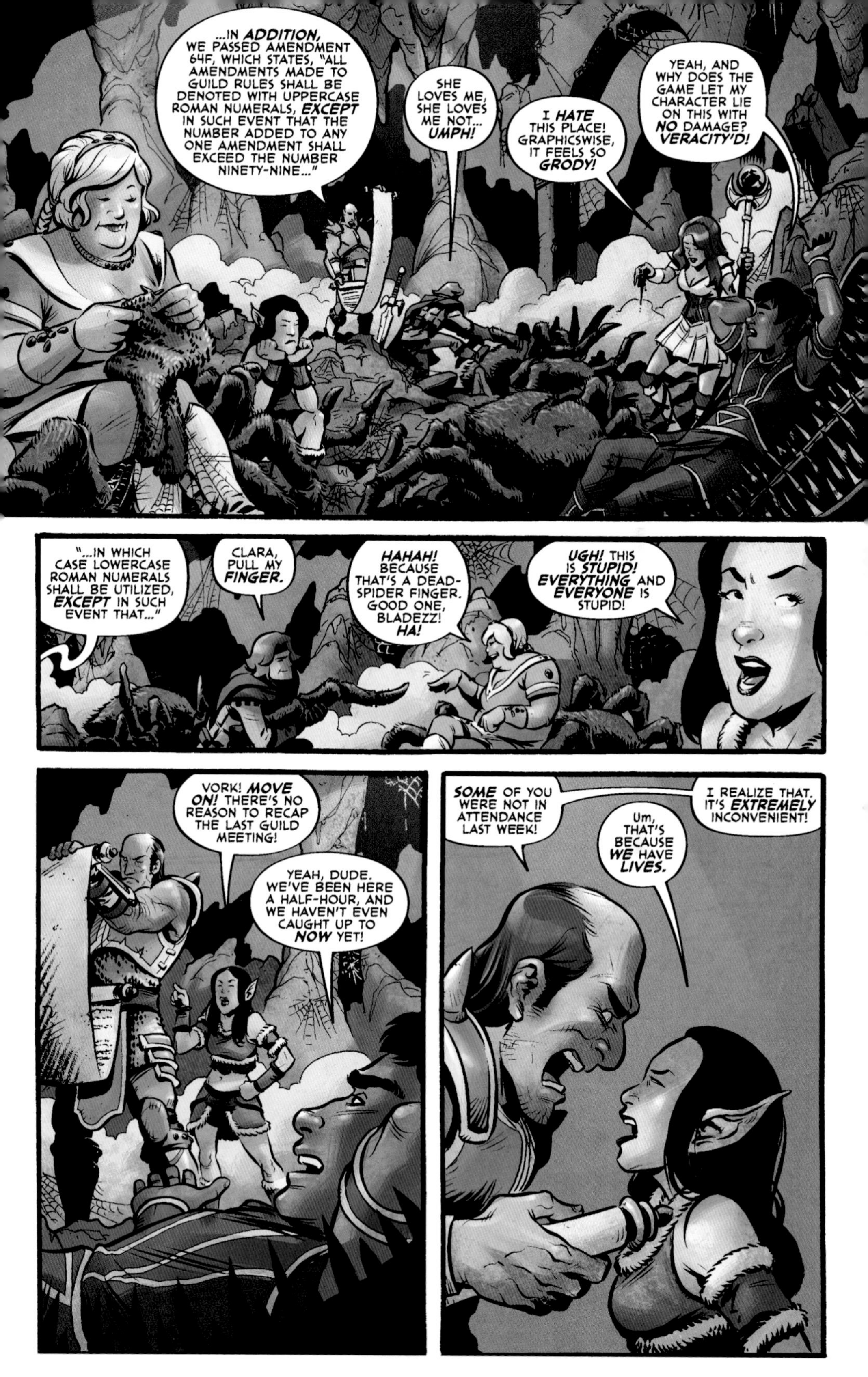
...IN ADDITION, WE PASSED AMENDMENT 64F, WHICH STATES, "ALL AMENDMENTS MADE TO GUILD RULES SHALL BE DENOTED WITH UPPERCASE ROMAN NUMERALS, EXCEPT IN SUCH EVENT THAT THE NUMBER ADDED TO ANY ONE AMENDMENT SHALL EXCEED THE NUMBER NINETY-NINE..."
SHE LOVES ME, SHE LOVES ME NOT... UMPH!
I HATE THIS PLACE! GRAPHICSWISE, IT FEELS SO GRODY!
YEAH, AND WHY DOES THE GAME LET MY CHARACTER LIE ON THIS WITH NO DAMAGE? VERACITY'D!
"...IN WHICH CASE LOWERCASE ROMAN NUMERALS SHALL BE UTILIZED, EXCEPT IN SUCH EVENT THAT..."
CLARA, PULL MY FINGER.
HAHAH! BECAUSE THAT'S A DEAD-SPIDER FINGER. GOOD ONE, BLADEZZ! HA!
UGH! THIS IS STUPID! EVERYTHING AND EVERYONE IS STUPID!
VORK! MOVE ON! THERE'S NO REASON TO RECAP THE LAST GUILD MEETING!
YEAH, DUDE. WE'VE BEEN HERE A HALF-HOUR, AND WE HAVEN'T EVEN CAUGHT UP TO NOW YET!
SOME OF YOU WERE NOT IN ATTENDANCE LAST WEEK!
I REALIZE THAT. IT'S EXTREMELY INCONVENIENT!
Um, THAT'S BECAUSE WE HAVE LIVES.

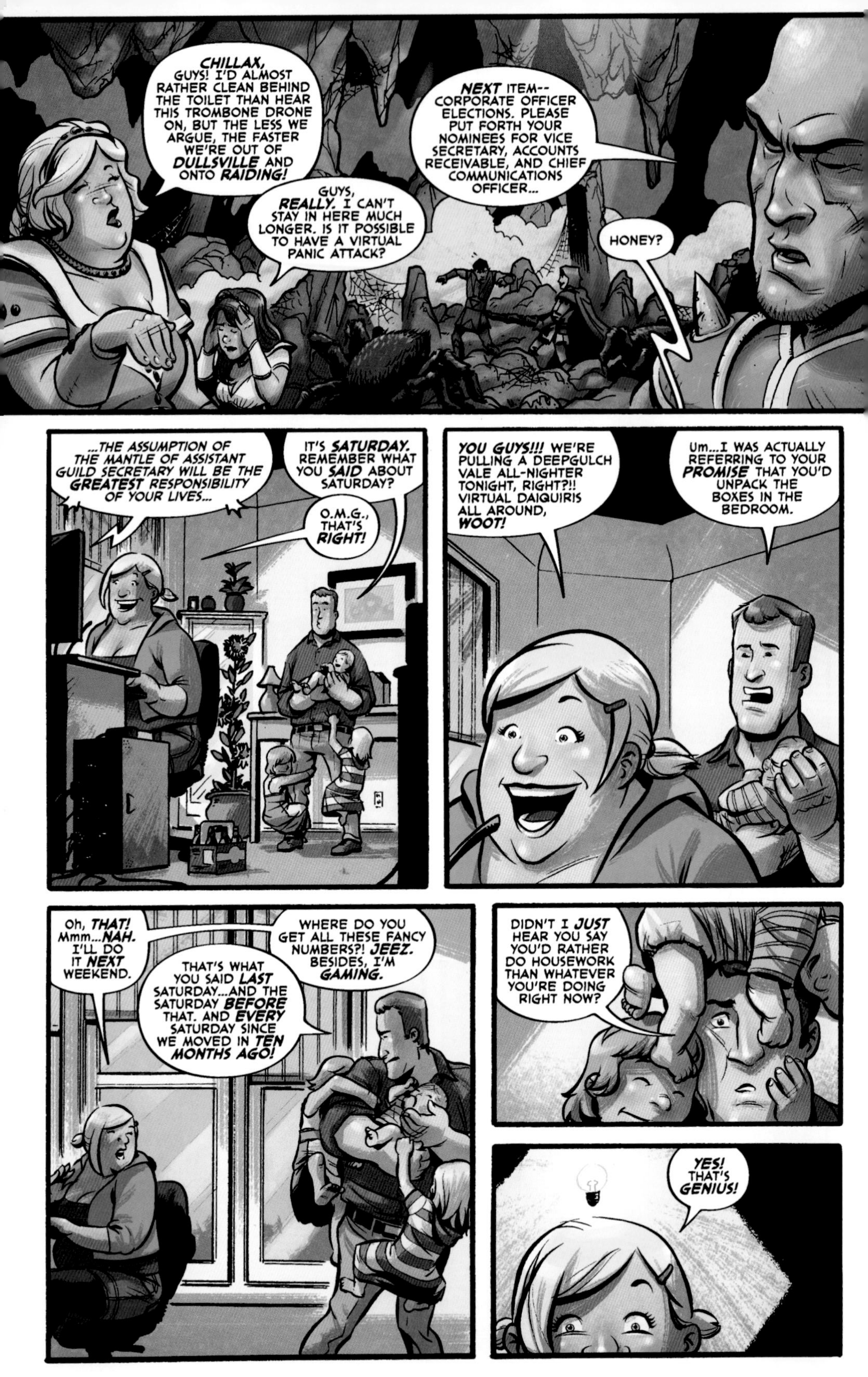
CHILLAX, GUYS! I'D ALMOST RATHER CLEAN BEHIND THE TOILET THAN HEAR THIS TROMBONE DRONE ON, BUT THE LESS WE ARGUE, THE FASTER WE'RE OUT OF DULLSVILLE AND ONTO RAIDING!
GUYS, REALLY. I CAN'T STAY IN HERE MUCH LONGER. IS IT POSSIBLE TO HAVE A VIRTUAL PANIC ATTACK?
NEXT ITEM-- CORPORATE OFFICER ELECTIONS. PLEASE PUT FORTH YOUR NOMINEES FOR VICE SECRETARY, ACCOUNTS RECEIVABLE, AND CHIEF COMMUNICATIONS OFFICER...
HONEY?
...THE ASSUMPTION OF THE MANTLE OF ASSISTANT GUILD SECRETARY WILL BE THE GREATEST RESPONSIBILITY OF YOUR LIVES...
IT'S SATURDAY. REMEMBER WHAT YOU SAID ABOUT SATURDAY?
O.M.G., THAT'S RIGHT!
YOU GUYS!!! WE'RE PULLING A DEEPGULCH VALE ALL-NIGHTER TONIGHT, RIGHT?!! VIRTUAL DAIQUIRIS ALL AROUND, WOOT!
Um...I WAS ACTUALLY REFERRING TO YOUR PROMISE THAT YOU'D UNPACK THE BOXES IN THE BEDROOM.
Oh, THAT! Mmm...NAH. I'LL DO IT NEXT WEEKEND.
THAT'S WHAT YOU SAID LAST SATURDAY...AND THE SATURDAY BEFORE THAT. AND EVERY SATURDAY SINCE WE MOVED IN TEN MONTHS AGO!
WHERE DO YOU GET ALL THESE FANCY NUMBERS?! JEEZ. BESIDES, I'M GAMING.
DIDN'T I JUST HEAR YOU SAY YOU'D RATHER DO HOUSEWORK THAN WHATEVER YOU'RE DOING RIGHT NOW?
YES! THAT'S GENIUS!

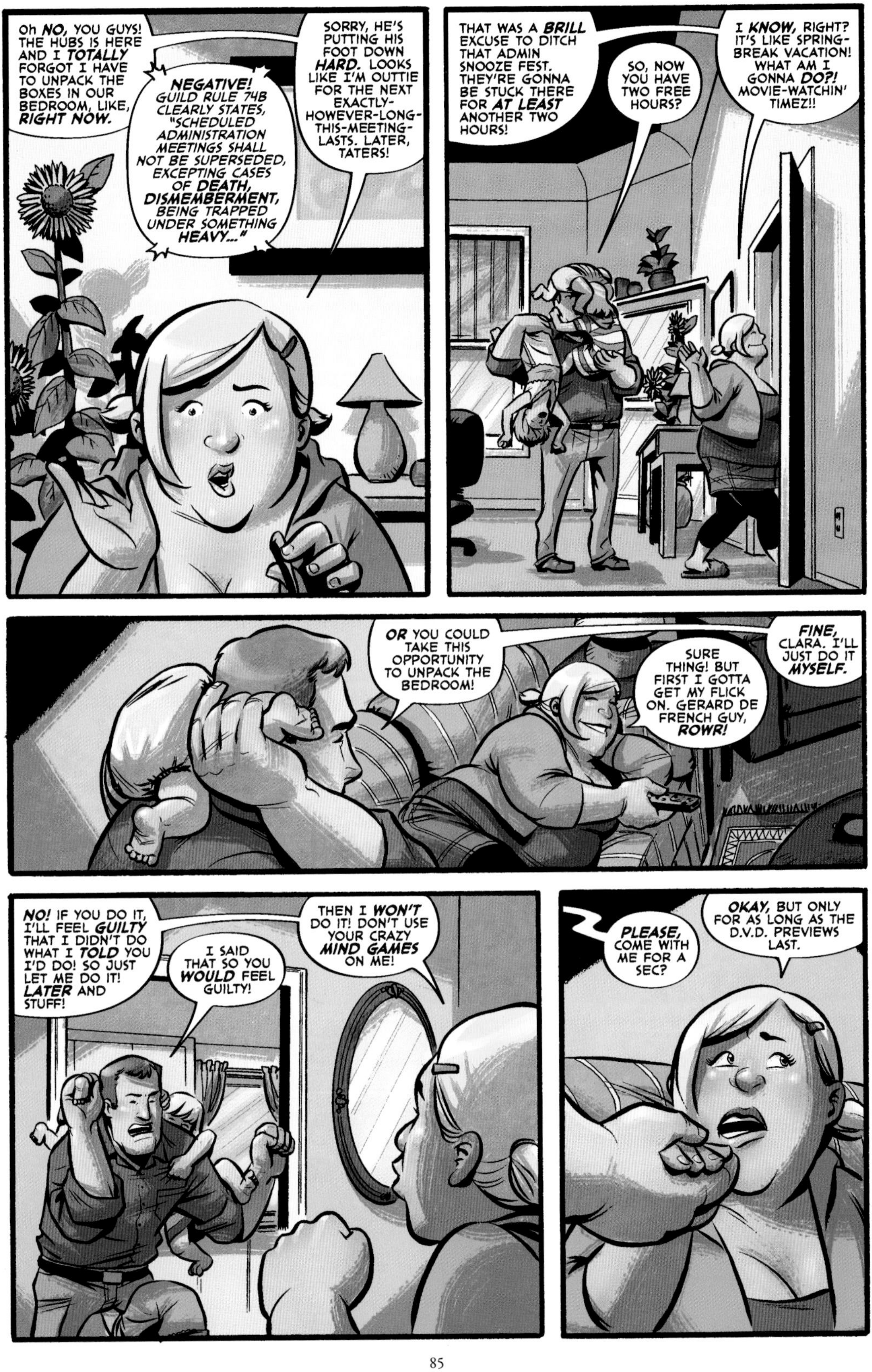

Oh NO, YOU GUYS! THE HUBS IS HERE AND I TOTALLY FORGOT I HAVE TO UNPACK THE BOXES IN OUR BEDROOM, LIKE, RIGHT NOW.
NEGATIVE! GUILD RULE 74B CLEARLY STATES, "SCHEDULED ADMINISTRATION MEETINGS SHALL NOT BE SUPERSEDED, EXCEPTING CASES OF DEATH, DISMEMBERMENT, BEING TRAPPED UNDER SOMETHING HEAVY..."
SORRY, HE'S PUTTING HIS FOOT DOWN HARD. LOOKS LIKE I'M OUTTIE FOR THE NEXT EXACTLY-HOWEVER-LONG-THIS-MEETING-LASTS. LATER, TATERS!
THAT WAS A BRILL EXCUSE TO DITCH THAT ADMIN SNOOZE FEST. THEY'RE GONNA BE STUCK THERE FOR AT LEAST ANOTHER TWO HOURS!
SO, NOW YOU HAVE TWO FREE HOURS?
I KNOW, RIGHT? IT'S LIKE SPRING-BREAK VACATION! WHAT AM I GONNA DO?! MOVIE-WATCHIN' TIMEZ!!
OR YOU COULD TAKE THIS OPPORTUNITY TO UNPACK THE BEDROOM!
SURE THING! BUT FIRST I GOTTA GET MY FLICK ON. GERARD DE FRENCH GUY, ROWR!
FINE, CLARA. I'LL JUST DO IT MYSELF.
NO! IF YOU DO IT, I'LL FEEL GUILTY THAT I DIDN'T DO WHAT I TOLD YOU I'D DO! SO JUST LET ME DO IT! LATER AND STUFF!
I SAID THAT SO YOU WOULD FEEL GUILTY!
THEN I WON'T DO IT! DON'T USE YOUR CRAZY MIND GAMES ON ME!
PLEASE, COME WITH ME FOR A SEC?
OKAY, BUT ONLY FOR AS LONG AS THE D.V.D. PREVIEWS LAST.

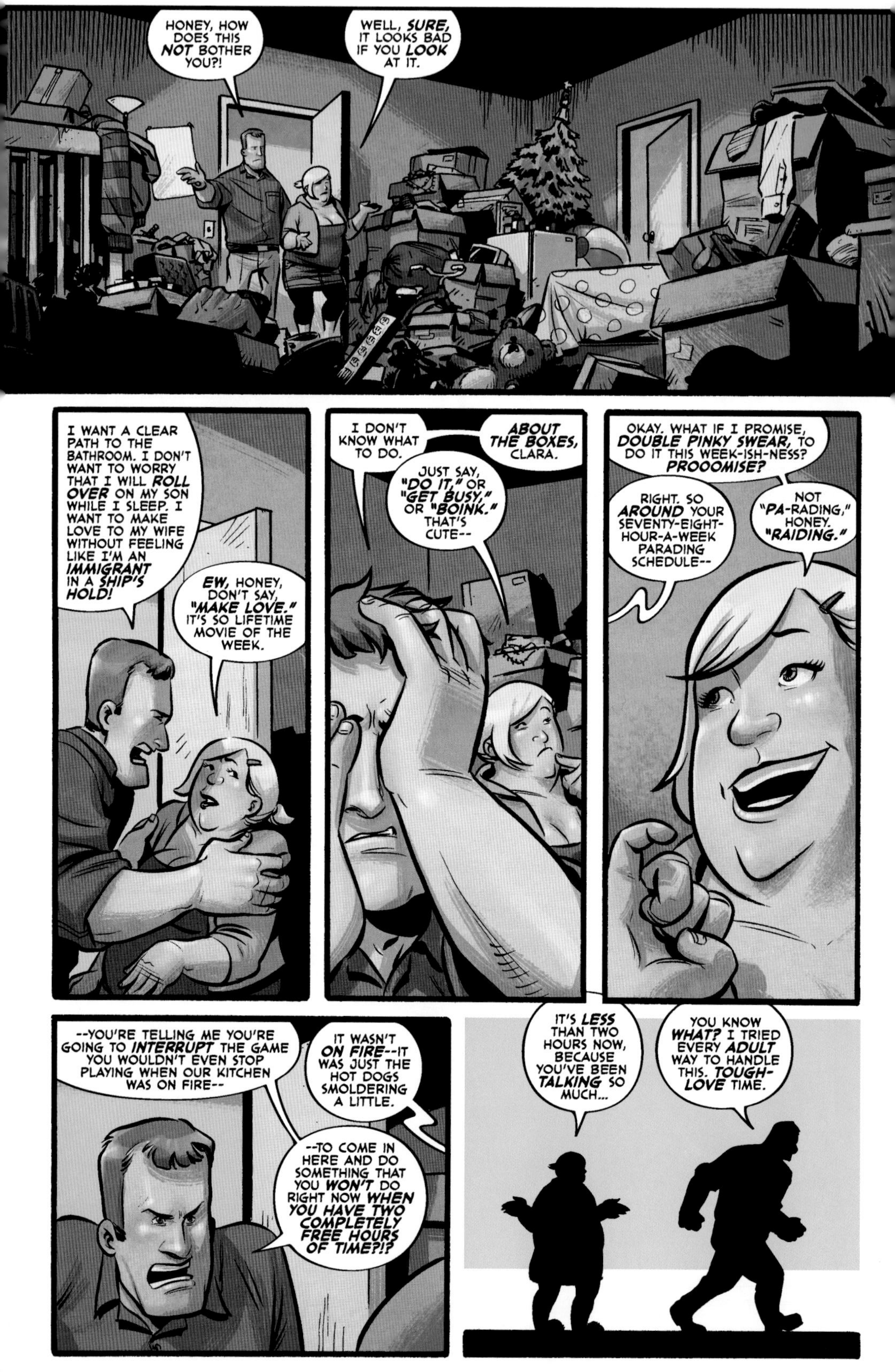
HONEY, HOW DOES THIS NOT BOTHER YOU?!
WELL, SURE, IT LOOKS BAD IF YOU LOOK AT IT.
I WANT A CLEAR PATH TO THE BATHROOM. I DON'T WANT TO WORRY THAT I WILL ROLL OVER ON MY SON WHILE I SLEEP. I WANT TO MAKE LOVE TO MY WIFE WITHOUT FEELING LIKE I'M AN IMMIGRANT IN A SHIP'S HOLD!
EW, HONEY, DON'T SAY, "MAKE LOVE." IT'S SO LIFETIME MOVIE OF THE WEEK.
I DON'T KNOW WHAT TO DO.
ABOUT THE BOXES, CLARA.
JUST SAY, "DO IT," OR "GET BUSY," OR "BOINK." THAT'S CUTE--
OKAY. WHAT IF I PROMISE, DOUBLE PINKY SWEAR, TO DO IT THIS WEEK-ISH-NESS? PROOOMISE?
RIGHT. SO AROUND YOUR SEVENTY-EIGHT-HOUR-A-WEEK PARADING SCHEDULE--
NOT "PA-RADING," HONEY. "RAIDING."
--YOU'RE TELLING ME YOU'RE GOING TO INTERRUPT THE GAME YOU WOULDN'T EVEN STOP PLAYING WHEN OUR KITCHEN WAS ON FIRE--
IT WASN'T ON FIRE--IT WAS JUST THE HOT DOGS SMOLDERING A LITTLE.
--TO COME IN HERE AND DO SOMETHING THAT YOU WON'T DO RIGHT NOW WHEN YOU HAVE TWO COMPLETELY FREE HOURS OF TIME?!?
IT'S LESS THAN TWO HOURS NOW, BECAUSE YOU'VE BEEN TALKING SO MUCH...
YOU KNOW WHAT? I TRIED EVERY ADULT WAY TO HANDLE THIS. TOUGH-LOVE TIME.

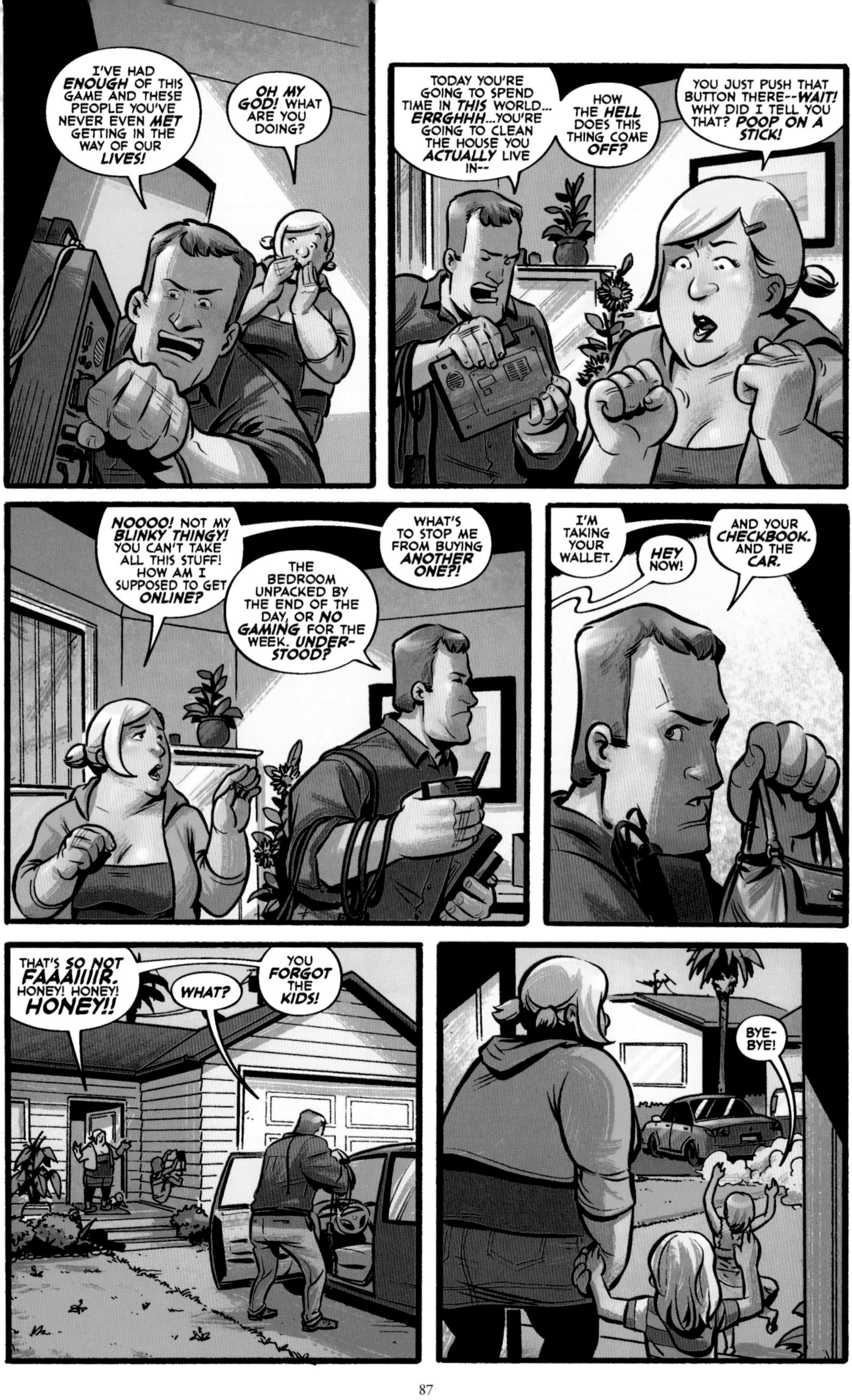
I'VE HAD ENOUGH OF THIS GAME AND THESE PEOPLE YOU'VE NEVER EVEN MET GETTING IN THE WAY OF OUR LIVES!
OH MY GOD! WHAT ARE YOU DOING?
TODAY YOU'RE GOING TO SPEND TIME IN THIS WORLD... ERRGHHH...YOU'RE GOING TO CLEAN THE HOUSE YOU ACTUALLY LIVE IN--
HOW THE HELL DOES THIS THING COME OFF?
YOU JUST PUSH THAT BUTTON THERE--WAIT! WHY DID I TELL YOU THAT? POOP ON A STICK!
THE BEDROOM UNPACKED BY THE END OF THE DAY, OR NO GAMING FOR THE WEEK. UNDERSTOOD?
NOOOO! NOT MY BLINKY THINGY! YOU CAN'T TAKE ALL THIS STUFF! HOW AM I SUPPOSED TO GET ONLINE?
WHAT'S TO STOP ME FROM BUYING ANOTHER ONE?!
I'M TAKING YOUR WALLET.
HEY NOW!
AND YOUR CHECKBOOK. AND THE CAR.
THAT'S SO NOT FAAAIIIIR. HONEY! HONEY! HONEY!!
WHAT?
YOU FORGOT THE KIDS!
BYE-BYE!

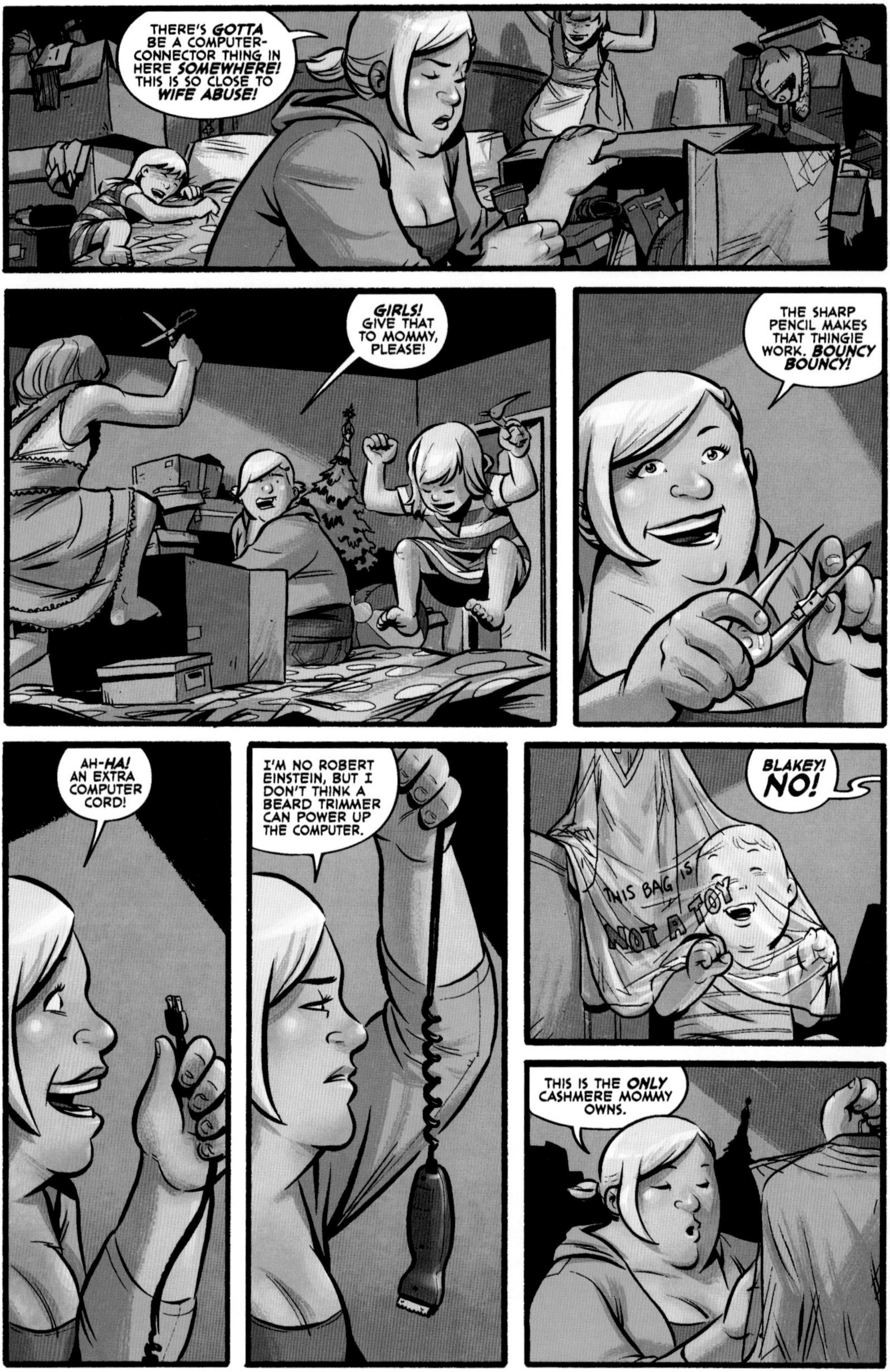
THERE'S GOTTA BE A COMPUTER-CONNECTOR THING IN HERE SOMEWHERE! THIS IS SO CLOSE TO WIFE ABUSE!
GIRLS! GIVE THAT TO MOMMY, PLEASE!
THE SHARP PENCIL MAKES THAT THINGIE WORK. BOUNCY BOUNCY!
AH-HA! AN EXTRA COMPUTER CORD!
I'M NO ROBERT EINSTEIN, BUT I DON'T THINK A BEARD TRIMMER CAN POWER UP THE COMPUTER.
BLAKEY! NO!
THIS BAG IS NOT A TOY
THIS IS THE ONLY CASHMERE MOMMY OWNS.

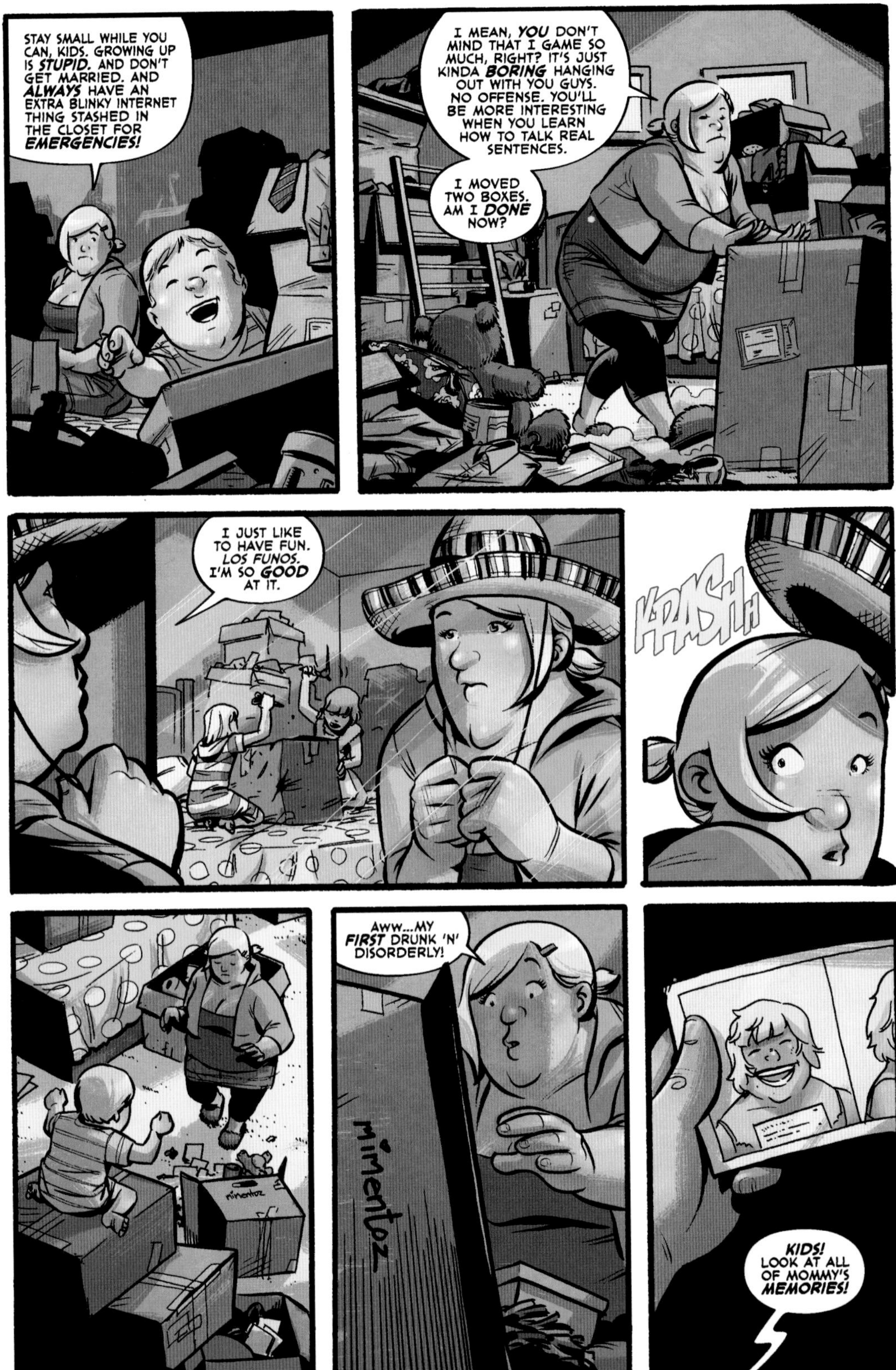
STAY SMALL WHILE YOU CAN, KIDS. GROWING UP IS STUPID. AND DON'T GET MARRIED. AND ALWAYS HAVE AN EXTRA BLINKY INTERNET THING STASHED IN THE CLOSET FOR EMERGENCIES!
I MEAN, YOU DON'T MIND THAT I GAME SO MUCH, RIGHT? IT'S JUST KINDA BORING HANGING OUT WITH YOU GUYS. NO OFFENSE. YOU'LL BE MORE INTERESTING WHEN YOU LEARN HOW TO TALK REAL SENTENCES.
I MOVED TWO BOXES. AM I DONE NOW?
I JUST LIKE TO HAVE FUN. LOS FUNOS. I'M SO GOOD AT IT.
KRASHH
AWW...MY FIRST DRUNK 'N' DISORDERLY!
mimentoz
KIDS! LOOK AT ALL OF MOMMY'S MEMORIES!

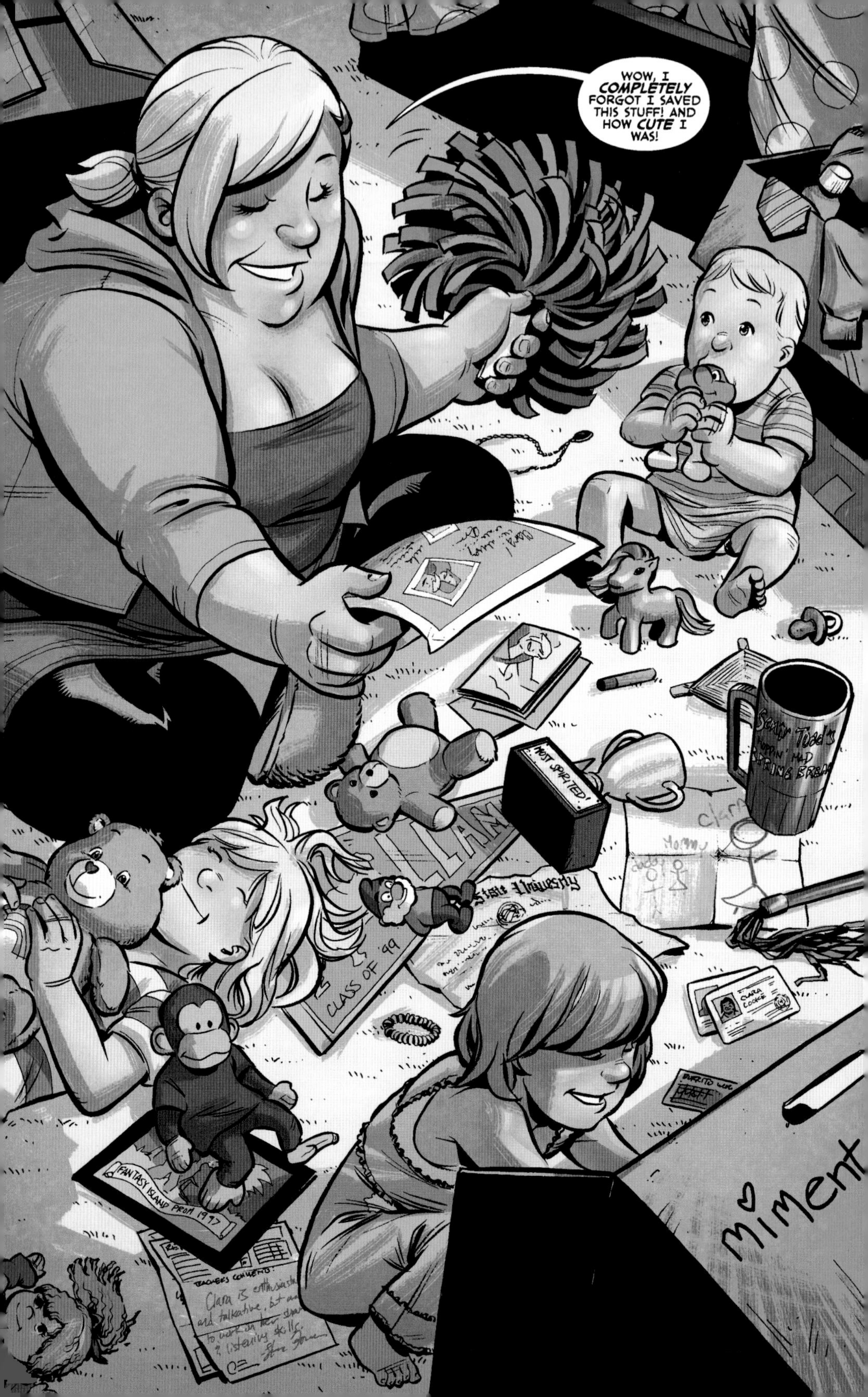

WOW, I COMPLETELY FORGOT I SAVED THIS STUFF! AND HOW CUTE I WAS!
MOST SPIRITED!
CLASS OF '99
FANTASY ISLAND PROM 1997
TEACHER'S COMMENTS:
CLARA COOKE

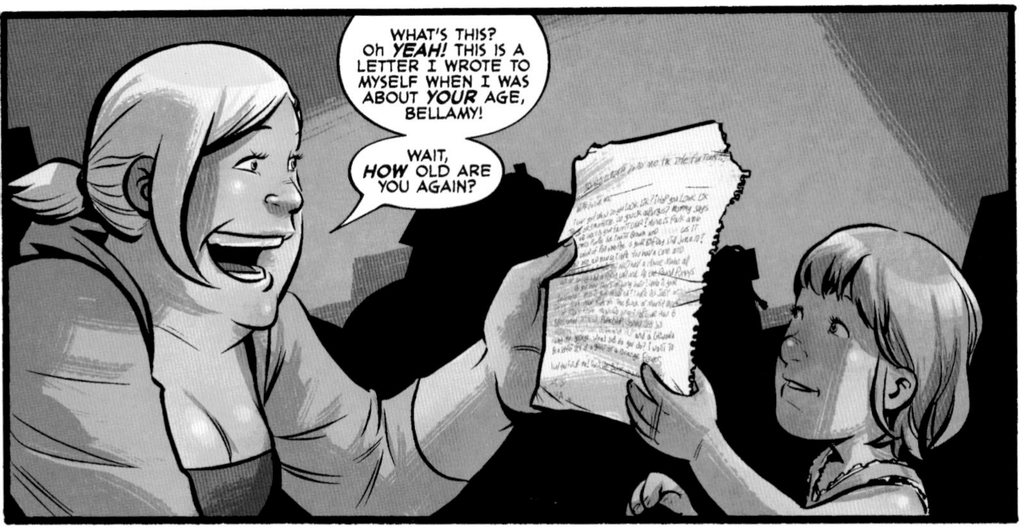
WHAT'S THIS? Oh YEAH! THIS IS A LETTER I WROTE TO MYSELF WHEN I WAS ABOUT YOUR AGE, BELLAMY!
WAIT, HOW OLD ARE YOU AGAIN?

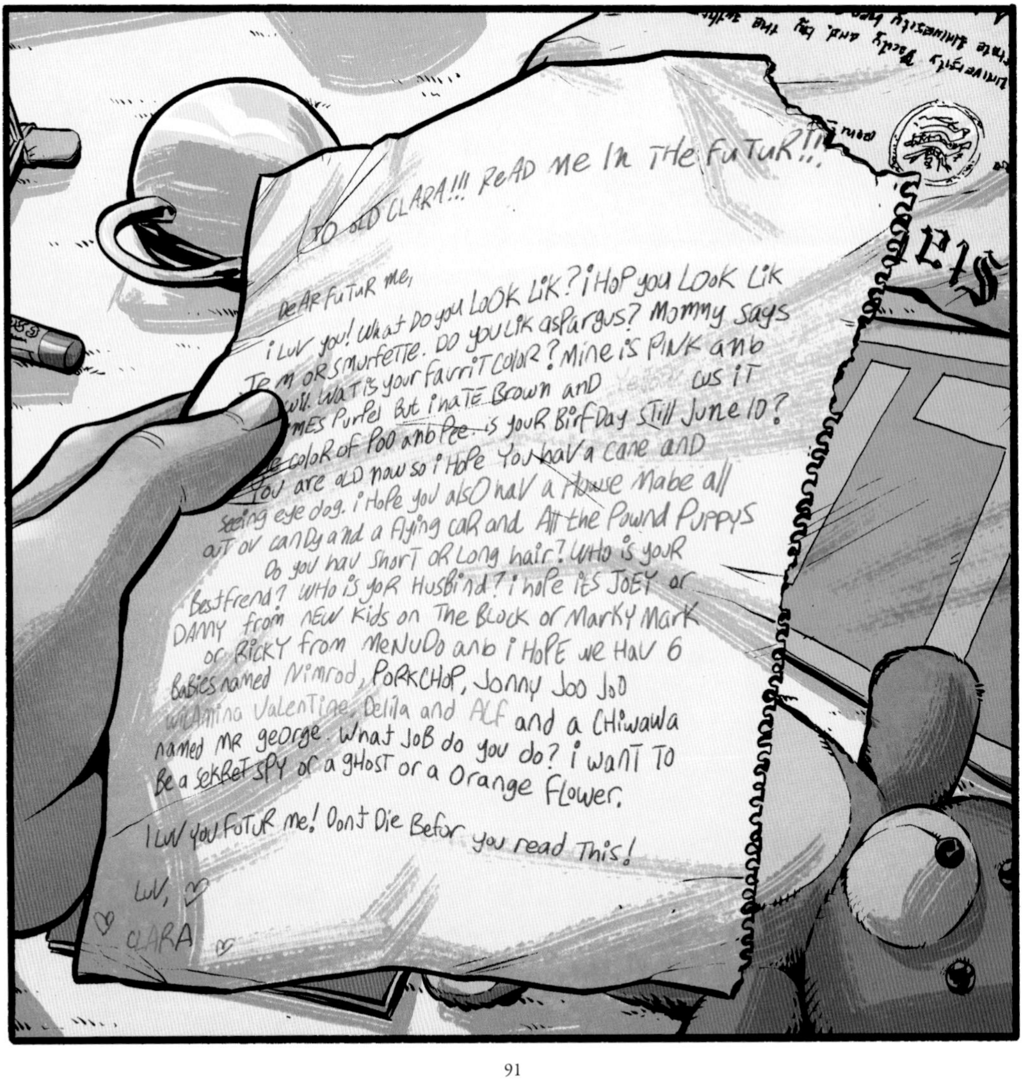
TO OLD CLARA!!! READ me IN THE FuTuR!!!
DeAR FuTuR me,
i Luv you! What Do you LOOK Lik? i HoP you LOOK Lik
Jem OR Smurfette. Do you Lik aspargus? Mommy says
ew. WaT is your favriT color? Mine is PiNK and
MES Purpel But i haTE Brown and cus iT
color of Poo and Pee. is youR BirfDay STill June 10?
You are oLD now so i Hope You hav a cane and
seeing eye dog. i Hope you alsO hav a House mabe all
ouT ov canDy and a flying caR and All the Pound Puppys
Do you hav ShorT oR Long hair? WHo is youR
Bestfrend? WHo is yoR HusBind? i hope its JOEY or
DANNY from NEW Kids on The BLock or MarKY Mark
or RICKY from MeNuDo and i HoPE we Hav 6
Babies named Nimrod, PORKCHOP, Jonny Joo Joo
Wilamina Valentine, Delila and ALF and a CHiwawa
named MR george. What JOB do you do? i wanT TO
Be a SeKReT SPY or a gHOST or a Orange Flower.
I Luv you FuTuR me! Don't Die Befor you read This!
Luv,
CLARA

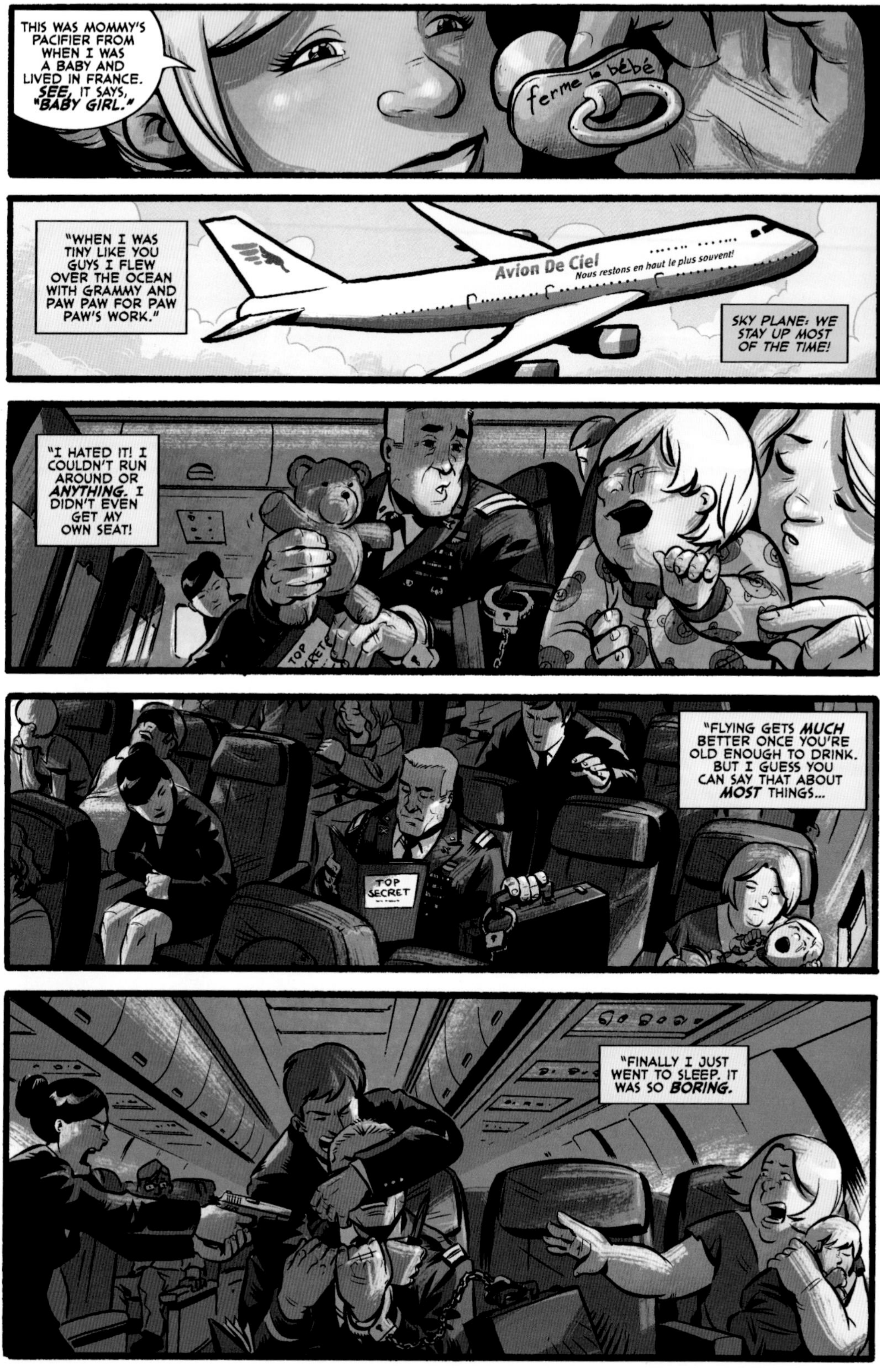

THIS WAS MOMMY'S PACIFIER FROM WHEN I WAS A BABY AND LIVED IN FRANCE. SEE, IT SAYS, "BABY GIRL."
ferme le bébé
"WHEN I WAS TINY LIKE YOU GUYS I FLEW OVER THE OCEAN WITH GRAMMY AND PAW PAW FOR PAW PAW'S WORK."
Avion De Ciel
Nous restons en haut le plus souvent!
SKY PLANE: WE STAY UP MOST OF THE TIME!
"I HATED IT! I COULDN'T RUN AROUND OR ANYTHING. I DIDN'T EVEN GET MY OWN SEAT!
TOP SECRET
"FLYING GETS MUCH BETTER ONCE YOU'RE OLD ENOUGH TO DRINK. BUT I GUESS YOU CAN SAY THAT ABOUT MOST THINGS...
TOP SECRET
"FINALLY I JUST WENT TO SLEEP. IT WAS SO BORING.

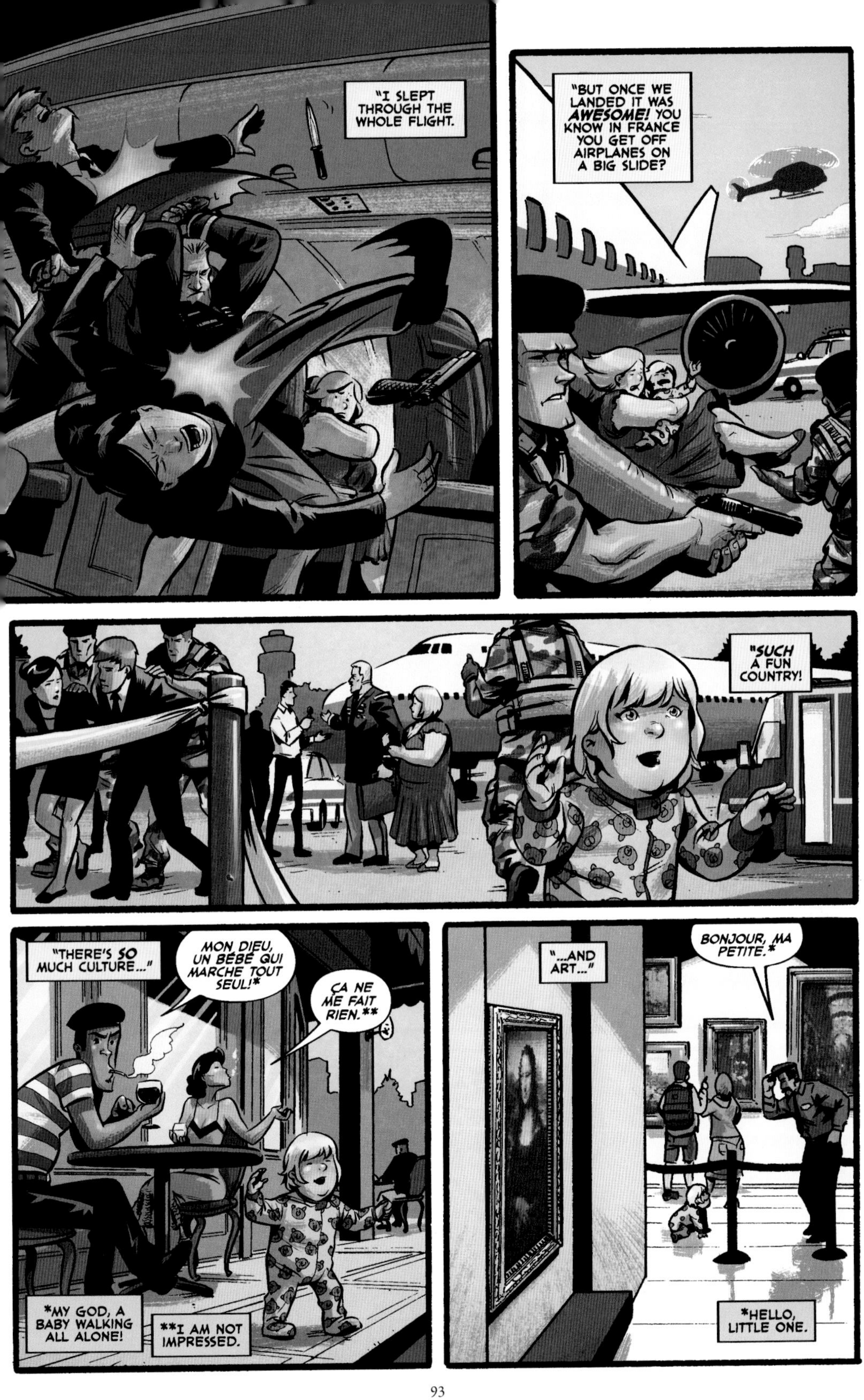
"I SLEPT THROUGH THE WHOLE FLIGHT.
"BUT ONCE WE LANDED IT WAS AWESOME! YOU KNOW IN FRANCE YOU GET OFF AIRPLANES ON A BIG SLIDE?
"SUCH A FUN COUNTRY!
"THERE'S SO MUCH CULTURE..."
MON DIEU, UN BÉBÉ QUI MARCHE TOUT SEUL!*
ÇA NE ME FAIT RIEN.**
*MY GOD, A BABY WALKING ALL ALONE!
**I AM NOT IMPRESSED.
"...AND ART..."
BONJOUR, MA PETITE.*
*HELLO, LITTLE ONE.

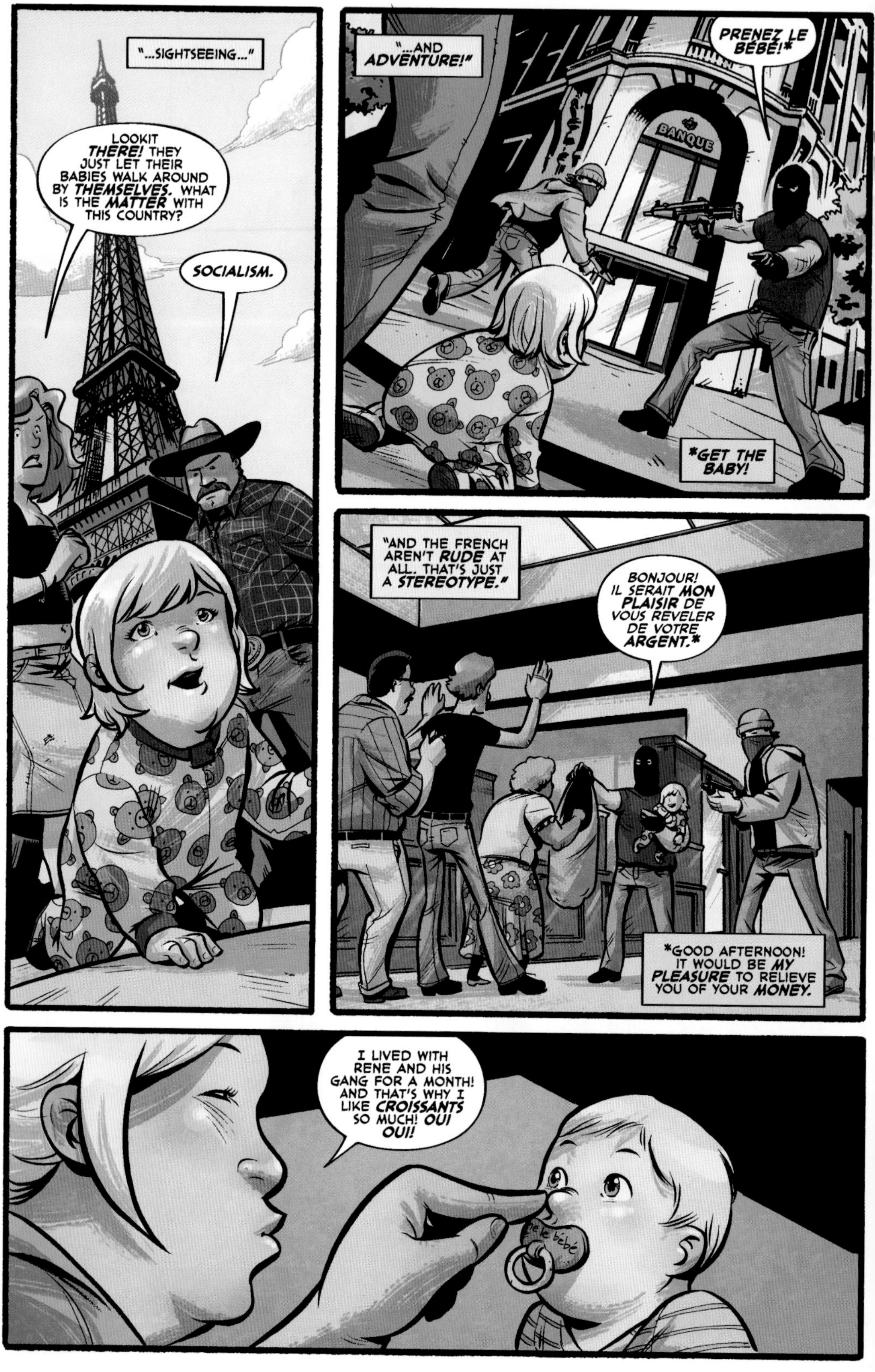
"...SIGHTSEEING..."
LOOKIT THERE! THEY JUST LET THEIR BABIES WALK AROUND BY THEMSELVES. WHAT IS THE MATTER WITH THIS COUNTRY?
SOCIALISM.
"...AND ADVENTURE!"
PRENEZ LE BÉBÉ!*
BANQUE
*GET THE BABY!
"AND THE FRENCH AREN'T RUDE AT ALL. THAT'S JUST A STEREOTYPE."
BONJOUR! IL SERAIT MON PLAISIR DE VOUS REVELER DE VOTRE ARGENT.*
*GOOD AFTERNOON! IT WOULD BE MY PLEASURE TO RELIEVE YOU OF YOUR MONEY.
I LIVED WITH RENE AND HIS GANG FOR A MONTH! AND THAT'S WHY I LIKE CROISSANTS SO MUCH! OUI OUI!

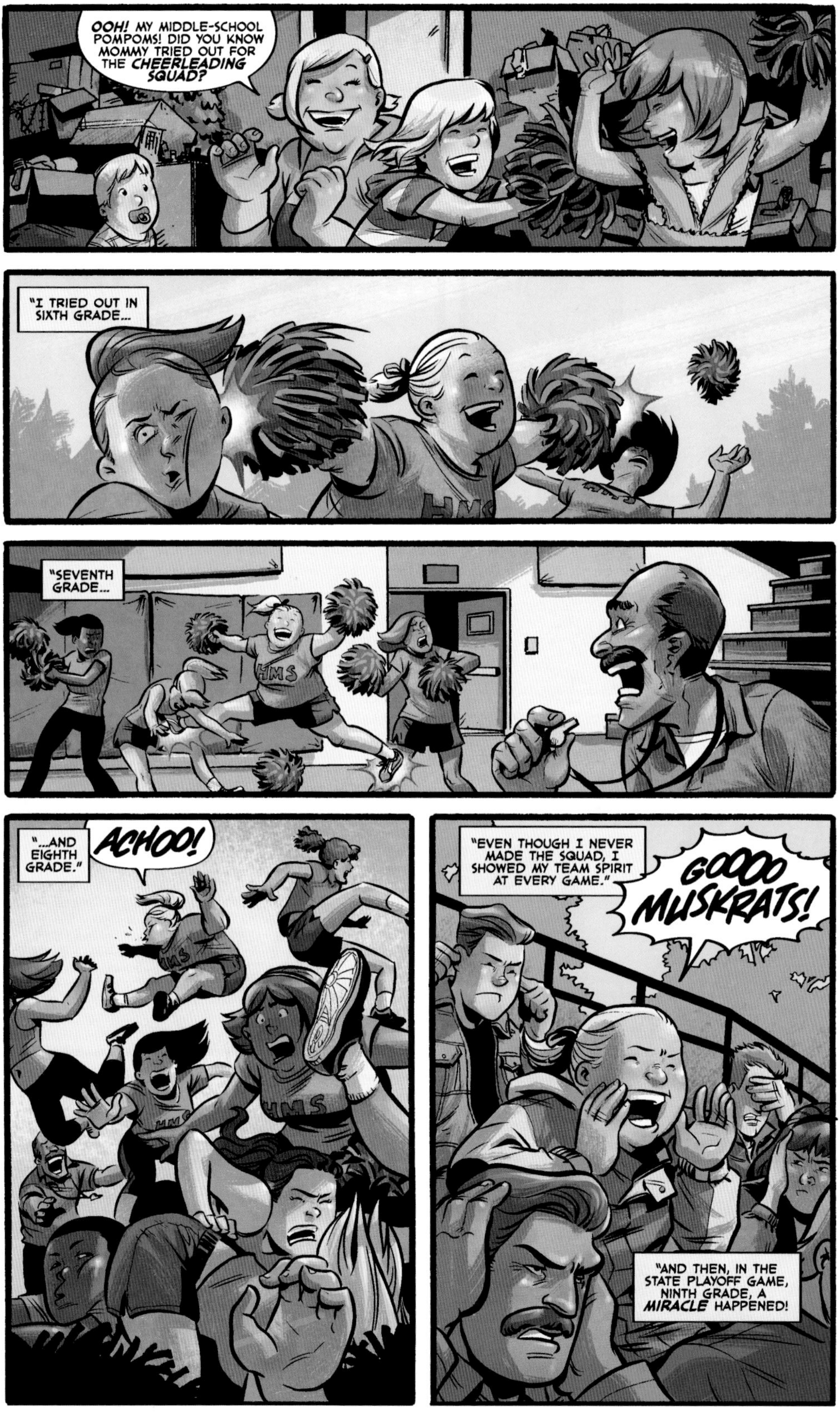
OOH! MY MIDDLE-SCHOOL POMPOMS! DID YOU KNOW MOMMY TRIED OUT FOR THE CHEERLEADING SQUAD?
"I TRIED OUT IN SIXTH GRADE...
"SEVENTH GRADE...
"...AND EIGHTH GRADE."
ACHOO!
"EVEN THOUGH I NEVER MADE THE SQUAD, I SHOWED MY TEAM SPIRIT AT EVERY GAME."
GOOOO MUSKRATS!
"AND THEN, IN THE STATE PLAYOFF GAME, NINTH GRADE, A MIRACLE HAPPENED!

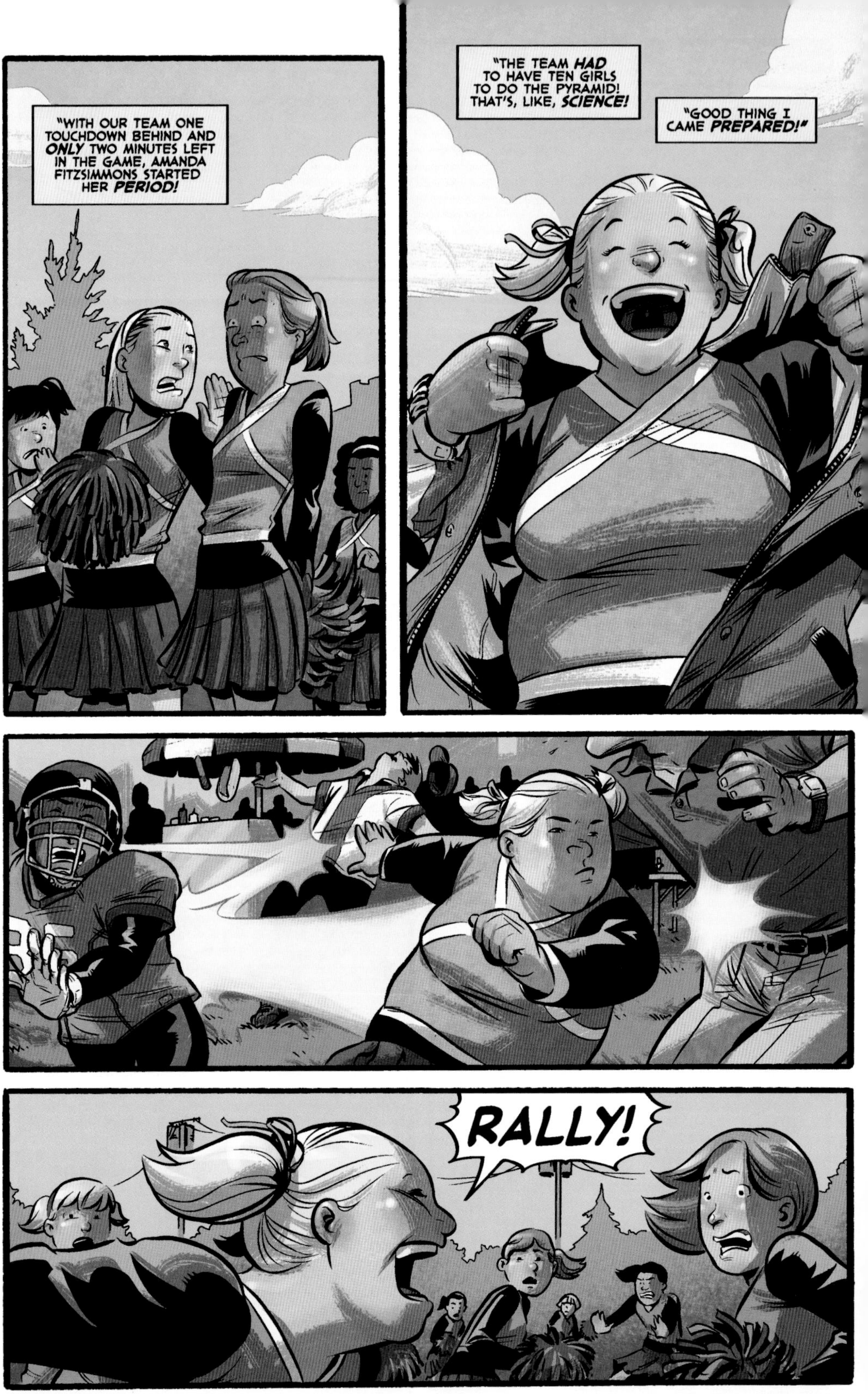
"WITH OUR TEAM ONE TOUCHDOWN BEHIND AND ONLY TWO MINUTES LEFT IN THE GAME, AMANDA FITZSIMMONS STARTED HER PERIOD!
"THE TEAM HAD TO HAVE TEN GIRLS TO DO THE PYRAMID! THAT'S, LIKE, SCIENCE!
"GOOD THING I CAME PREPARED!"
RALLY!

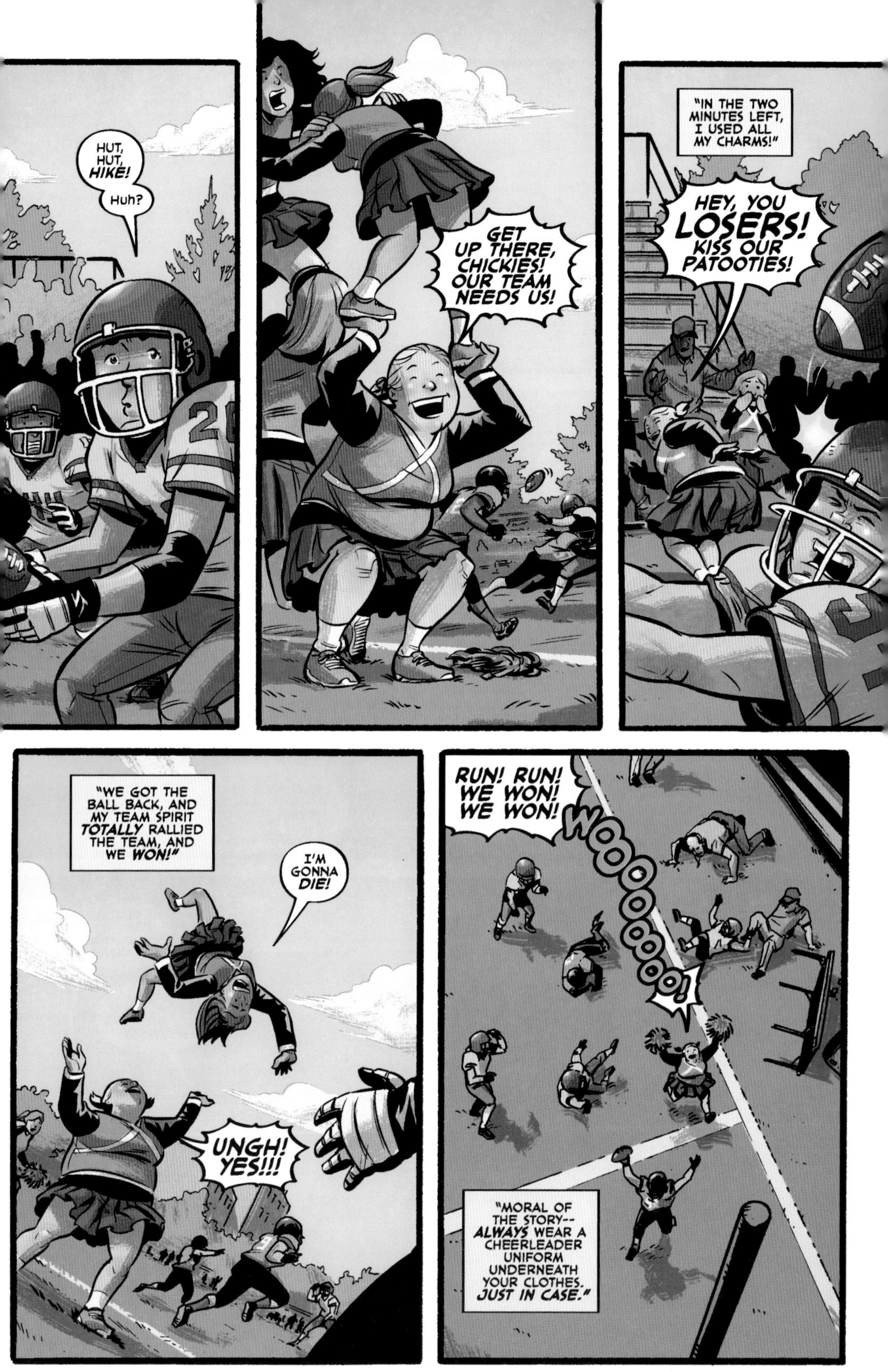

HUT, HUT, HIKE!
Huh?
GET UP THERE, CHICKIES! OUR TEAM NEEDS US!
"IN THE TWO MINUTES LEFT, I USED ALL MY CHARMS!"
HEY, YOU LOSERS! KISS OUR PATOOTIES!
"WE GOT THE BALL BACK, AND MY TEAM SPIRIT TOTALLY RALLIED THE TEAM, AND WE WON!"
I'M GONNA DIE!
UNGH! YES!!!
RUN! RUN! WE WON! WE WON!
WOOOOOOOO!
"MORAL OF THE STORY--ALWAYS WEAR A CHEERLEADER UNIFORM UNDERNEATH YOUR CLOTHES. JUST IN CASE."

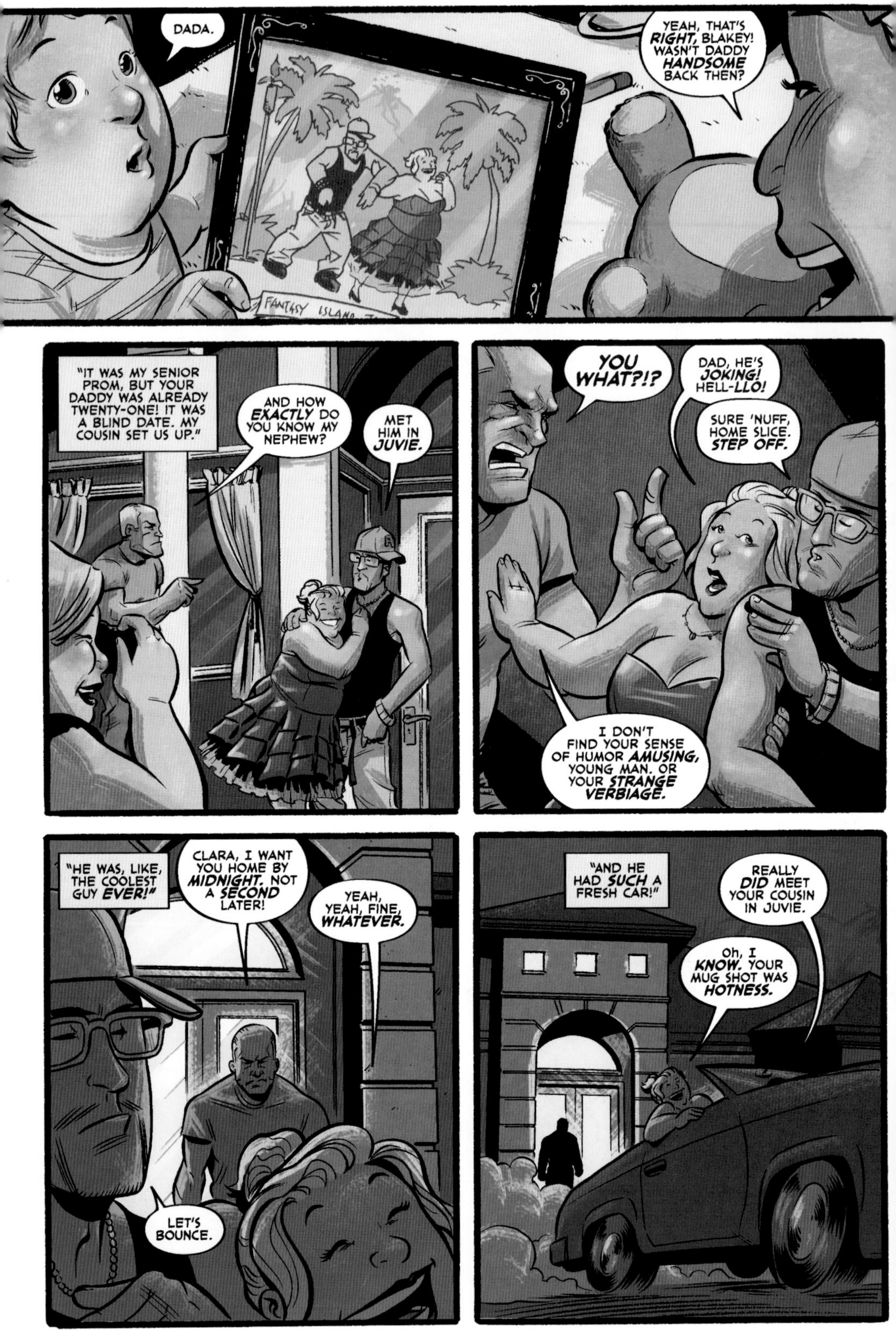
DADA.
YEAH, THAT'S RIGHT, BLAKEY! WASN'T DADDY HANDSOME BACK THEN?
FANTASY ISLAND
"IT WAS MY SENIOR PROM, BUT YOUR DADDY WAS ALREADY TWENTY-ONE! IT WAS A BLIND DATE. MY COUSIN SET US UP."
AND HOW EXACTLY DO YOU KNOW MY NEPHEW?
MET HIM IN JUVIE.
YOU WHAT?!?
DAD, HE'S JOKING! HELL-LLO!
SURE 'NUFF, HOME SLICE. STEP OFF.
I DON'T FIND YOUR SENSE OF HUMOR AMUSING, YOUNG MAN. OR YOUR STRANGE VERBIAGE.
"HE WAS, LIKE, THE COOLEST GUY EVER!"
CLARA, I WANT YOU HOME BY MIDNIGHT. NOT A SECOND LATER!
YEAH, YEAH, FINE, WHATEVER.
LET'S BOUNCE.
"AND HE HAD SUCH A FRESH CAR!"
REALLY DID MEET YOUR COUSIN IN JUVIE.
Oh, I KNOW. YOUR MUG SHOT WAS HOTNESS.

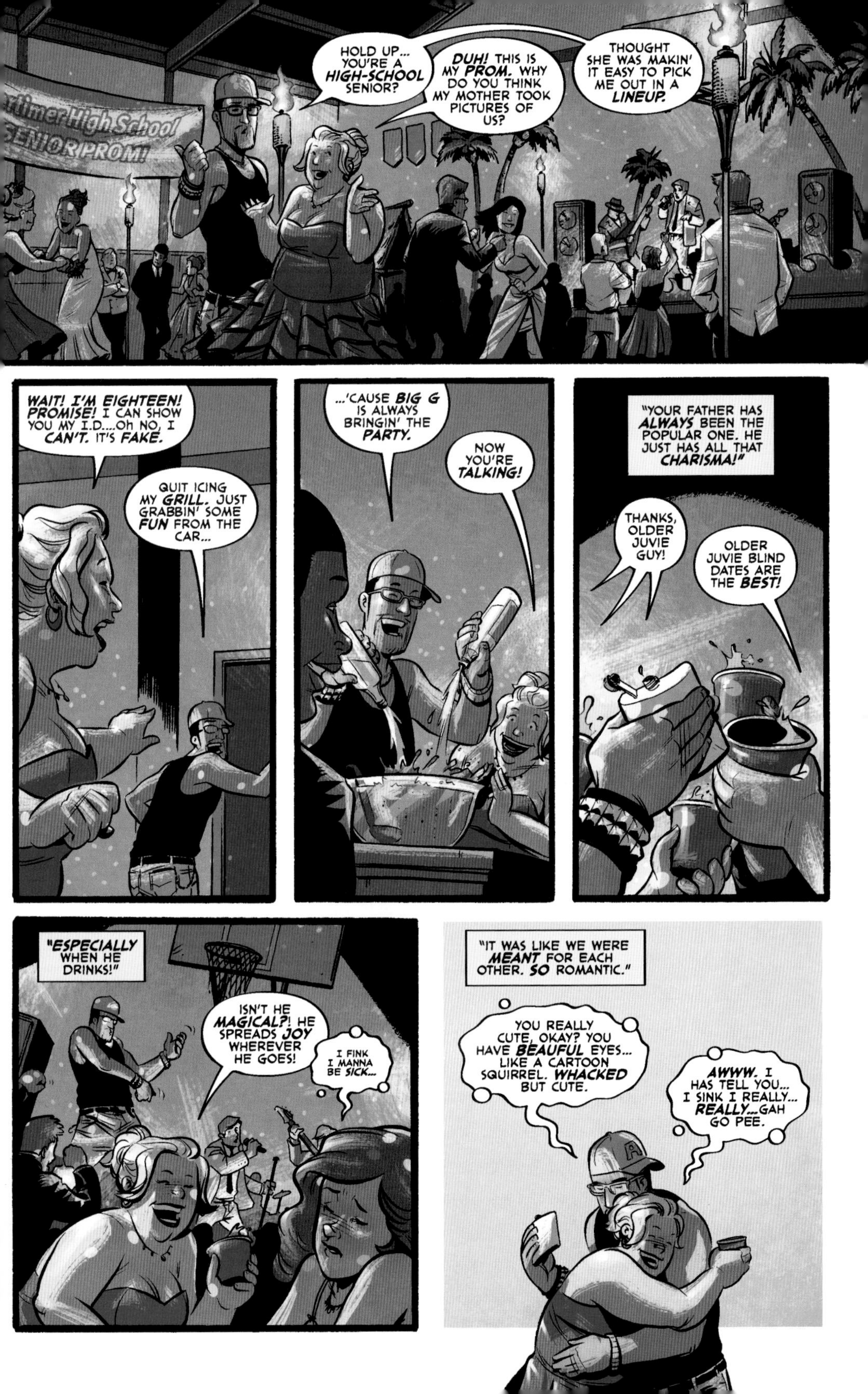

Mortimer High School SENIOR PROM!
HOLD UP... YOU'RE A HIGH-SCHOOL SENIOR?
DUH! THIS IS MY PROM. WHY DO YOU THINK MY MOTHER TOOK PICTURES OF US?
THOUGHT SHE WAS MAKIN' IT EASY TO PICK ME OUT IN A LINEUP.
WAIT! I'M EIGHTEEN! PROMISE! I CAN SHOW YOU MY I.D....Oh NO, I CAN'T. IT'S FAKE.
QUIT ICING MY GRILL. JUST GRABBIN' SOME FUN FROM THE CAR...
...'CAUSE BIG G IS ALWAYS BRINGIN' THE PARTY.
NOW YOU'RE TALKING!
"YOUR FATHER HAS ALWAYS BEEN THE POPULAR ONE. HE JUST HAS ALL THAT CHARISMA!"
THANKS, OLDER JUVIE GUY!
OLDER JUVIE BLIND DATES ARE THE BEST!
"ESPECIALLY WHEN HE DRINKS!"
ISN'T HE MAGICAL?! HE SPREADS JOY WHEREVER HE GOES!
I FINK I MANNA BE SICK...
"IT WAS LIKE WE WERE MEANT FOR EACH OTHER. SO ROMANTIC."
YOU REALLY CUTE, OKAY? YOU HAVE BEAUFUL EYES... LIKE A CARTOON SQUIRREL. WHACKED BUT CUTE.
AWWW. I HAS TELL YOU... I SINK I REALLY... REALLY...GAH GO PEE.

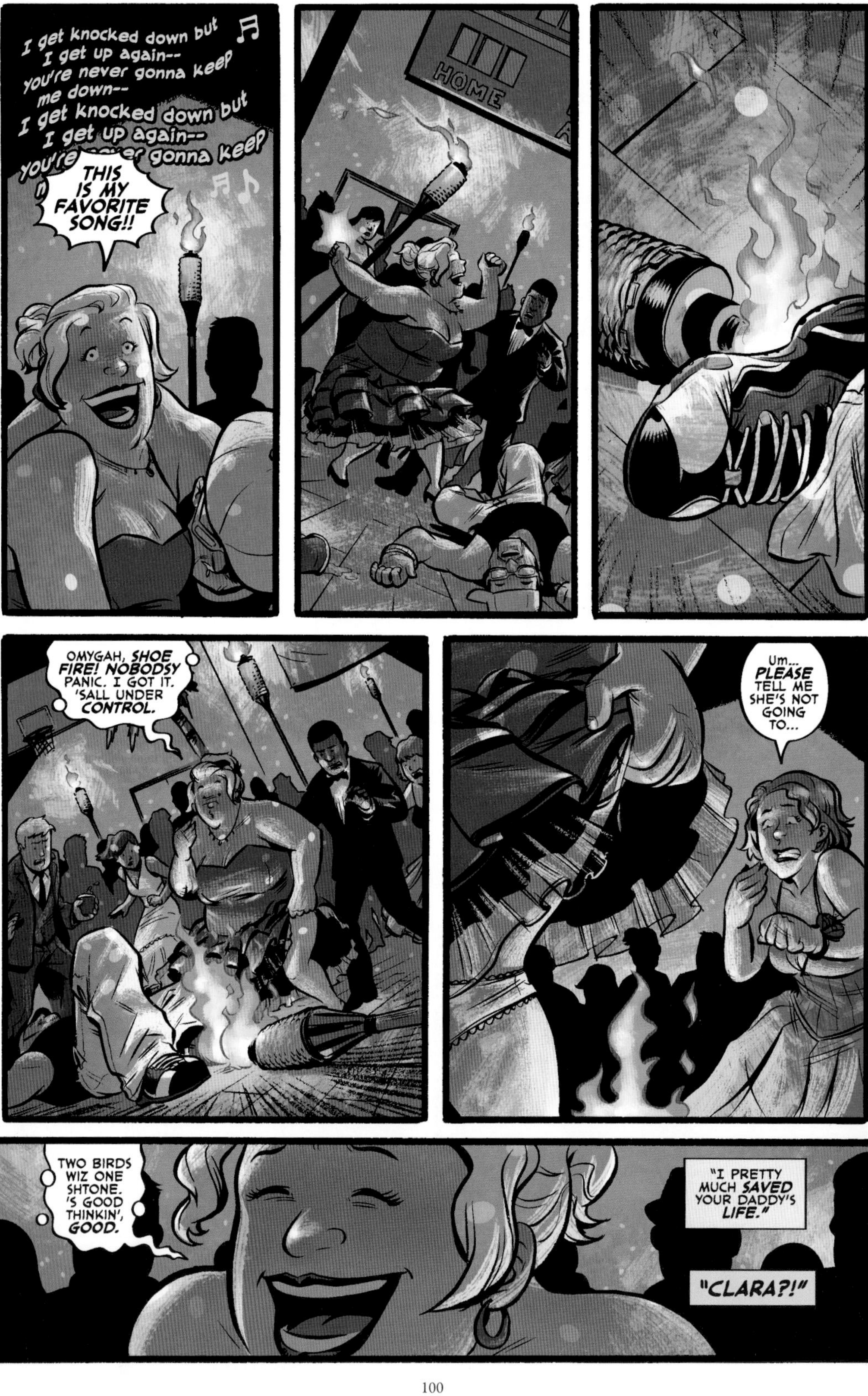
I get knocked down but
I get up again--
you're never gonna keep
me down--
I get knocked down but
I get up again--
you're ver gonna keep
THIS IS MY FAVORITE SONG!!
HOME
OMYGAH, SHOE FIRE! NOBODSY PANIC. I GOT IT. 'SALL UNDER CONTROL.
Um... PLEASE TELL ME SHE'S NOT GOING TO...
TWO BIRDS WIZ ONE SHTONE. 'S GOOD THINKIN', GOOD.
"I PRETTY MUCH SAVED YOUR DADDY'S LIFE."
"CLARA?!"

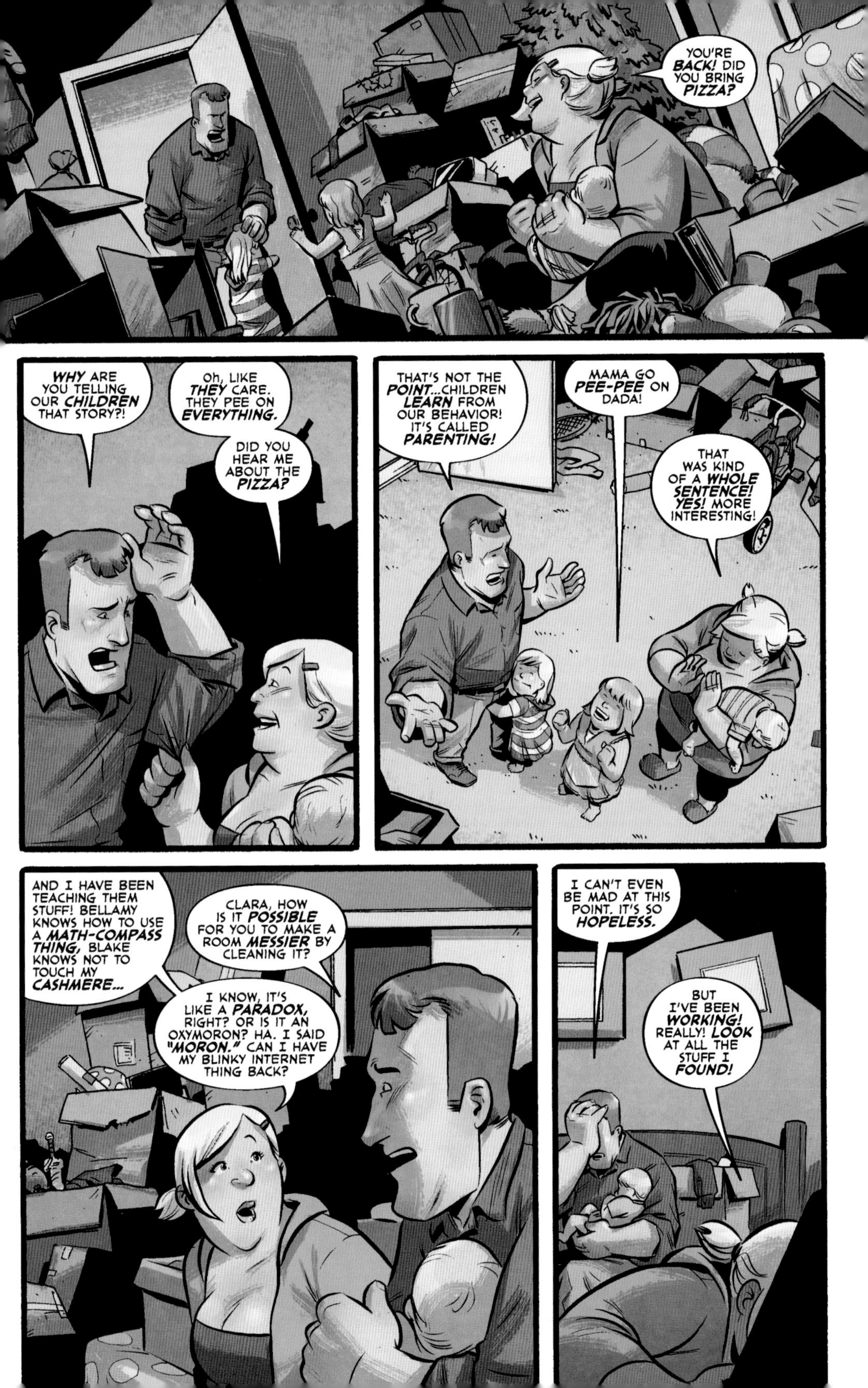
YOU'RE BACK! DID YOU BRING PIZZA?
WHY ARE YOU TELLING OUR CHILDREN THAT STORY?!
Oh, LIKE THEY CARE. THEY PEE ON EVERYTHING.
DID YOU HEAR ME ABOUT THE PIZZA?
THAT'S NOT THE POINT...CHILDREN LEARN FROM OUR BEHAVIOR! IT'S CALLED PARENTING!
MAMA GO PEE-PEE ON DADA!
THAT WAS KIND OF A WHOLE SENTENCE! YES! MORE INTERESTING!
AND I HAVE BEEN TEACHING THEM STUFF! BELLAMY KNOWS HOW TO USE A MATH-COMPASS THING, BLAKE KNOWS NOT TO TOUCH MY CASHMERE...
CLARA, HOW IS IT POSSIBLE FOR YOU TO MAKE A ROOM MESSIER BY CLEANING IT?
I KNOW, IT'S LIKE A PARADOX, RIGHT? OR IS IT AN OXYMORON? HA. I SAID "MORON." CAN I HAVE MY BLINKY INTERNET THING BACK?
I CAN'T EVEN BE MAD AT THIS POINT. IT'S SO HOPELESS.
BUT I'VE BEEN WORKING! REALLY! LOOK AT ALL THE STUFF I FOUND!

REMEMBER, THIS WAS OUR *FIRST* CONCERT TOGETHER!

FXL PRESENTS
TOAD THE WET SPROCKET
HOOTIE & THE BLOWFISH '01
WED AUG 13, 2001 7:30 PM

FROM OUR HONEYMOON TRIP! MOST ROMANTIC WEEKEND *EVER*.

WHAT'S *THIS*?

THE JUNK COVER THAT BROKE TO MAKE *BELLAMY!* I SAVED MEMENTOS OF ALL OUR KIDS' *CONCEPTIONS!*

HERE'S GABY'S...

In Loving Memory
Abraham Beane 1927-2003

...d at Holy Love Church
...W. Dogwood Lane.
...4

YOU WERE *INSATIABLE* AFTER YOUR GRANDPA'S FUNERAL.

THEY SAY GRIEF IMPACTS DIFFERENT PEOPLE IN *DIFFERENT* WAYS.

AND THIS IS FROM THE NIGHT WE MADE *BLAKEY.* IF YOU WANT, WE CAN POP IT IN THE PLAYER TO JOSTLE YOUR--

CLARA! NOT IN FRONT OF THE *KIDS!*

LUSTY & BUSTY

I CAN'T BELIEVE YOU *KEPT* THIS STUFF.

HOW COULD I *RESIST?* BLOND JESUS WAS A *HOT* LOOK FOR YOU.

YEAH, IT WASN'T BAD... HEY *LOOK,* THE KIDS' BABY BOOKS!

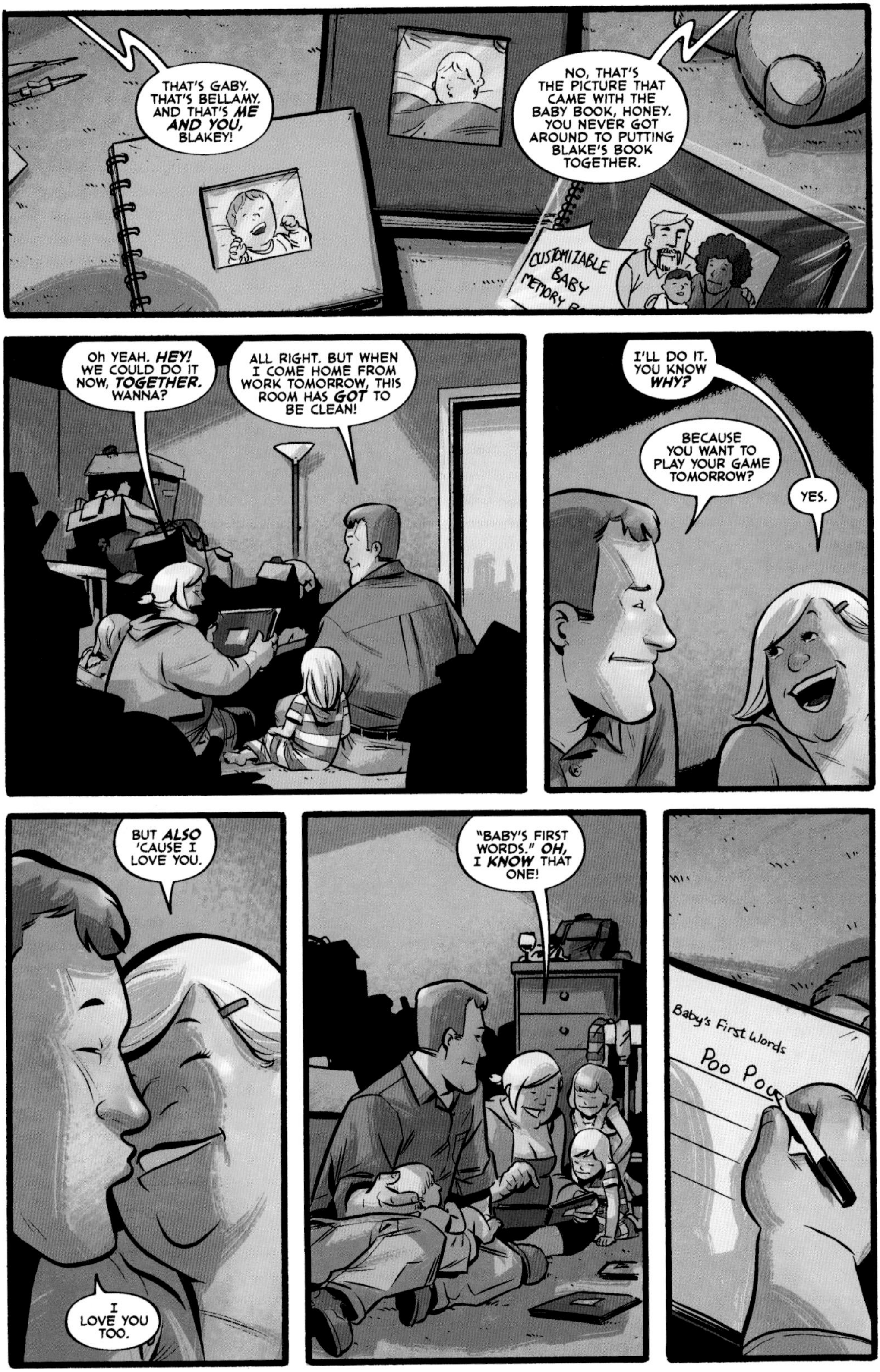
THAT'S GABY. THAT'S BELLAMY. AND THAT'S ME AND YOU, BLAKEY!
NO, THAT'S THE PICTURE THAT CAME WITH THE BABY BOOK, HONEY. YOU NEVER GOT AROUND TO PUTTING BLAKE'S BOOK TOGETHER.
CUSTOMIZABLE BABY MEMORY B
Oh YEAH. HEY! WE COULD DO IT NOW, TOGETHER. WANNA?
ALL RIGHT. BUT WHEN I COME HOME FROM WORK TOMORROW, THIS ROOM HAS GOT TO BE CLEAN!
I'LL DO IT. YOU KNOW WHY?
BECAUSE YOU WANT TO PLAY YOUR GAME TOMORROW?
YES.
BUT ALSO 'CAUSE I LOVE YOU.
I LOVE YOU TOO.
"BABY'S FIRST WORDS." OH, I KNOW THAT ONE!
Baby's First Words
Poo Po

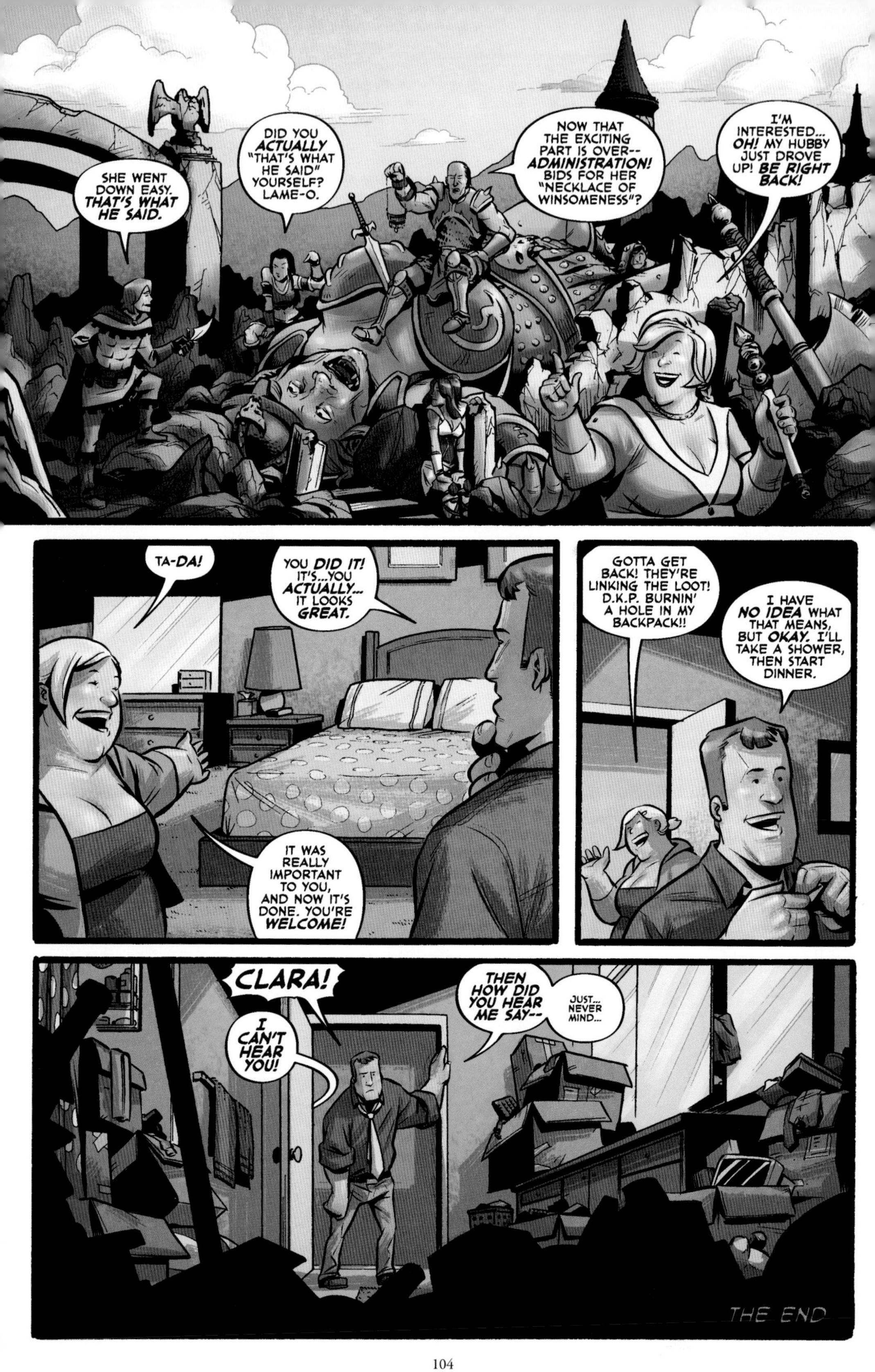
SHE WENT DOWN EASY. THAT'S WHAT HE SAID.
DID YOU ACTUALLY "THAT'S WHAT HE SAID" YOURSELF? LAME-O.
NOW THAT THE EXCITING PART IS OVER-- ADMINISTRATION! BIDS FOR HER "NECKLACE OF WINSOMENESS"?
I'M INTERESTED... OH! MY HUBBY JUST DROVE UP! BE RIGHT BACK!
TA-DA!
YOU DID IT! IT'S...YOU ACTUALLY... IT LOOKS GREAT.
IT WAS REALLY IMPORTANT TO YOU, AND NOW IT'S DONE. YOU'RE WELCOME!
GOTTA GET BACK! THEY'RE LINKING THE LOOT! D.K.P. BURNIN' A HOLE IN MY BACKPACK!!
I HAVE NO IDEA WHAT THAT MEANS, BUT OKAY. I'LL TAKE A SHOWER, THEN START DINNER.
CLARA!
I CAN'T HEAR YOU!
THEN HOW DID YOU HEAR ME SAY--
JUST... NEVER MIND...
THE END

CHAPTER FIVE
ZABOO

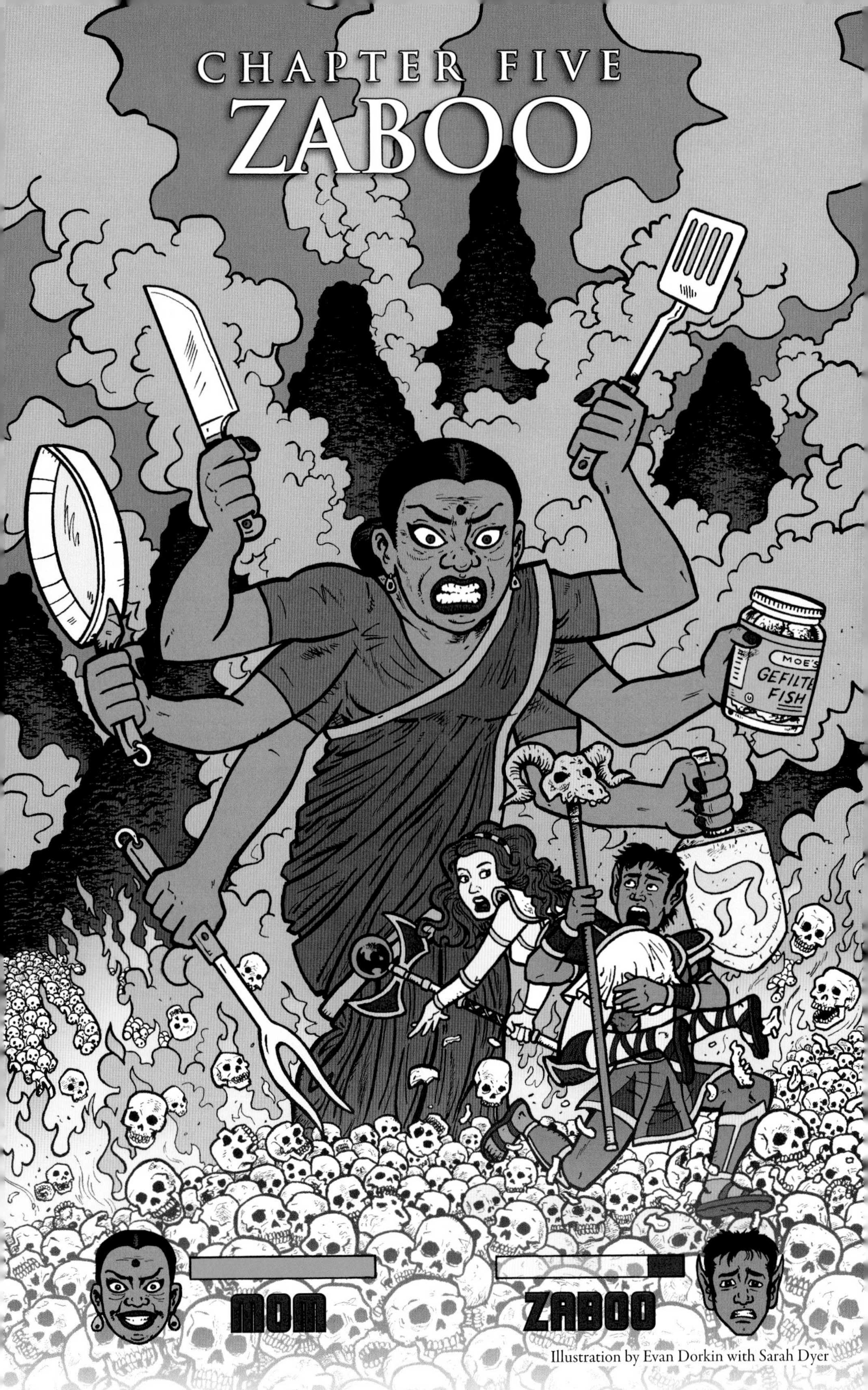
MOE'S
GEFILTE
FISH
MOM
ZABOO

Illustration by Evan Dorkin with Sarah Dyer

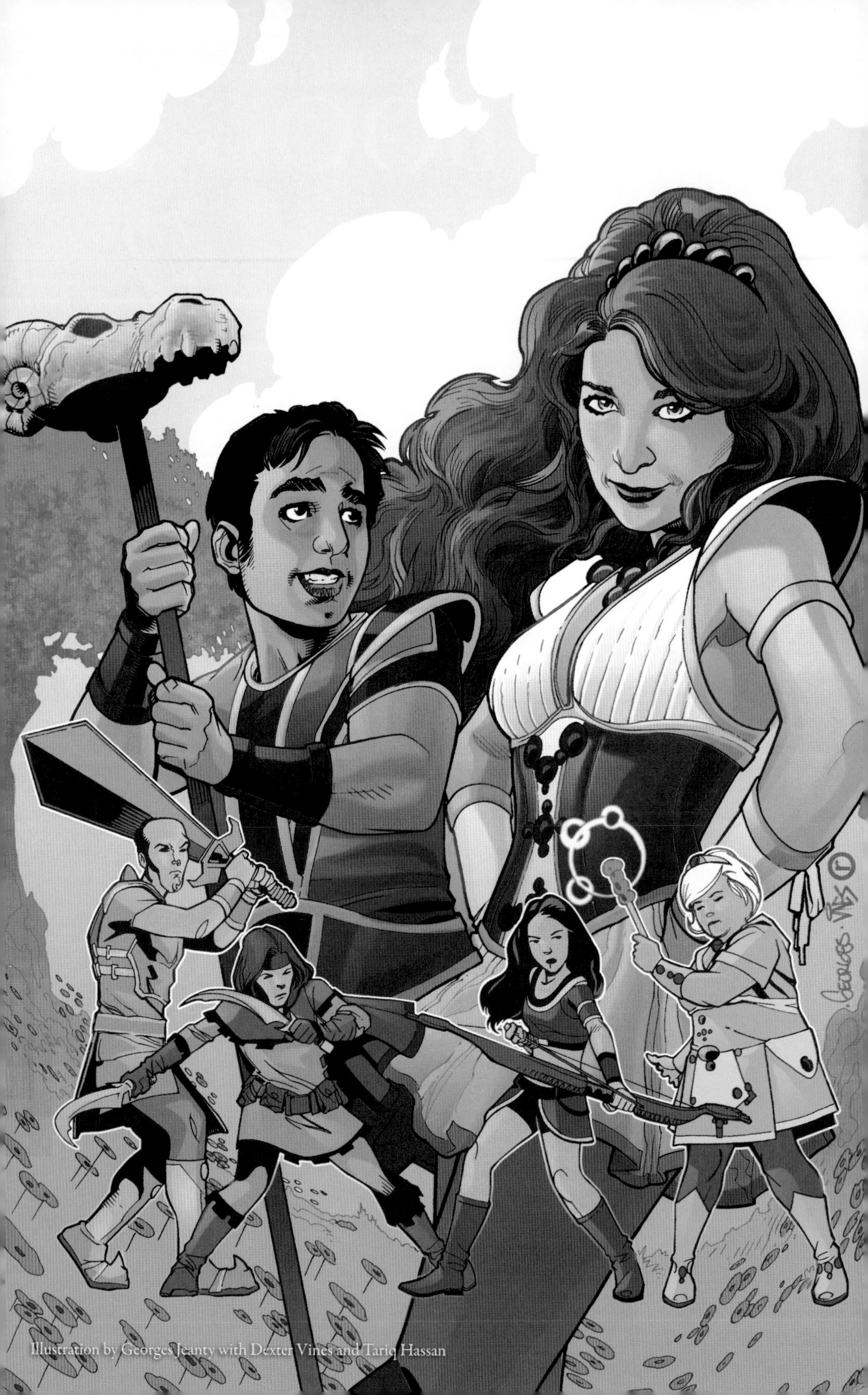

Illustration by Georges Jeanty with Dexter Vines and Tariq Hassan

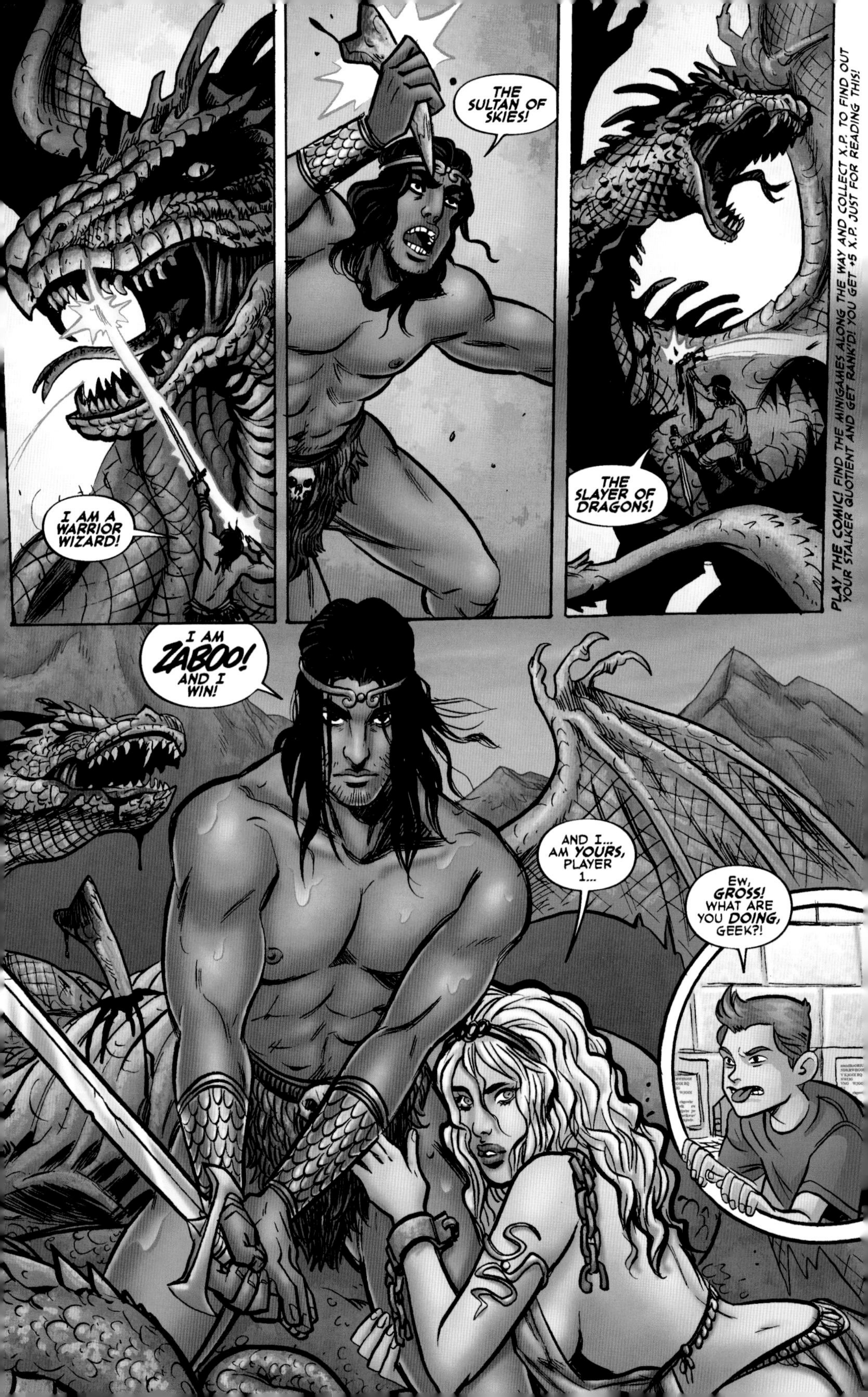
I AM A WARRIOR WIZARD!
THE SULTAN OF SKIES!
THE SLAYER OF DRAGONS!
I AM ZABOO! AND I WIN!
AND I... AM YOURS, PLAYER 1...
EW, GROSS! WHAT ARE YOU DOING, GEEK?!

PLAY THE COMIC! FIND THE MINIGAMES ALONG THE WAY AND COLLECT X.P. TO FIND OUT YOUR STALKER QUOTIENT AND GET RANK'D! YOU GET +5 X.P. JUST FOR READING THIS!

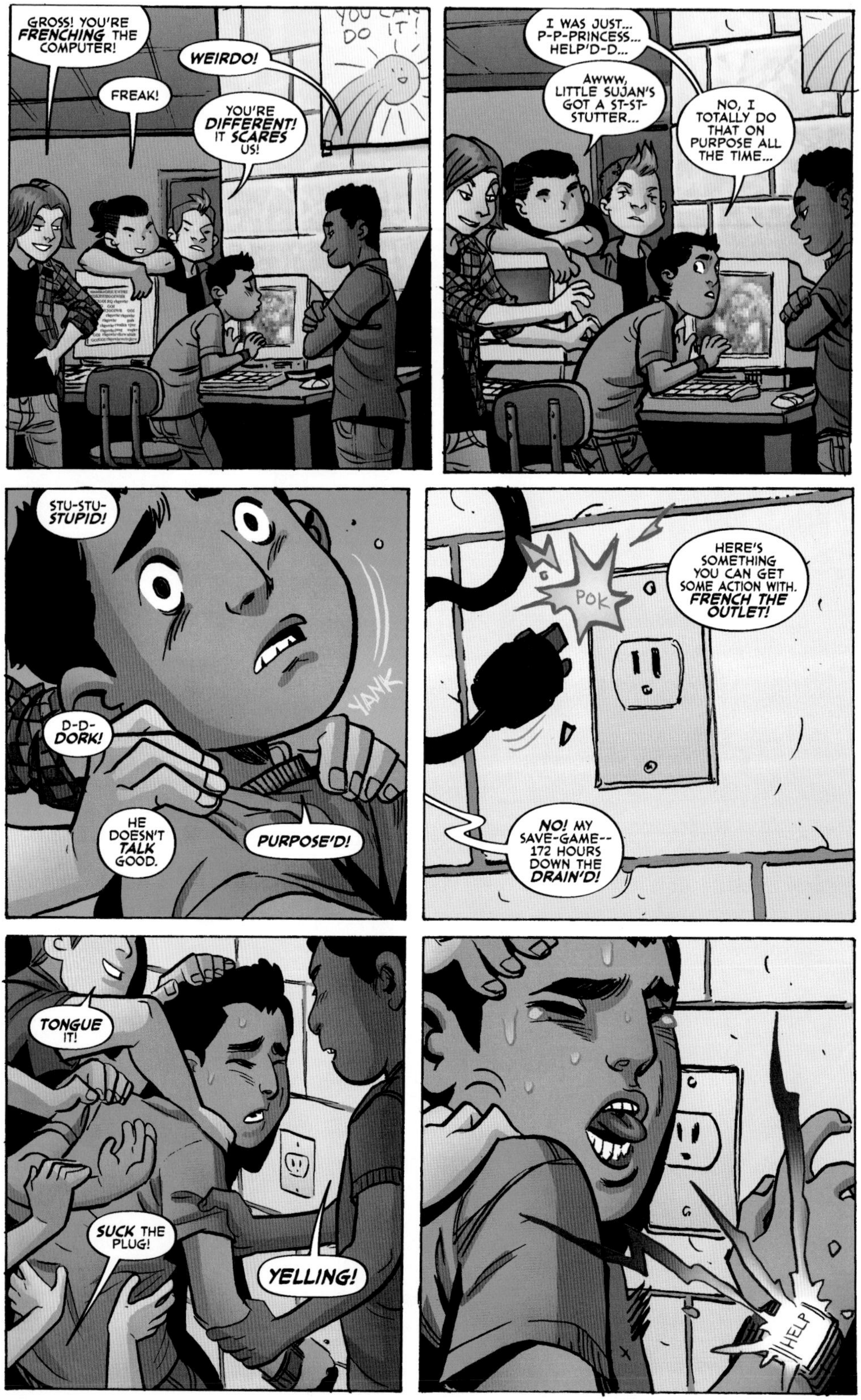
GROSS! YOU'RE FRENCHING THE COMPUTER!
FREAK!
WEIRDO!
YOU'RE DIFFERENT! IT SCARES US!
YOU CAN DO IT!
I WAS JUST... P-P-PRINCESS... HELP'D-D...
AWWW, LITTLE SUJAN'S GOT A ST-ST-STUTTER...
NO, I TOTALLY DO THAT ON PURPOSE ALL THE TIME...
STU-STU-STUPID!
D-D-DORK!
HE DOESN'T TALK GOOD.
PURPOSE'D!
YANK
POK
HERE'S SOMETHING YOU CAN GET SOME ACTION WITH. FRENCH THE OUTLET!
NO! MY SAVE-GAME-- 172 HOURS DOWN THE DRAIN'D!
TONGUE IT!
SUCK THE PLUG!
YELLING!
HELP

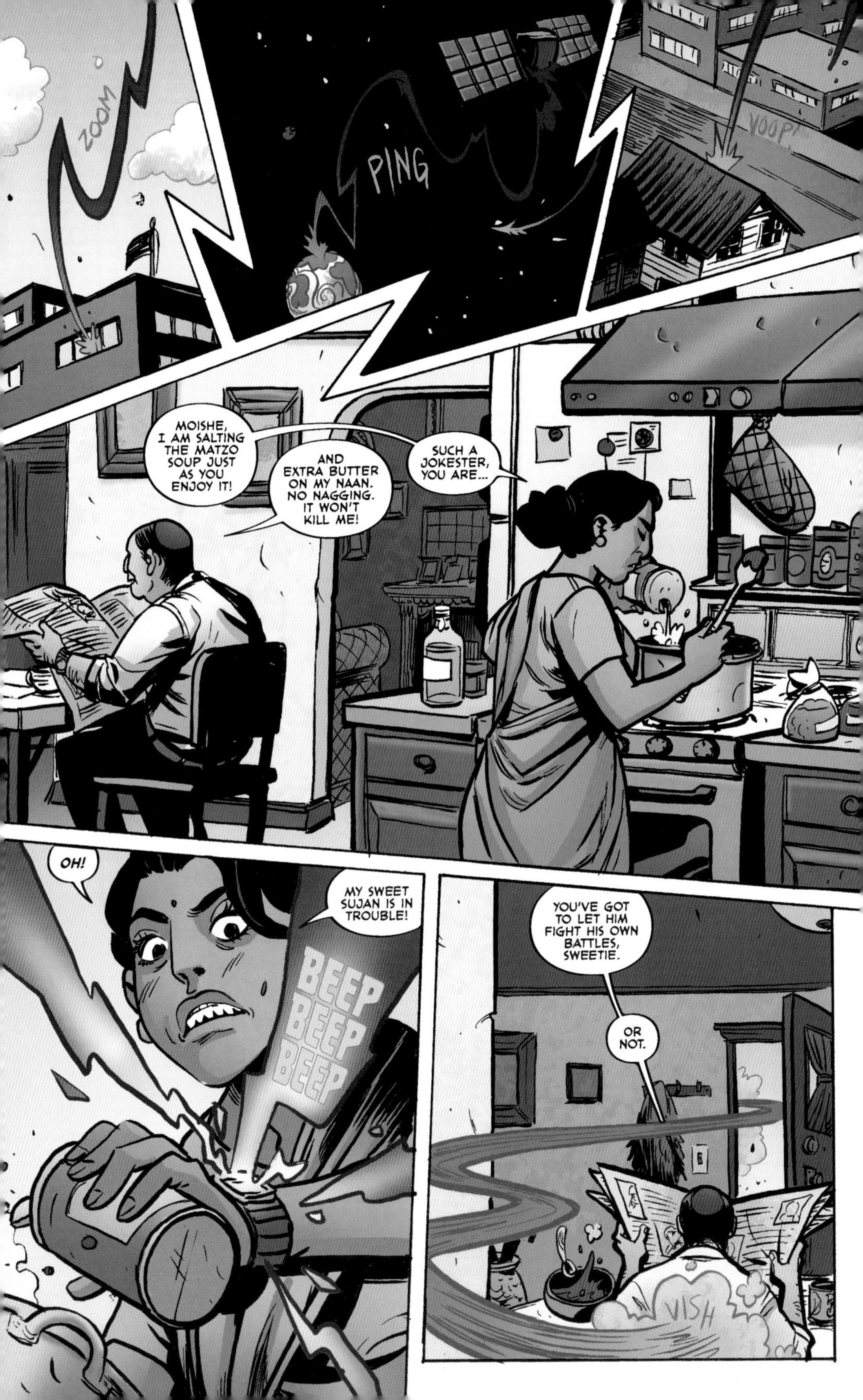
ZOOM
PING
VOOP!
MOISHE, I AM SALTING THE MATZO SOUP JUST AS YOU ENJOY IT!
AND EXTRA BUTTER ON MY NAAN. NO NAGGING. IT WON'T KILL ME!
SUCH A JOKESTER, YOU ARE...
OH!
MY SWEET SUJAN IS IN TROUBLE!
BEEP BEEP BEEP
YOU'VE GOT TO LET HIM FIGHT HIS OWN BATTLES, SWEETIE.
OR NOT.
VISH

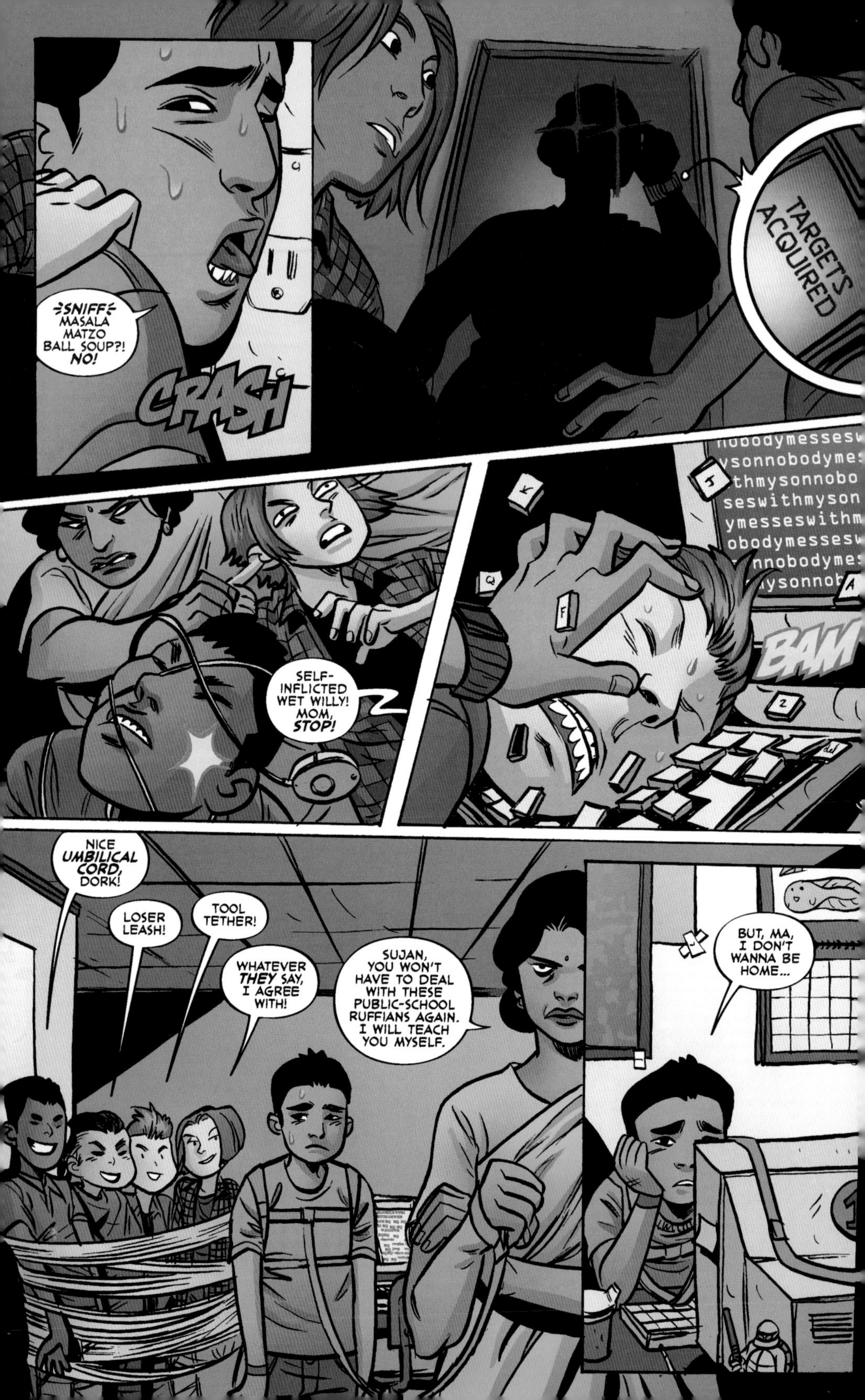
SNIFF MASALA MATZO BALL SOUP?! NO!
CRASH
TARGETS ACQUIRED
SELF-INFLICTED WET WILLY! MOM, STOP!
nobodymessesw
ysonnobodymes
ithmysonnobo
seswithmyson
ymesseswithm
obodymessesw
nnobodymes
ysonnob
BAM
NICE UMBILICAL CORD, DORK!
LOSER LEASH!
TOOL TETHER!
WHATEVER THEY SAY, I AGREE WITH!
SUJAN, YOU WON'T HAVE TO DEAL WITH THESE PUBLIC-SCHOOL RUFFIANS AGAIN. I WILL TEACH YOU MYSELF.
BUT, MA, I DON'T WANNA BE HOME...

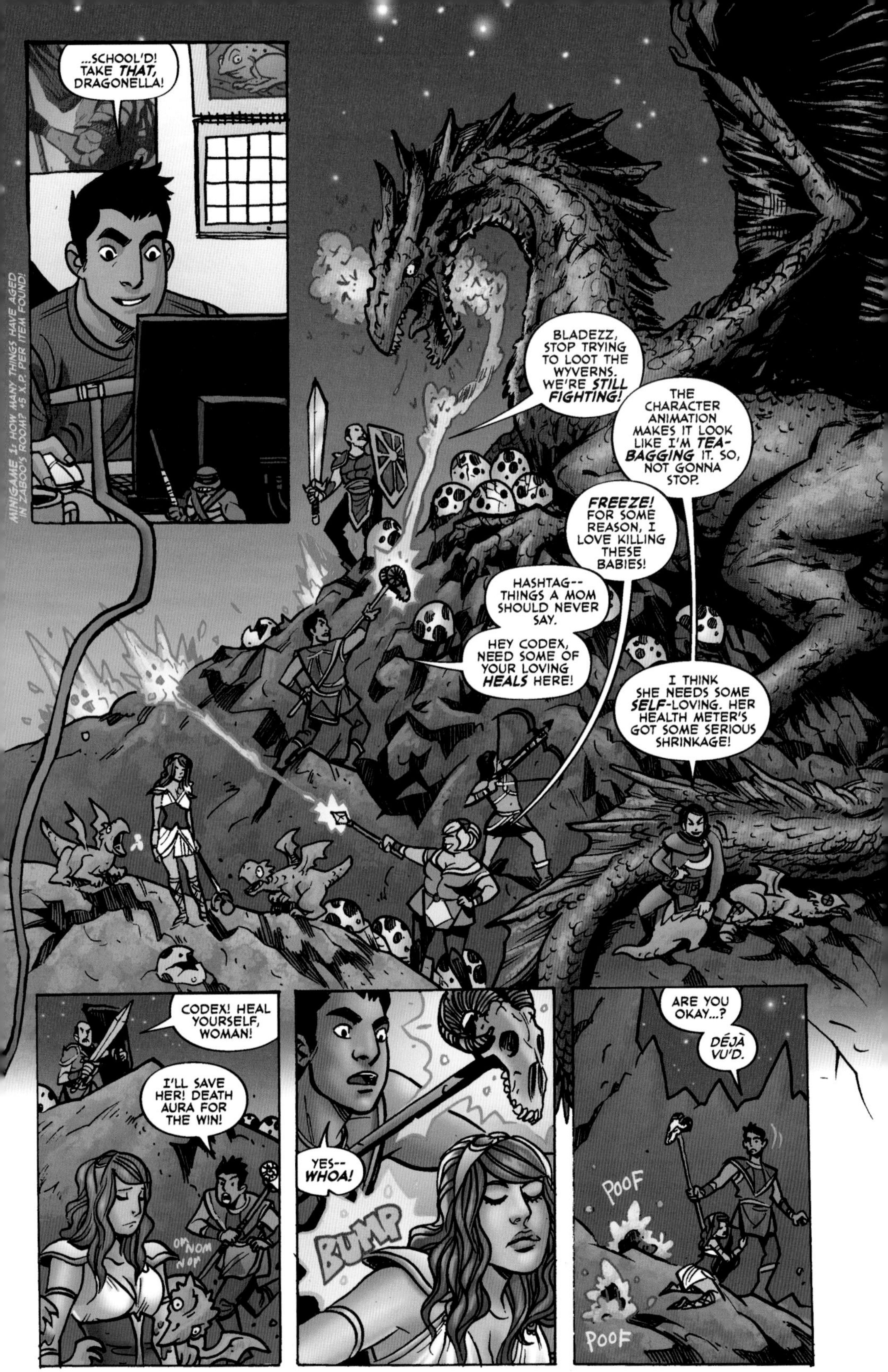

...SCHOOL'D! TAKE THAT, DRAGONELLA!
MINIGAME 1: HOW MANY THINGS HAVE AGED IN ZABOO'S ROOM? +5 X.P. PER ITEM FOUND!
BLADEZZ, STOP TRYING TO LOOT THE WYVERNS. WE'RE STILL FIGHTING!
THE CHARACTER ANIMATION MAKES IT LOOK LIKE I'M TEA-BAGGING IT. SO, NOT GONNA STOP.
FREEZE! FOR SOME REASON, I LOVE KILLING THESE BABIES!
HASHTAG-- THINGS A MOM SHOULD NEVER SAY.
HEY CODEX, NEED SOME OF YOUR LOVING HEALS HERE!
I THINK SHE NEEDS SOME SELF-LOVING. HER HEALTH METER'S GOT SOME SERIOUS SHRINKAGE!
CODEX! HEAL YOURSELF, WOMAN!
I'LL SAVE HER! DEATH AURA FOR THE WIN!
OM NOM NOM
YES-- WHOA!
BUMP
ARE YOU OKAY...?
DÉJÀ VU'D.
POOF
POOF

CODEX, WERE YOU A.F.K.?

NO. SORRY, I JUST LOST THE WILL TO LIVE FOR A MOMENT AND STOPPED CLICKING.

Ha-ha, JUST KIDDING.

TAK TAK TAK

YOU'VE BEEN SO OUT OF IT LATELY! SPACE CADET'D.

I DON'T WANNA TALK ABOUT IT.

LET'S CHAT IN A PRIVATE CHANNEL. THERE, YOU DON'T HAVE TO BE SHY...

Mmm... OKAY.

don't have a job, rent's overdue, my therapist told me yesterday that I suck at getting therapy. How does suck at paying for advice?! I spend rangers like you, and all I can thin is where I'm gonna be in ten year d some neck poppin ry. Never m

WOW. Uh, CONFIDANT'D.

What can I do to help?! We're not just strangers!

I think I'll just log off for a while. It's not like you can come rescue me from my real-life wyverns. ;)

Oh, CRAP, NOT AGAIN.

THAT WAS SUPPOSED TO BE A REGULAR PLAIN COLON SMILE, NOT A...Oh, WHATEVER.

LOGGING!

SHE KEEPS WINKY-ING ME. WE REALLY ARE TOGETHER. GASP'D!

GASP'D!

TAK TAK TAK

TAK TAK

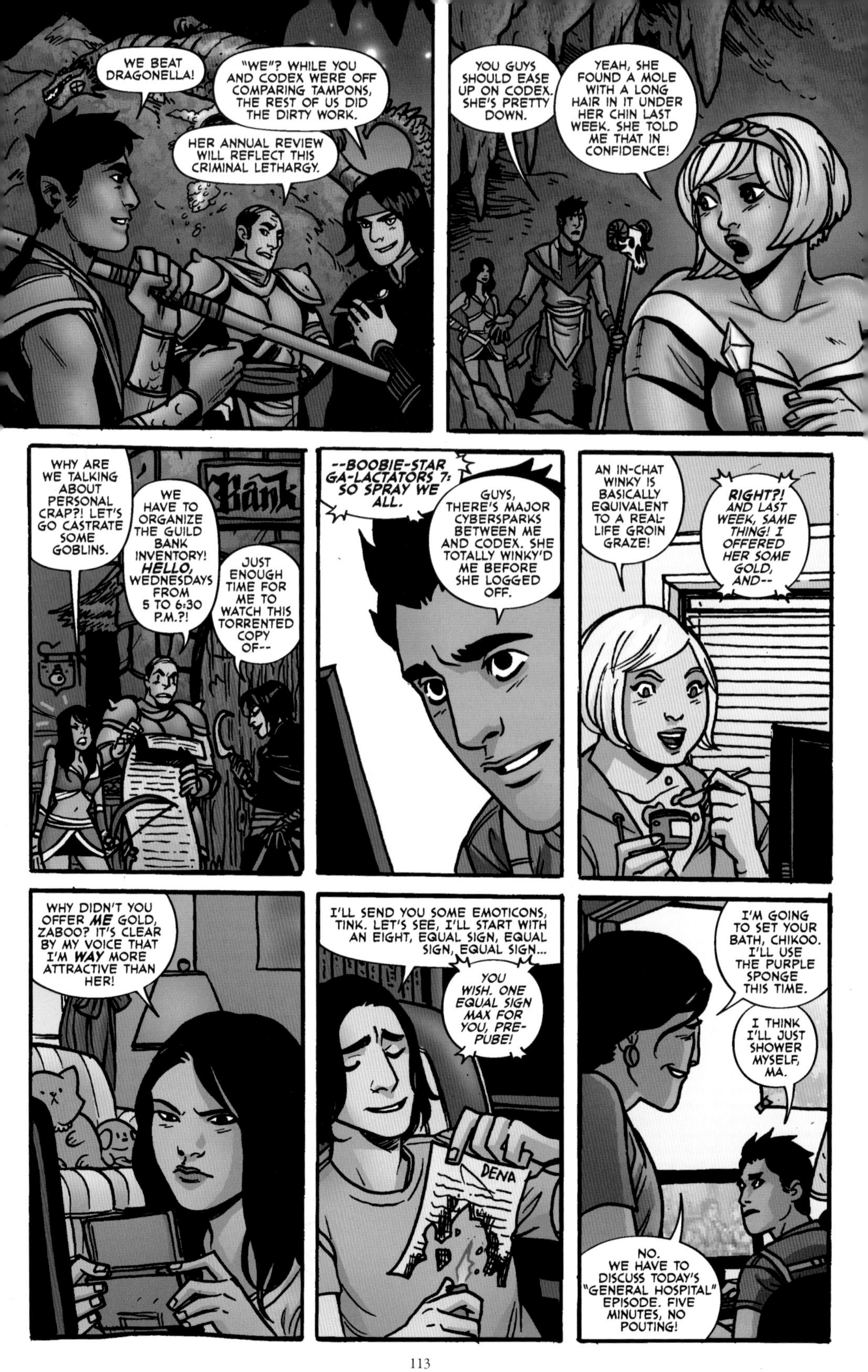
WE BEAT DRAGONELLA!
"WE"? WHILE YOU AND CODEX WERE OFF COMPARING TAMPONS, THE REST OF US DID THE DIRTY WORK.
HER ANNUAL REVIEW WILL REFLECT THIS CRIMINAL LETHARGY.
YOU GUYS SHOULD EASE UP ON CODEX. SHE'S PRETTY DOWN.
YEAH, SHE FOUND A MOLE WITH A LONG HAIR IN IT UNDER HER CHIN LAST WEEK. SHE TOLD ME THAT IN CONFIDENCE!
WHY ARE WE TALKING ABOUT PERSONAL CRAP?! LET'S GO CASTRATE SOME GOBLINS.
WE HAVE TO ORGANIZE THE GUILD BANK INVENTORY! HELLO, WEDNESDAYS FROM 5 TO 6:30 P.M.?!
BANK
JUST ENOUGH TIME FOR ME TO WATCH THIS TORRENTED COPY OF--
--BOOBIE-STAR GA-LACTATORS 7: SO SPRAY WE ALL.
GUYS, THERE'S MAJOR CYBERSPARKS BETWEEN ME AND CODEX. SHE TOTALLY WINKY'D ME BEFORE SHE LOGGED OFF.
AN IN-CHAT WINKY IS BASICALLY EQUIVALENT TO A REAL-LIFE GROIN GRAZE!
RIGHT?! AND LAST WEEK, SAME THING! I OFFERED HER SOME GOLD, AND--
WHY DIDN'T YOU OFFER ME GOLD, ZABOO? IT'S CLEAR BY MY VOICE THAT I'M WAY MORE ATTRACTIVE THAN HER!
I'LL SEND YOU SOME EMOTICONS, TINK. LET'S SEE, I'LL START WITH AN EIGHT, EQUAL SIGN, EQUAL SIGN, EQUAL SIGN...
YOU WISH. ONE EQUAL SIGN MAX FOR YOU, PRE-PUBE!
DENA
I'M GOING TO SET YOUR BATH, CHIKOO. I'LL USE THE PURPLE SPONGE THIS TIME.
I THINK I'LL JUST SHOWER MYSELF, MA.
NO. WE HAVE TO DISCUSS TODAY'S "GENERAL HOSPITAL" EPISODE. FIVE MINUTES, NO POUTING!

PROFILES -> PEOPLE -> FAMILY -> **CODEX**
DECEASED | GUILD | VORK
ANIMALS | SCHOOL | CLARA
| JUST MET | BLADEZZ
| FAMOUS | TINK
| EVERY1 ELSE |

CODEX
415-952-6339
204 Clovervilestreet Lane
OTHER INFORMATION
Social Security Number:
Height, Weight, Measure
Menstruation Cycle: 2/1
Allergies: Dust, Cats, a
Employment History:
Degree... from Un

O.M.W., MY LOVE!

FAVORITE WEBSITES: LOL Cats, Pos
HOBBIES, INTERESTS, ACTIVITIES: Pla
FAVORITE/LEAST FAVORITE FOODS: C
FAVORITE/LEAST FAVORITE COLOR: R
MOST HOURS LOGGED ON THE GAM
MOST HOURS LOGGED OFF THE GAM
LAST MOVIE SEEN IN THEATERS: T
...ITE FANTASY NOVEL: Drago

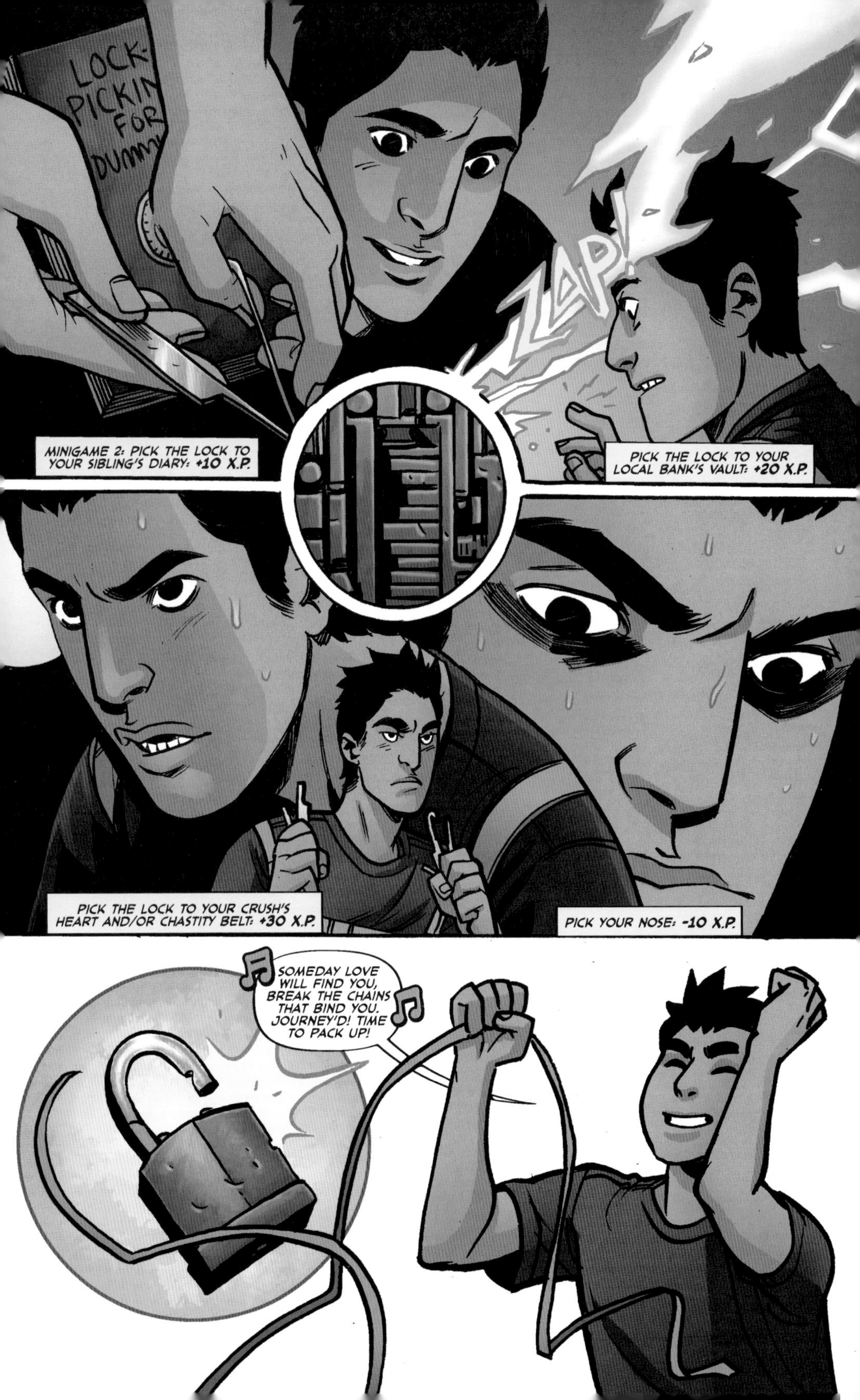
LOCK-PICKIN FOR DUMM
MINIGAME 2: PICK THE LOCK TO YOUR SIBLING'S DIARY: +10 X.P.
ZAP!
PICK THE LOCK TO YOUR LOCAL BANK'S VAULT: +20 X.P.
PICK THE LOCK TO YOUR CRUSH'S HEART AND/OR CHASTITY BELT: +30 X.P.
PICK YOUR NOSE: -10 X.P.
SOMEDAY LOVE WILL FIND YOU, BREAK THE CHAINS THAT BIND YOU. JOURNEY'D! TIME TO PACK UP!

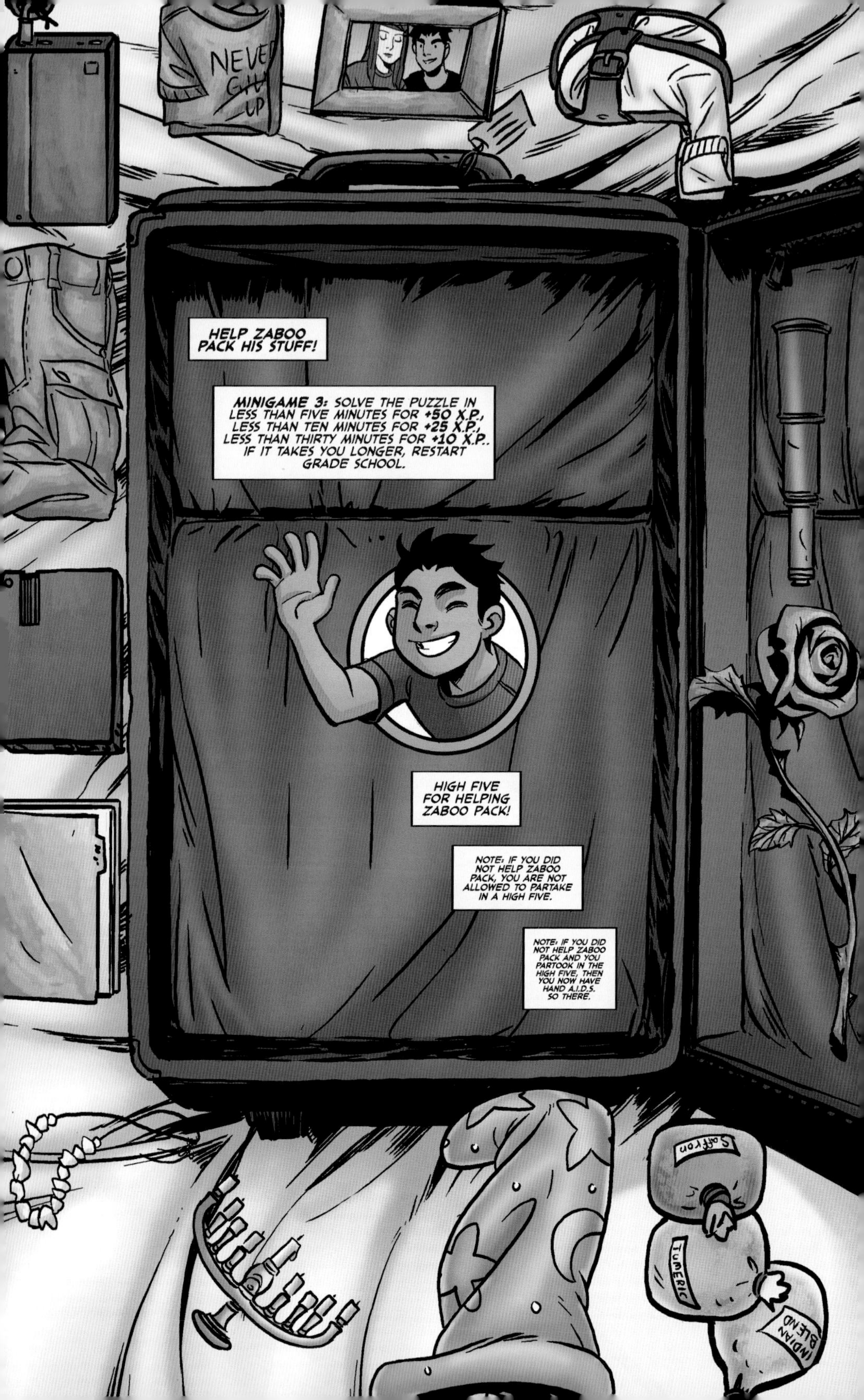
HELP ZABOO PACK HIS STUFF!
MINIGAME 3: SOLVE THE PUZZLE IN LESS THAN FIVE MINUTES FOR +50 X.P., LESS THAN TEN MINUTES FOR +25 X.P., LESS THAN THIRTY MINUTES FOR +10 X.P.. IF IT TAKES YOU LONGER, RESTART GRADE SCHOOL.
HIGH FIVE FOR HELPING ZABOO PACK!
NOTE: IF YOU DID NOT HELP ZABOO PACK, YOU ARE NOT ALLOWED TO PARTAKE IN A HIGH FIVE.
NOTE: IF YOU DID NOT HELP ZABOO PACK AND YOU PARTOOK IN THE HIGH FIVE, THEN YOU NOW HAVE HAND A.I.D.S. SO THERE.
NEVER GIVE UP
Saffron
TUMERIC
INDIAN BLEND

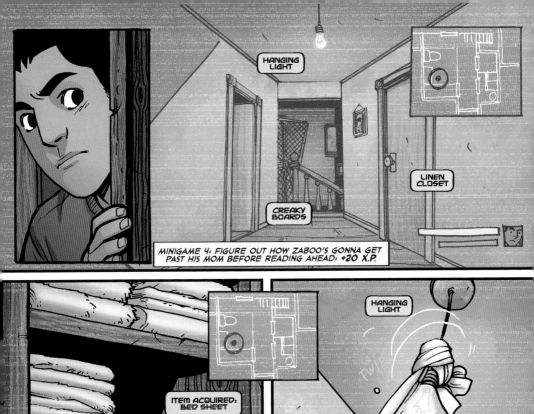

HANGING LIGHT

CREAKY BOARDS

LINEN CLOSET

MINIGAME 4: FIGURE OUT HOW ZABOO'S GONNA GET PAST HIS MOM BEFORE READING AHEAD: +20 X.P.

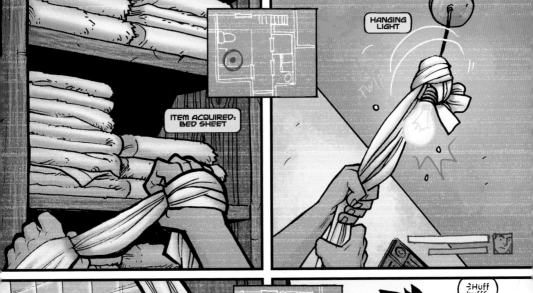

ITEM ACQUIRED: BED SHEET

HANGING LIGHT

FWIP

Huff huff

GOOD THING MOM'S INTO HIGH THREAD COUNT. ZABOOOO!

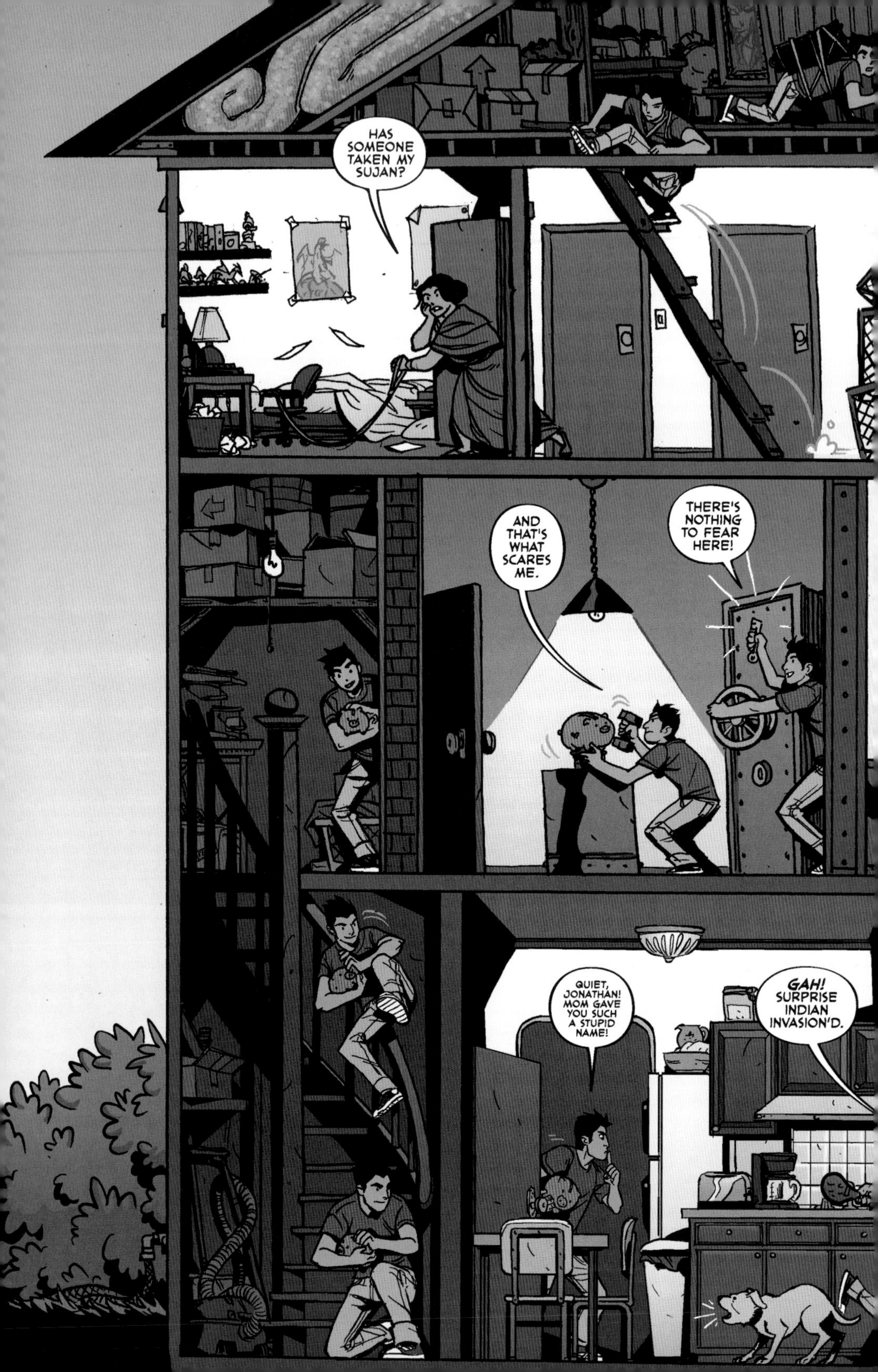
HAS SOMEONE TAKEN MY SUJAN?
AND THAT'S WHAT SCARES ME.
THERE'S NOTHING TO FEAR HERE!
QUIET, JONATHAN! MOM GAVE YOU SUCH A STUPID NAME!
GAH! SURPRISE INDIAN INVASION'D.

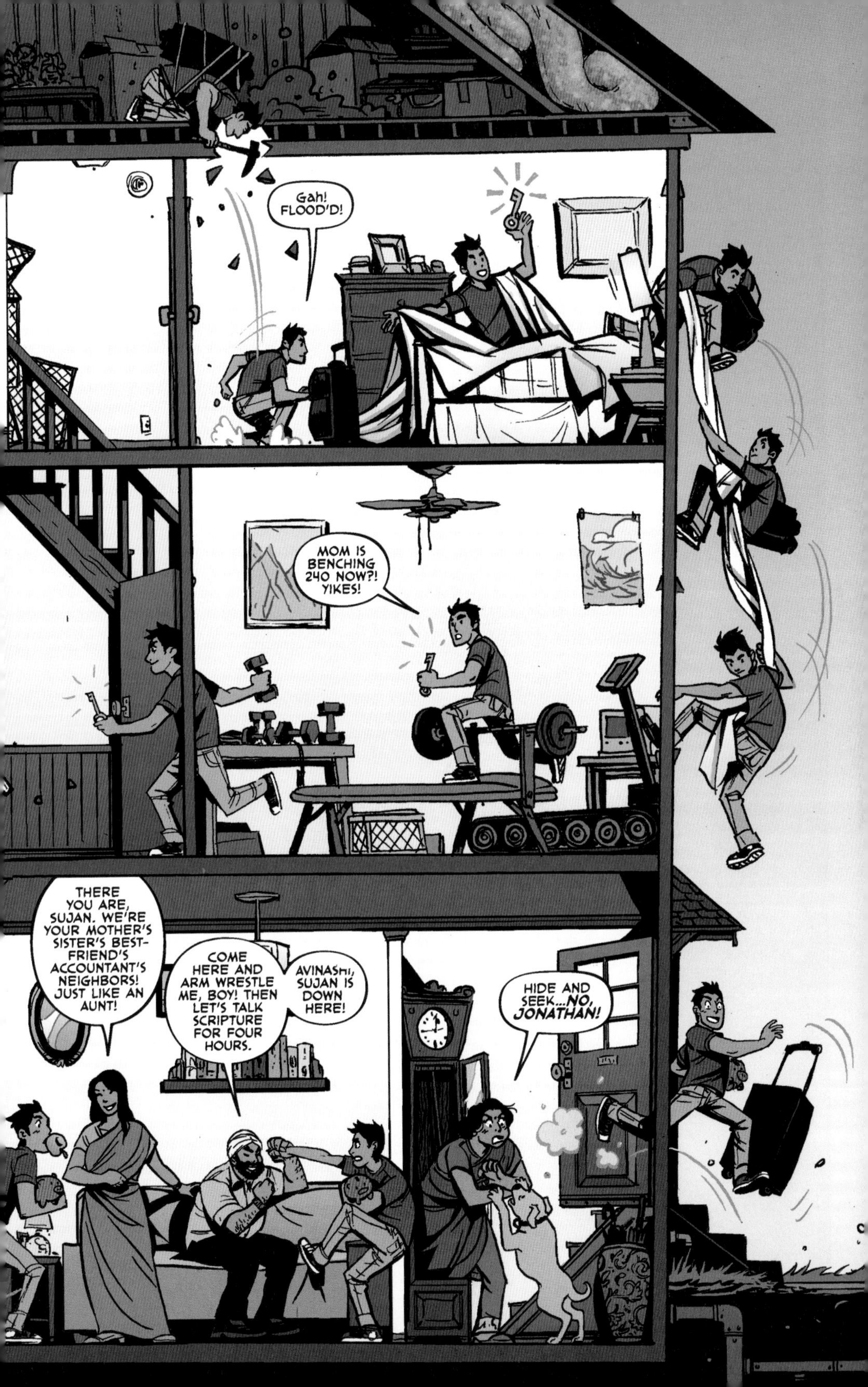

Gah! FLOOD'D!
MOM IS BENCHING 240 NOW?! YIKES!
THERE YOU ARE, SUJAN. WE'RE YOUR MOTHER'S SISTER'S BEST-FRIEND'S ACCOUNTANT'S NEIGHBORS! JUST LIKE AN AUNT!
COME HERE AND ARM WRESTLE ME, BOY! THEN LET'S TALK SCRIPTURE FOR FOUR HOURS.
AVINASHI, SUJAN IS DOWN HERE!
HIDE AND SEEK...NO, JONATHAN!

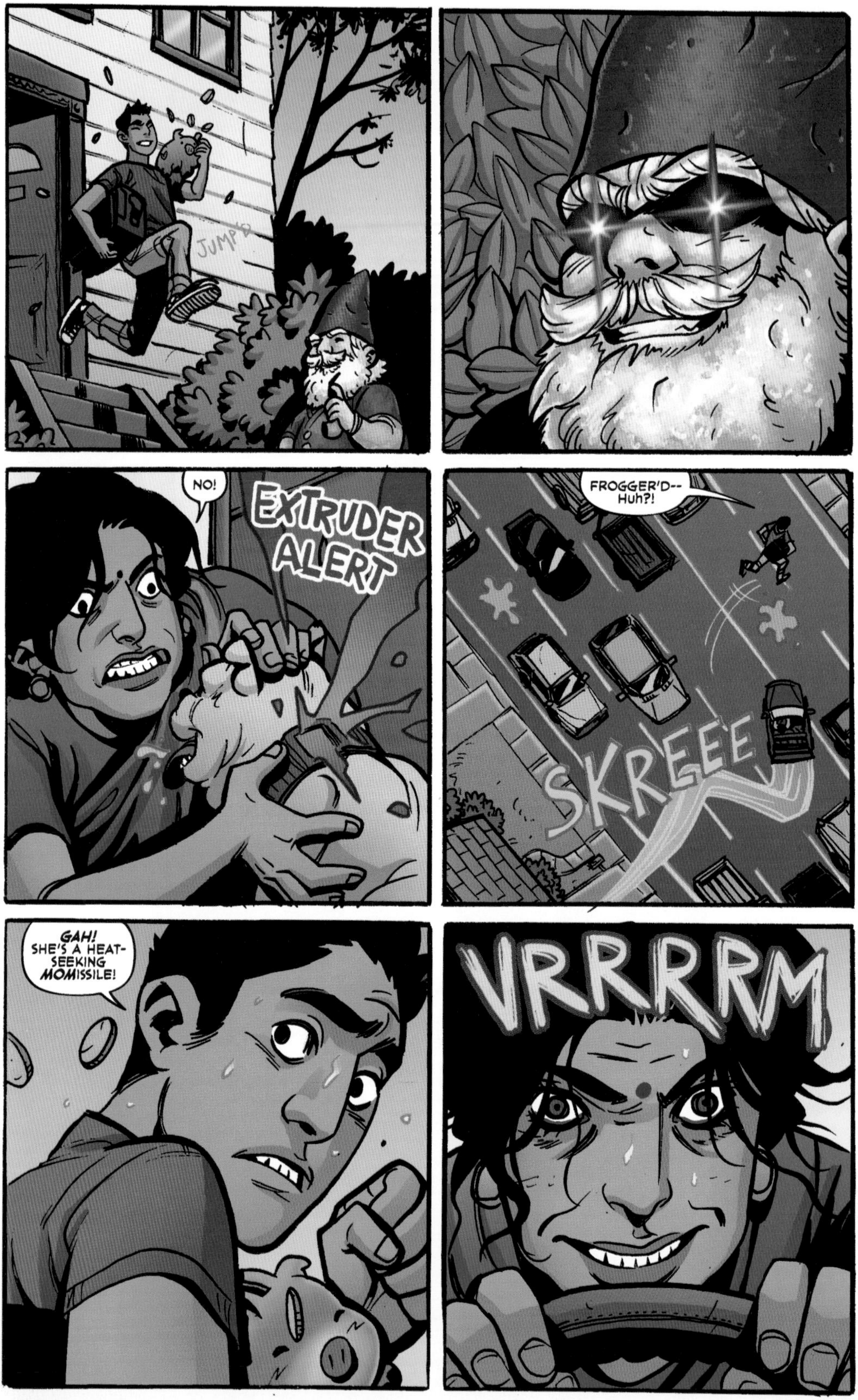
JUMP'D
NO!
EXTRUDER ALERT
FROGGER'D-- Huh?!
SKREEE
GAH! SHE'S A HEAT-SEEKING *MOM*ISSILE!
VRRRRM

X.P. BONUS: IF YOU'VE BEEN READING THIS COMIC WITH YOUR PANTS OFF, YOU GET +30 X.P. IF NOT, YOU MAY TAKE YOUR PANTS OFF NOW FOR +15 X.P.

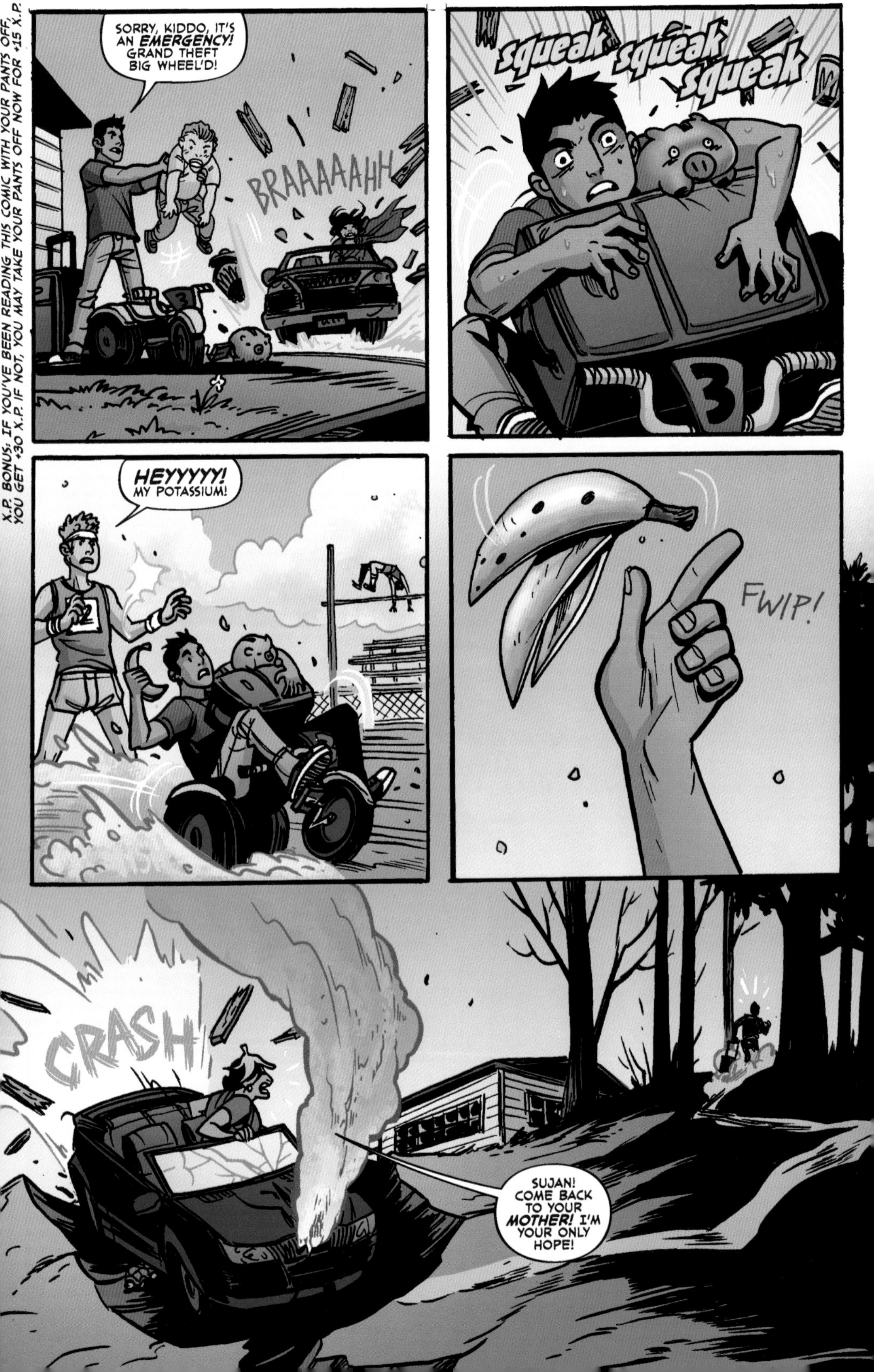
SORRY, KIDDO, IT'S AN **EMERGENCY!** GRAND THEFT BIG WHEEL'D!
BRAAAAAHH
squeak squeak squeak
HEYYYYY! MY POTASSIUM!
FWIP!
CRASH
SUJAN! COME BACK TO YOUR **MOTHER!** I'M YOUR ONLY HOPE!

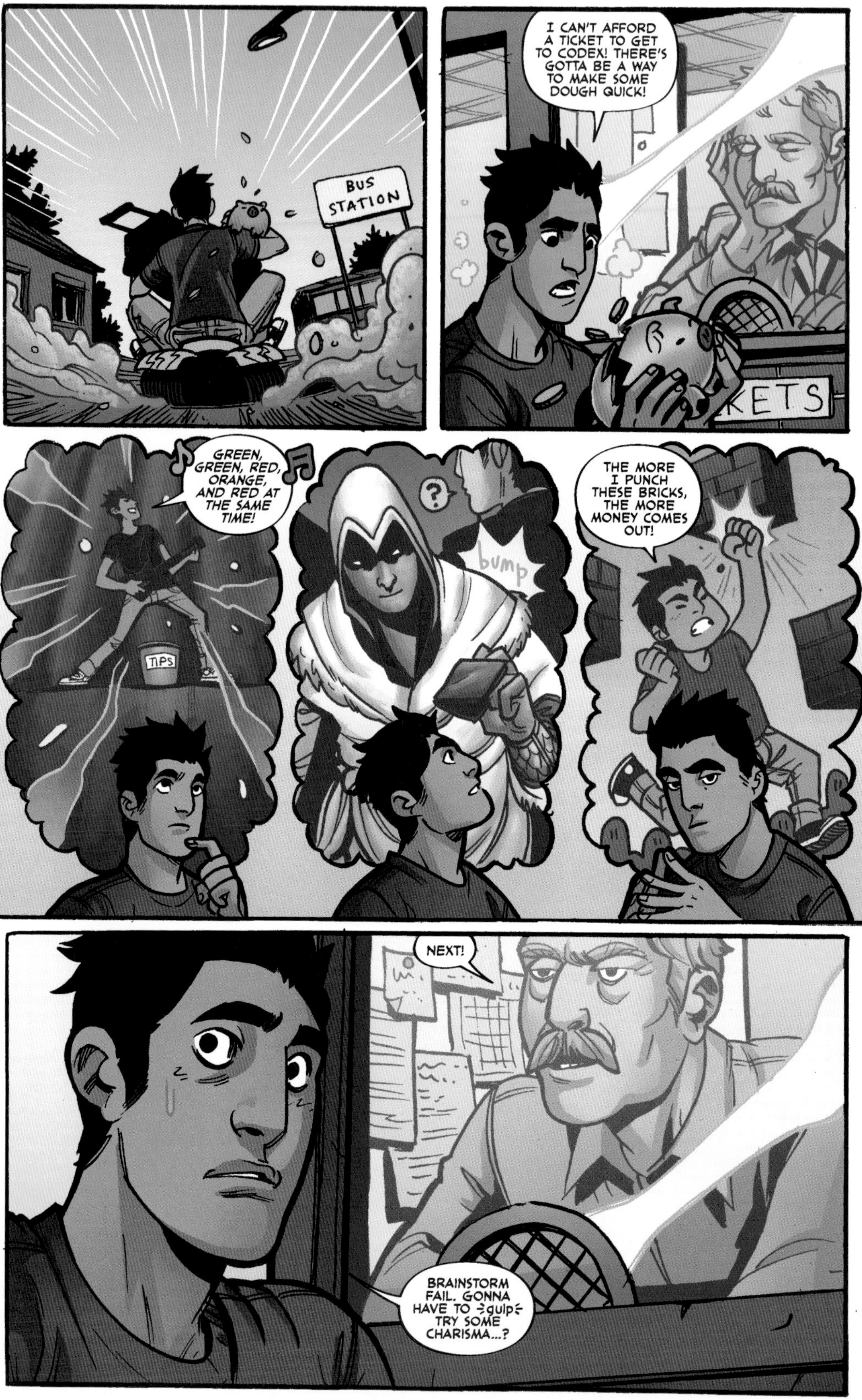
BUS STATION
I CAN'T AFFORD A TICKET TO GET TO CODEX! THERE'S GOTTA BE A WAY TO MAKE SOME DOUGH QUICK!
KETS
GREEN, GREEN, RED, ORANGE, AND RED AT THE SAME TIME!
TIPS
?
bump
THE MORE I PUNCH THESE BRICKS, THE MORE MONEY COMES OUT!
NEXT!
BRAINSTORM FAIL. GONNA HAVE TO ⪢gulp⪡ TRY SOME CHARISMA...?

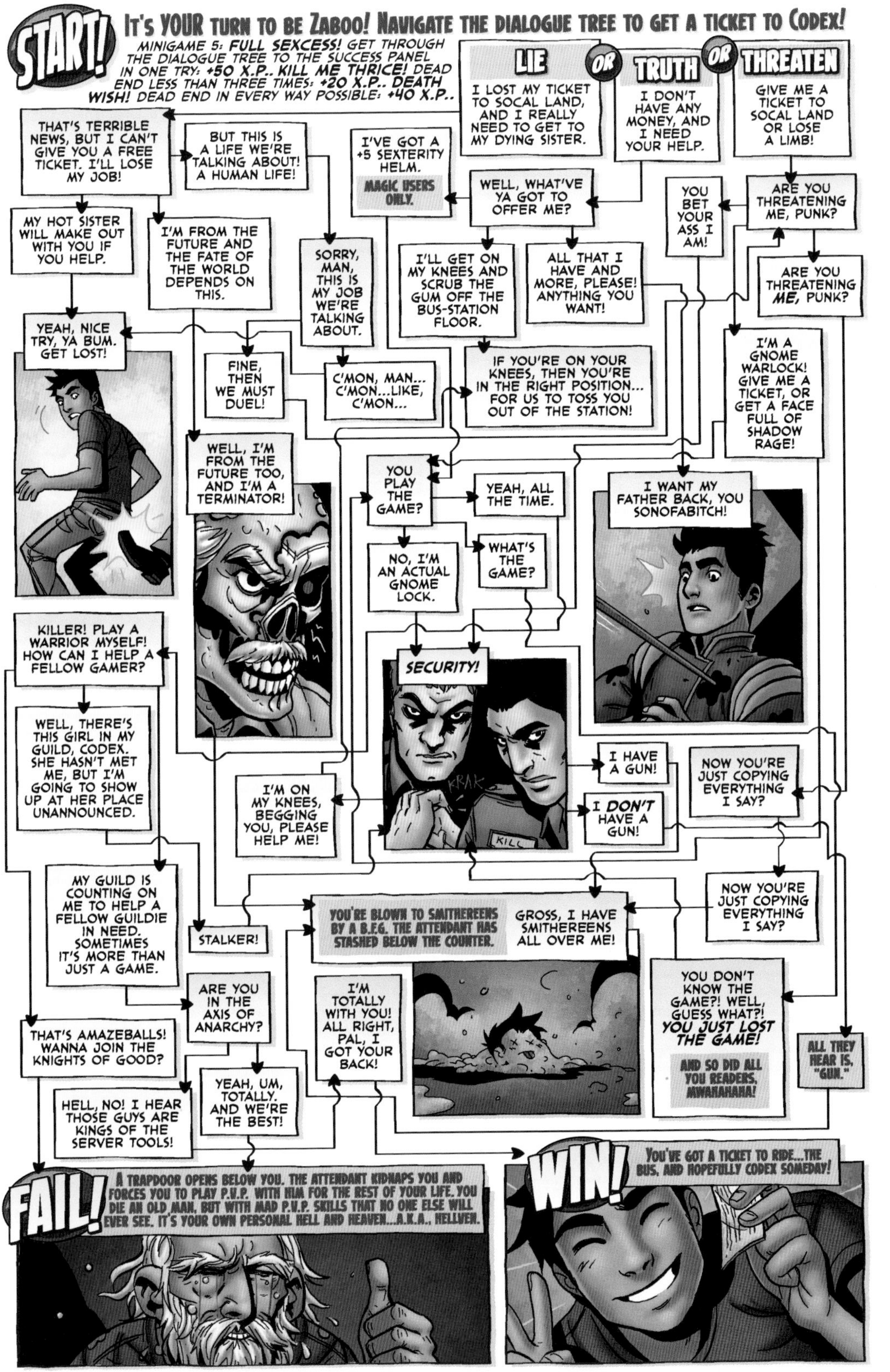
START!
It's YOUR turn to be Zaboo! Navigate the dialogue tree to get a ticket to Codex!
MINIGAME 5: FULL SEXCESS! GET THROUGH THE DIALOGUE TREE TO THE SUCCESS PANEL IN ONE TRY: +50 X.P.. KILL ME THRICE! DEAD END LESS THAN THREE TIMES: +20 X.P.. DEATH WISH! DEAD END IN EVERY WAY POSSIBLE: +40 X.P..
LIE
I LOST MY TICKET TO SOCAL LAND, AND I REALLY NEED TO GET TO MY DYING SISTER.
OR
TRUTH
I DON'T HAVE ANY MONEY, AND I NEED YOUR HELP.
OR
THREATEN
GIVE ME A TICKET TO SOCAL LAND OR LOSE A LIMB!
THAT'S TERRIBLE NEWS, BUT I CAN'T GIVE YOU A FREE TICKET. I'LL LOSE MY JOB!
BUT THIS IS A LIFE WE'RE TALKING ABOUT! A HUMAN LIFE!
I'VE GOT A +5 SEXTERITY HELM.
MAGIC USERS ONLY.
WELL, WHAT'VE YA GOT TO OFFER ME?
YOU BET YOUR ASS I AM!
ARE YOU THREATENING ME, PUNK?
MY HOT SISTER WILL MAKE OUT WITH YOU IF YOU HELP.
I'M FROM THE FUTURE AND THE FATE OF THE WORLD DEPENDS ON THIS.
SORRY, MAN, THIS IS MY JOB WE'RE TALKING ABOUT.
I'LL GET ON MY KNEES AND SCRUB THE GUM OFF THE BUS-STATION FLOOR.
ALL THAT I HAVE AND MORE, PLEASE! ANYTHING YOU WANT!
ARE YOU THREATENING ME, PUNK?
YEAH, NICE TRY, YA BUM. GET LOST!
FINE, THEN WE MUST DUEL!
C'MON, MAN... C'MON...LIKE, C'MON...
IF YOU'RE ON YOUR KNEES, THEN YOU'RE IN THE RIGHT POSITION... FOR US TO TOSS YOU OUT OF THE STATION!
I'M A GNOME WARLOCK! GIVE ME A TICKET, OR GET A FACE FULL OF SHADOW RAGE!
WELL, I'M FROM THE FUTURE TOO, AND I'M A TERMINATOR!
YOU PLAY THE GAME?
YEAH, ALL THE TIME.
I WANT MY FATHER BACK, YOU SONOFABITCH!
NO, I'M AN ACTUAL GNOME LOCK.
WHAT'S THE GAME?
KILLER! PLAY A WARRIOR MYSELF! HOW CAN I HELP A FELLOW GAMER?
SECURITY!
KRAK
WELL, THERE'S THIS GIRL IN MY GUILD, CODEX. SHE HASN'T MET ME, BUT I'M GOING TO SHOW UP AT HER PLACE UNANNOUNCED.
I HAVE A GUN!
NOW YOU'RE JUST COPYING EVERYTHING I SAY?
I'M ON MY KNEES, BEGGING YOU, PLEASE HELP ME!
I DON'T HAVE A GUN!
MY GUILD IS COUNTING ON ME TO HELP A FELLOW GUILDIE IN NEED. SOMETIMES IT'S MORE THAN JUST A GAME.
STALKER!
YOU'RE BLOWN TO SMITHEREENS BY A B.F.G. THE ATTENDANT HAS STASHED BELOW THE COUNTER.
GROSS, I HAVE SMITHEREENS ALL OVER ME!
NOW YOU'RE JUST COPYING EVERYTHING I SAY?
ARE YOU IN THE AXIS OF ANARCHY?
I'M TOTALLY WITH YOU! ALL RIGHT, PAL, I GOT YOUR BACK!
YOU DON'T KNOW THE GAME?! WELL, GUESS WHAT?! YOU JUST LOST THE GAME!
AND SO DID ALL YOU READERS. MWAHAHAHA!
THAT'S AMAZEBALLS! WANNA JOIN THE KNIGHTS OF GOOD?
ALL THEY HEAR IS, "GUN."
HELL, NO! I HEAR THOSE GUYS ARE KINGS OF THE SERVER TOOLS!
YEAH, UM, TOTALLY. AND WE'RE THE BEST!
WIN!
You've got a ticket to ride...the bus, and hopefully Codex someday!
FAIL!
A TRAPDOOR OPENS BELOW YOU. THE ATTENDANT KIDNAPS YOU AND FORCES YOU TO PLAY P.V.P. WITH HIM FOR THE REST OF YOUR LIFE. YOU DIE AN OLD MAN, BUT WITH MAD P.V.P. SKILLS THAT NO ONE ELSE WILL EVER SEE. IT'S YOUR OWN PERSONAL HELL AND HEAVEN...A.K.A., HELLVEN.

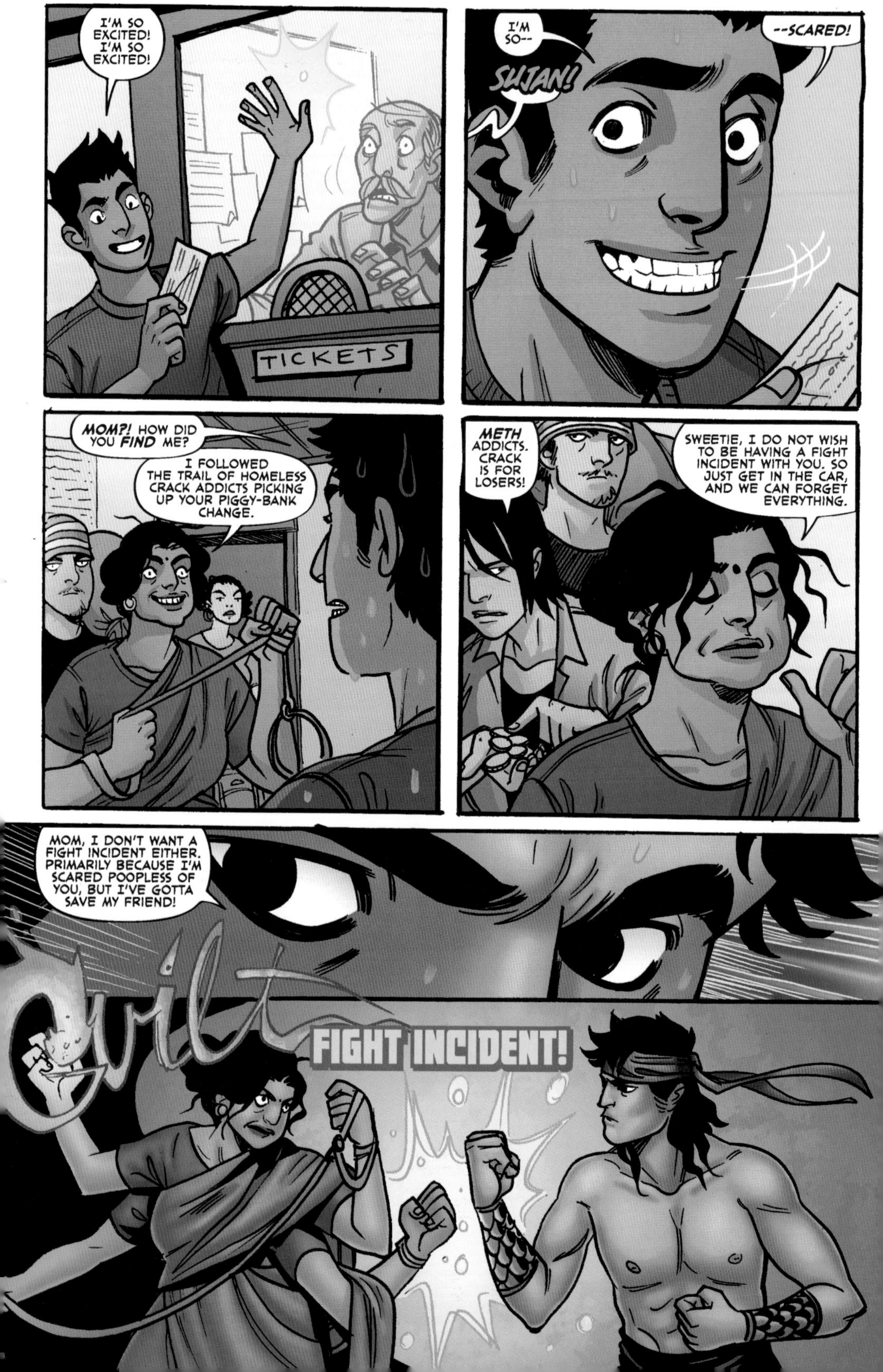

I'M SO EXCITED! I'M SO EXCITED!
TICKETS
I'M SO--
SUJAN!
--SCARED!
MOM?! HOW DID YOU FIND ME?
I FOLLOWED THE TRAIL OF HOMELESS CRACK ADDICTS PICKING UP YOUR PIGGY-BANK CHANGE.
METH ADDICTS. CRACK IS FOR LOSERS!
SWEETIE, I DO NOT WISH TO BE HAVING A FIGHT INCIDENT WITH YOU. SO JUST GET IN THE CAR, AND WE CAN FORGET EVERYTHING.
MOM, I DON'T WANT A FIGHT INCIDENT EITHER. PRIMARILY BECAUSE I'M SCARED POOPLESS OF YOU, BUT I'VE GOTTA SAVE MY FRIEND!
FIGHT INCIDENT!

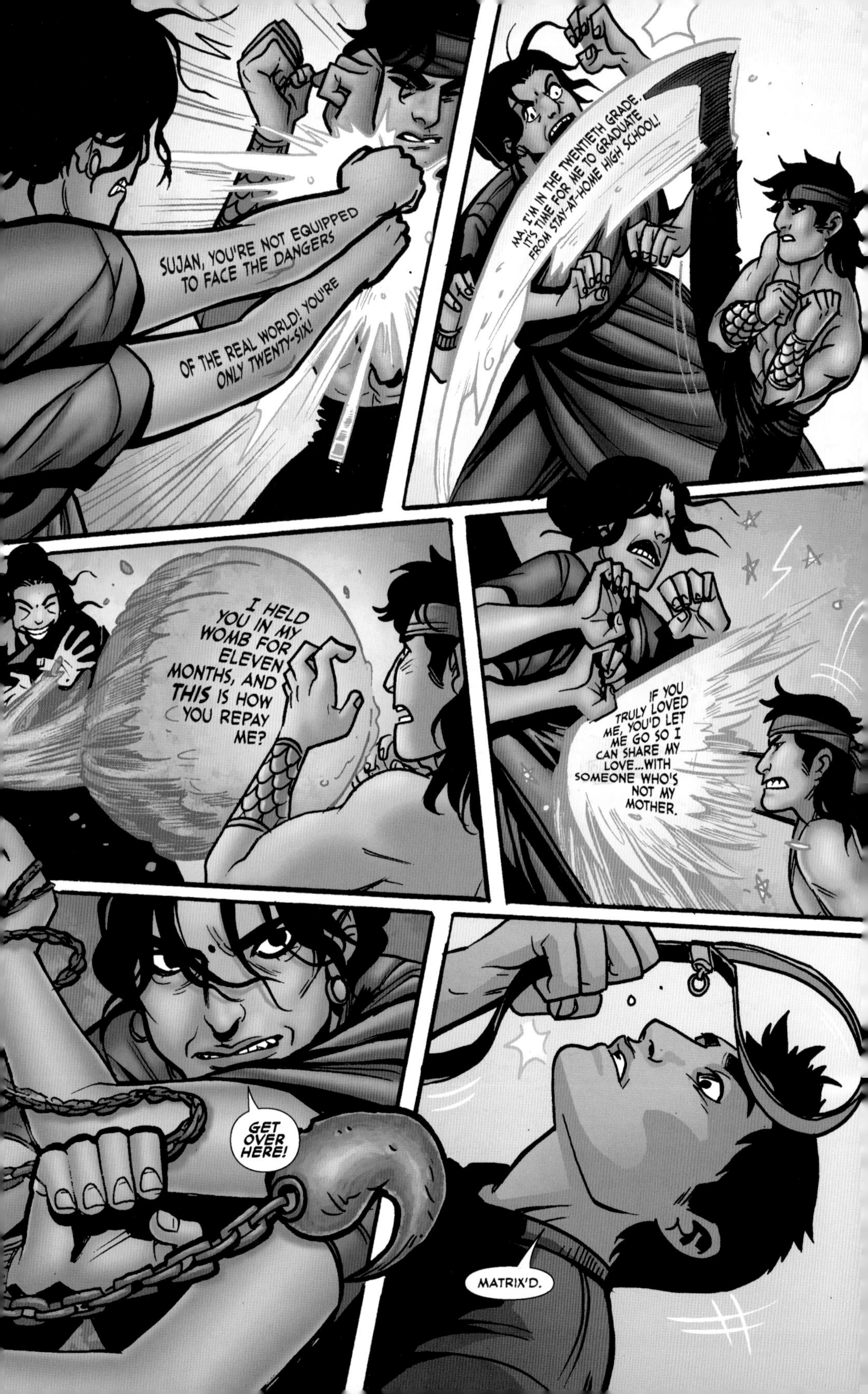
SUJAN, YOU'RE NOT EQUIPPED TO FACE THE DANGERS
OF THE REAL WORLD! YOU'RE ONLY TWENTY-SIX!
MA, I'M IN THE TWENTIETH GRADE. IT'S TIME FOR ME TO GRADUATE FROM STAY-AT-HOME HIGH SCHOOL!
I HELD YOU IN MY WOMB FOR ELEVEN MONTHS, AND THIS IS HOW YOU REPAY ME?
IF YOU TRULY LOVED ME, YOU'D LET ME GO SO I CAN SHARE MY LOVE...WITH SOMEONE WHO'S NOT MY MOTHER.
GET OVER HERE!
MATRIX'D.

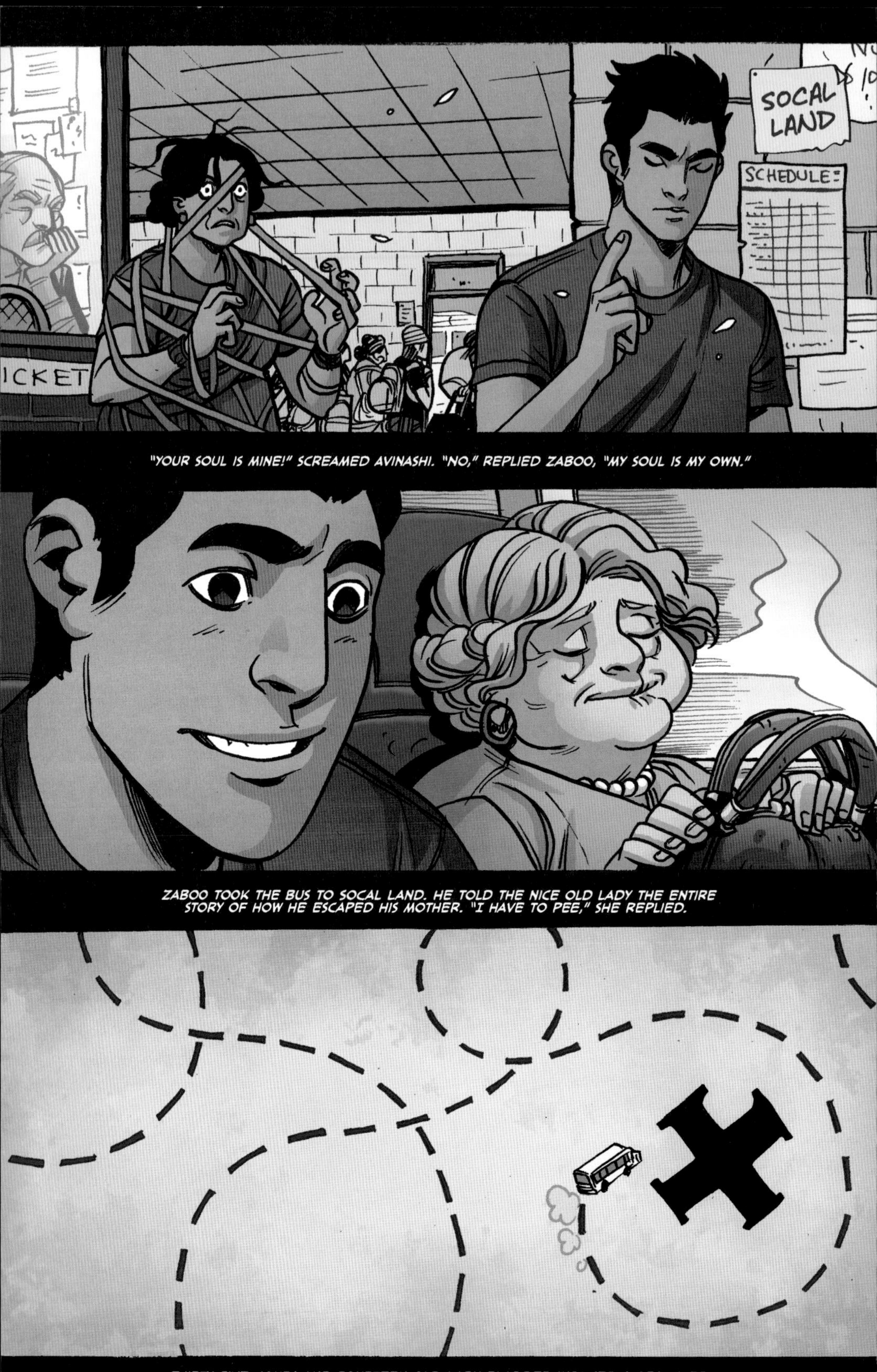
ICKET
SOCAL LAND
SCHEDULE
"YOUR SOUL IS MINE!" SCREAMED AVINASHI. "NO," REPLIED ZABOO, "MY SOUL IS MY OWN."
ZABOO TOOK THE BUS TO SOCAL LAND. HE TOLD THE NICE OLD LADY THE ENTIRE STORY OF HOW HE ESCAPED HIS MOTHER. "I HAVE TO PEE," SHE REPLIED.

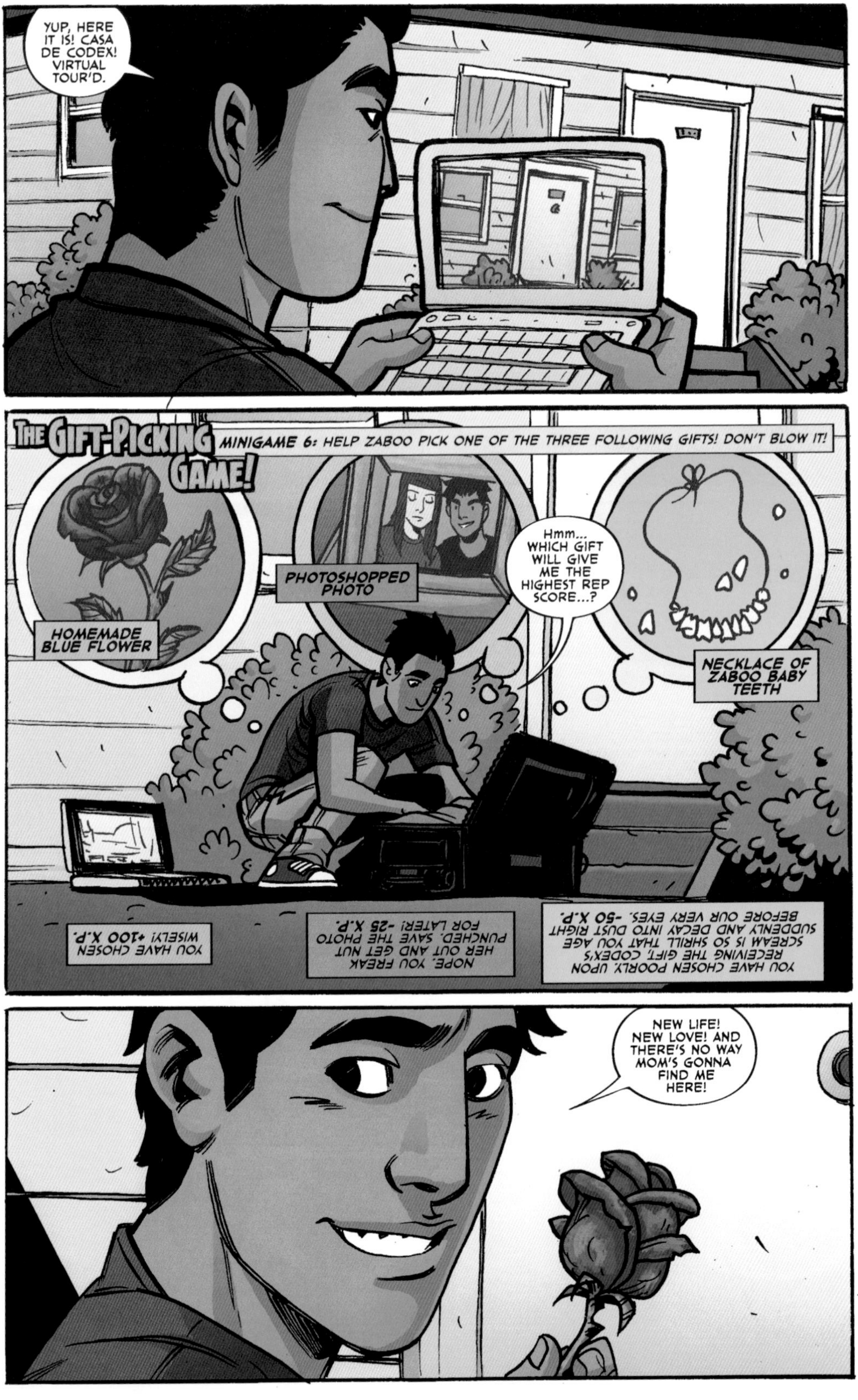
YUP, HERE IT IS! CASA DE CODEX! VIRTUAL TOUR'D.
THE GIFT-PICKING GAME!
MINIGAME 6: HELP ZABOO PICK ONE OF THE THREE FOLLOWING GIFTS! DON'T BLOW IT!
HOMEMADE BLUE FLOWER
PHOTOSHOPPED PHOTO
Hmm... WHICH GIFT WILL GIVE ME THE HIGHEST REP SCORE...?
NECKLACE OF ZABOO BABY TEETH
YOU HAVE CHOSEN POORLY. UPON RECEIVING THE GIFT, CODEX'S SCREAM IS SO SHRILL THAT YOU AGE SUDDENLY AND DECAY INTO DUST RIGHT BEFORE OUR VERY EYES. -50 X.P.
NOPE. YOU FREAK HER OUT AND GET NUT PUNCHED. SAVE THE PHOTO FOR LATER! -25 X.P.
YOU HAVE CHOSEN WISELY! +100 X.P.
NEW LIFE! NEW LOVE! AND THERE'S NO WAY MOM'S GONNA FIND ME HERE!

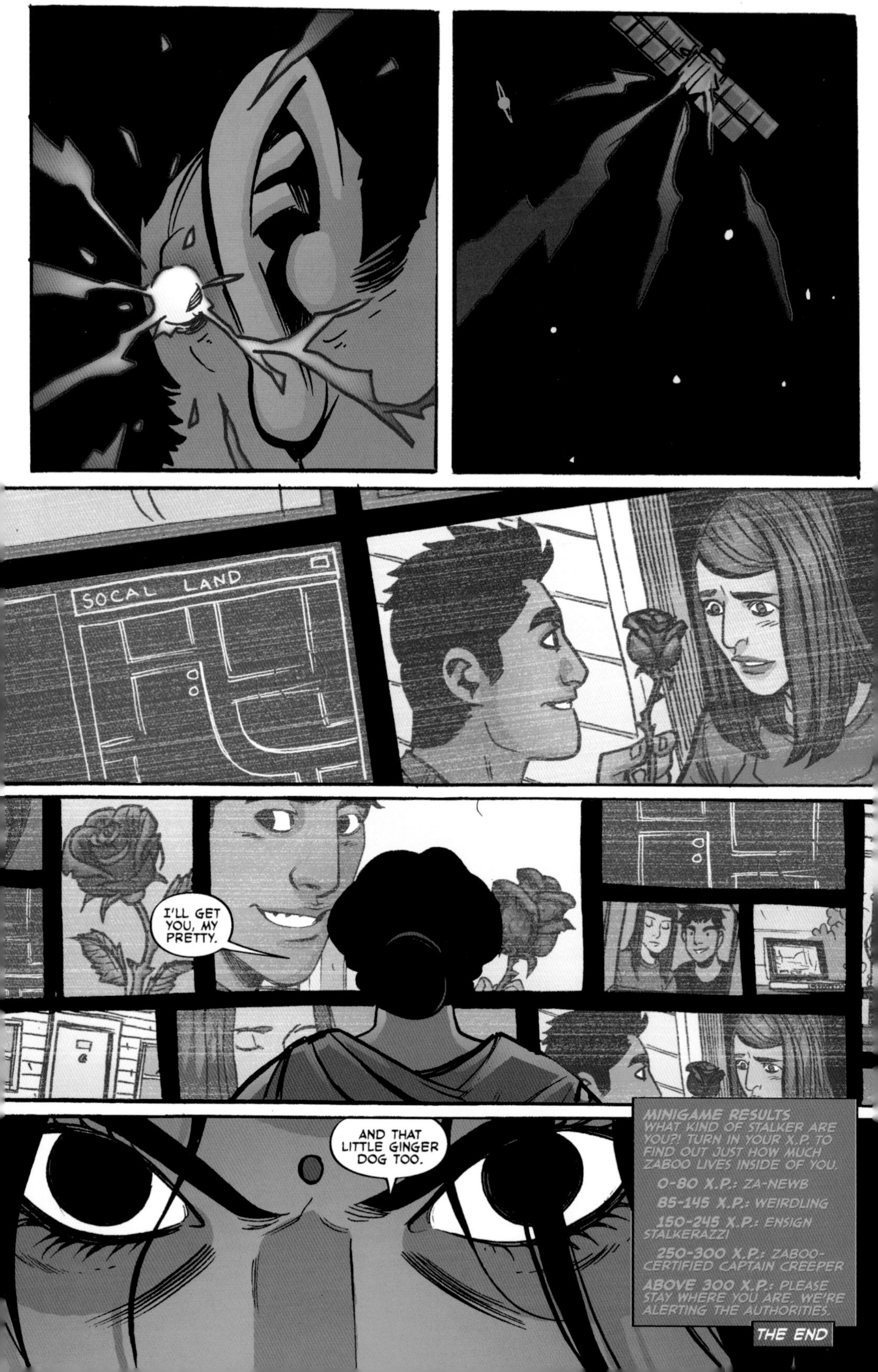
SOCAL LAND
I'LL GET YOU, MY PRETTY.
AND THAT LITTLE GINGER DOG TOO.
MINIGAME RESULTS
WHAT KIND OF STALKER ARE YOU?! TURN IN YOUR X.P. TO FIND OUT JUST HOW MUCH ZABOO LIVES INSIDE OF YOU.
0-80 X.P.: ZA-NEWB
85-145 X.P.: WEIRDLING
150-245 X.P.: ENSIGN STALKERAZZI
250-300 X.P.: ZABOO-CERTIFIED CAPTAIN CREEPER
ABOVE 300 X.P.: PLEASE STAY WHERE YOU ARE. WE'RE ALERTING THE AUTHORITIES.
THE END

SKETCHBOOK
Commentary by Scott Allie

Along with the crew of writers from the web series, a lot of artists contributed to this series of *Guild* stories. These pages present a look behind the scenes at their process and contributions.

Above: Ron Chan drew the ladies of *The Guild* as part of the sixth annual Women of Wonder Day celebration at Excalibur Books and Comics in Portland, Oregon. Women of Wonder is a growing national event to benefit domestic-violence programs. WomenOfWonderDay.com.

Loose cover pencils to *Vork* by Darick Robertson (compare to page 7).

Below: When Darick first drew Vork's grandfather on the roof, he drew the wings carefully constructed from cardboard, but Jeff Lewis thought it would be funnier (i.e., more pathetic) if they were just drawn on sheets of cardboard (see page 21).

Facing: Darick's pencils for the rave scene (see page 20).

DARK HORSE COMICS ART BOARD

TITLE: Vork ISSUE: 1 ARTIST: Robertson/Clark PAGE: 12

ALL "BLEED" ART MUST EXTEND TO THIS OUTERMOST DOTTED LINE.

TRIM MARKS INDICATE WHERE A PAGE IS CUT TO SIZE.

ALL LETTERING AND ESSENTIAL ART MUST FALL WITHIN THIS SOLID "LIVE AREA" BOX. THIS IS THE BORDER FOR A STANDARD, NON-BLEED COMIC BOOK PAGE.

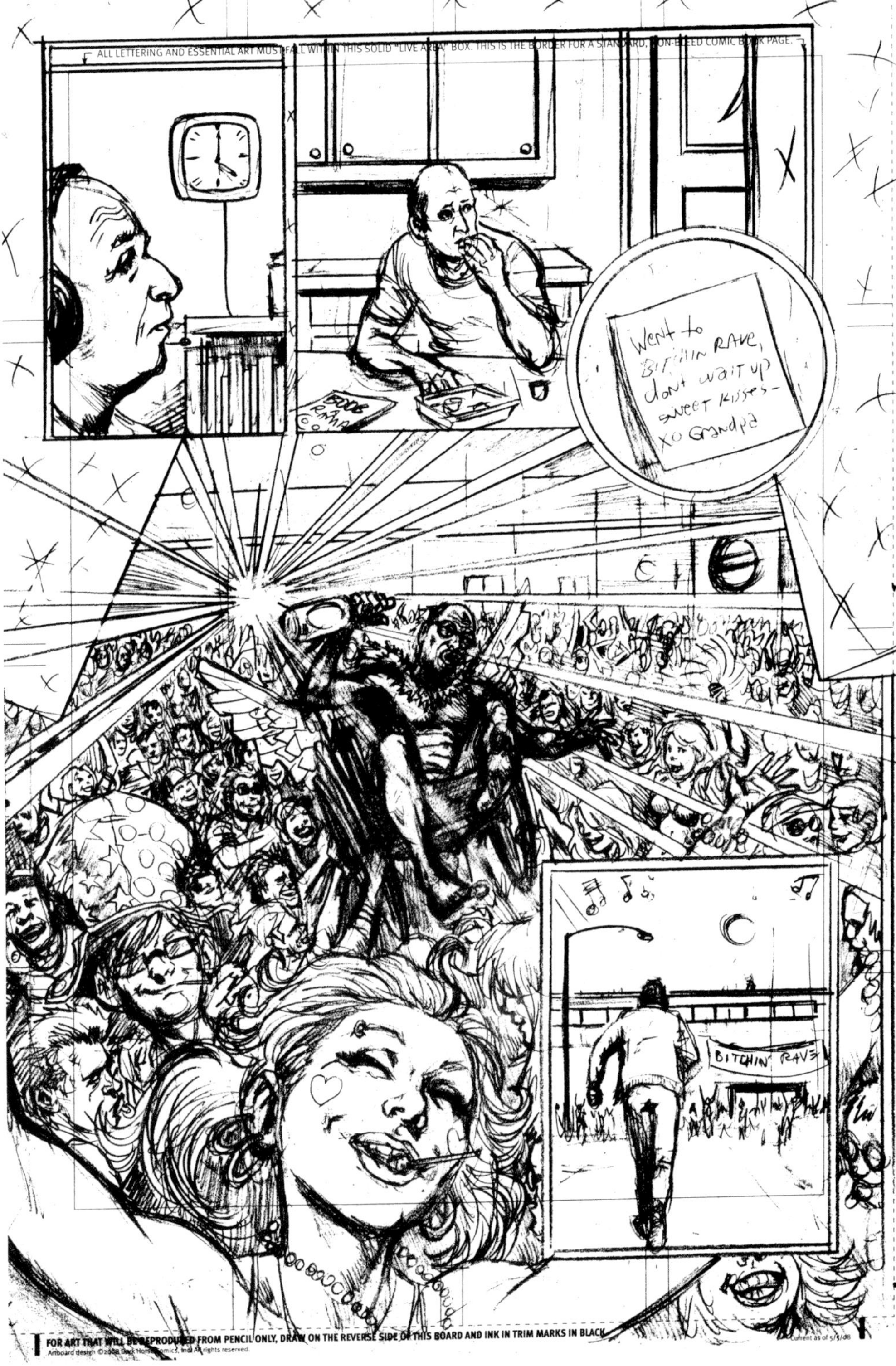
Went to
Bitchin Rave,
dont wait up
sweet kisses-
xo Grandpa
BITCHIN' RAVE

TO CREATE TWO-PAGE SPREAD, CUT ONE BOARD ALONG ITS RIGHT-HAND TRIM (INDICATED BY BLACK CROP MARKS), AND CUT ANOTHER BOARD ALONG ITS LEFT-HAND TRIM. BUTT CUT EDGES TOGETHER, TAPE ON BACK.

FOR ART THAT WILL BE REPRODUCED FROM PENCIL ONLY, DRAW ON THE REVERSE SIDE OF THIS BOARD AND INK IN TRIM MARKS IN BLACK.

Current as of 5/5/08

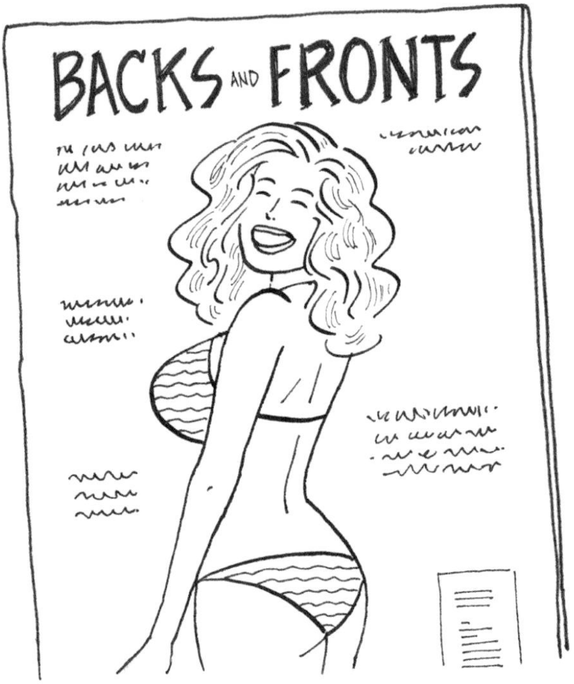
BACKS AND FRONTS

Gilbert Hernandez's sketches for the variant cover of *Vork*.

After Gilbert had drawn the cover, we asked him to add some porno mags from Grandpa's collection. Gilbert gave us this piece to patch in (see page 8).

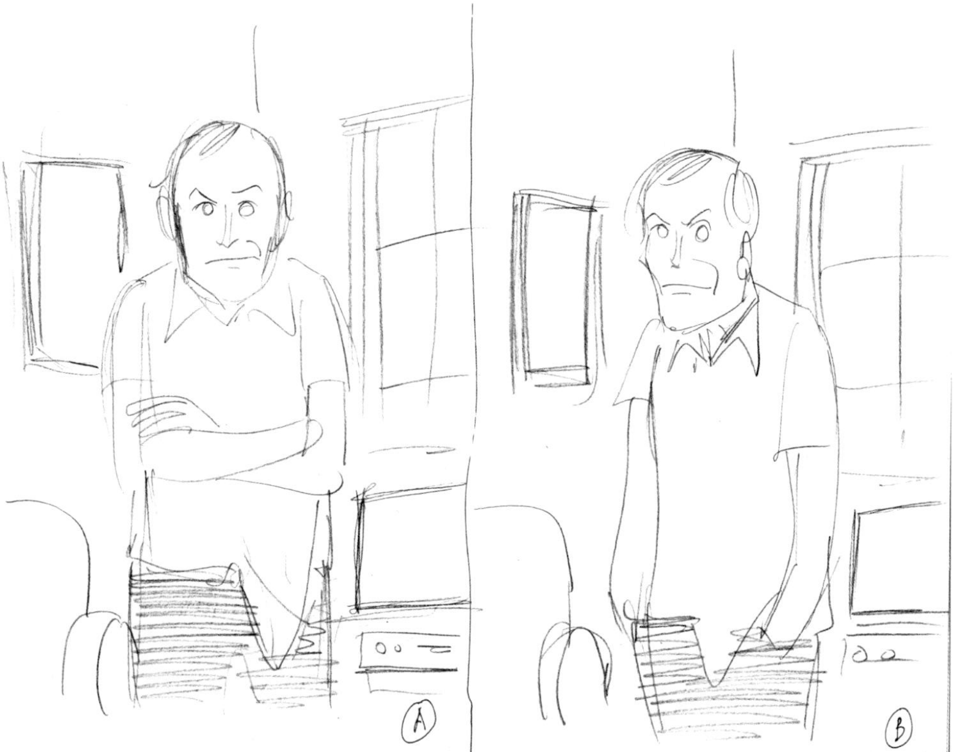
A
B

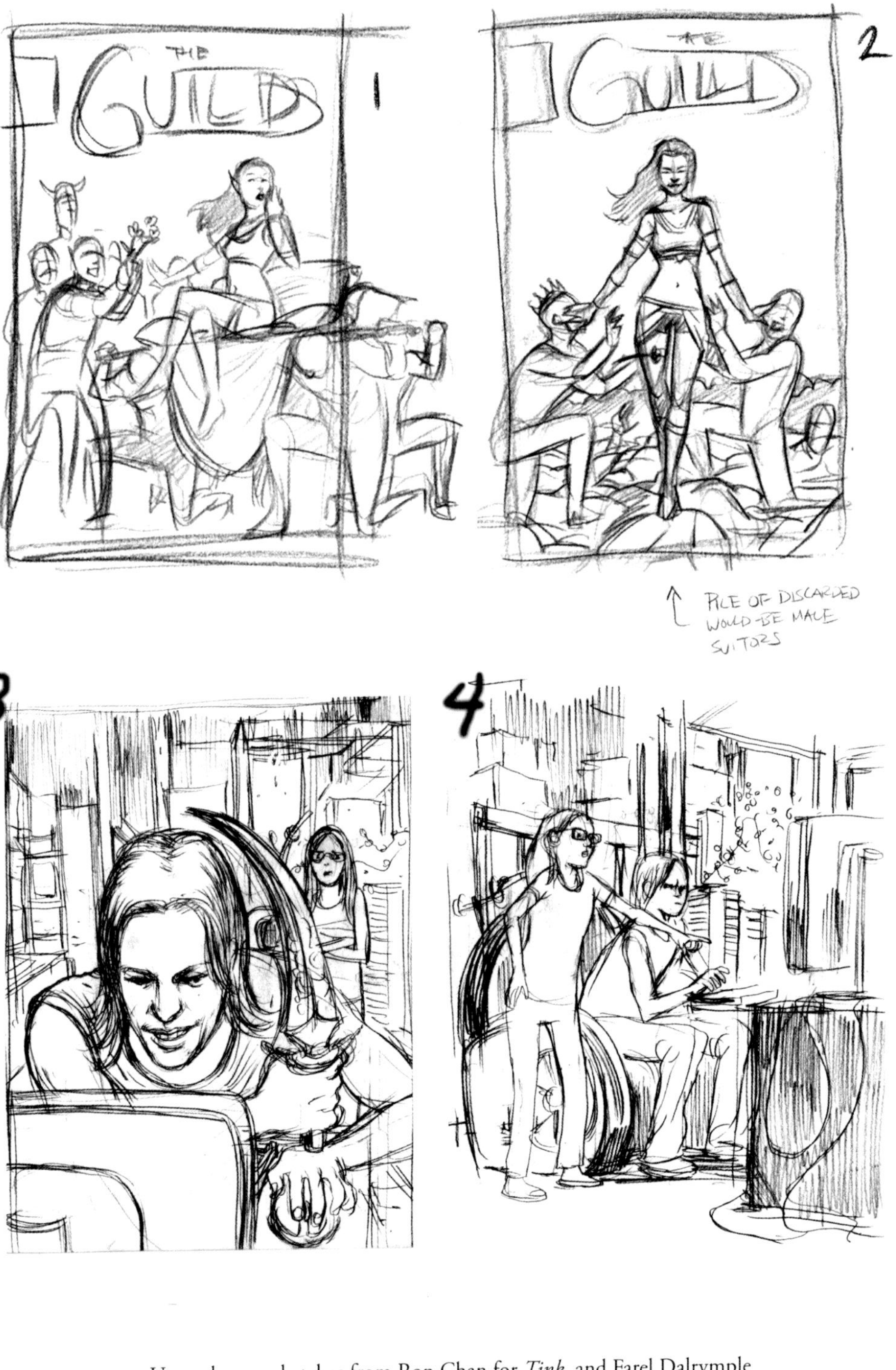
THE GUILD
1
THE GUILD
2
PILE OF DISCARDED WOULD-BE MALE SUITORS
3
4

Unused cover sketches from Ron Chan for *Tink*, and Farel Dalrymple for *Bladezz* (see final covers on pages 31 and 58 respectively).

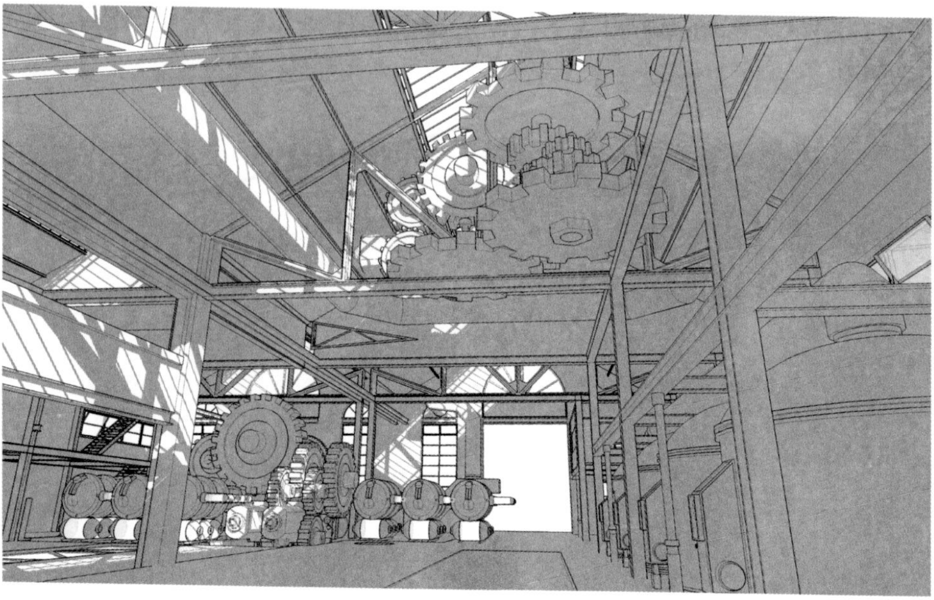

Kristian Donaldson, who penciled the bulk of the *Tink* one-shot, often creates 3-D models of the locations in his comics, from which he draws his backgrounds. For the few pages of *Tink* set in these locations, he created elaborate models of the factory (see pages 34–37) and Tink's room (pages 54–55). Kristian modeled far more details and views of the locations than we have room to include here.

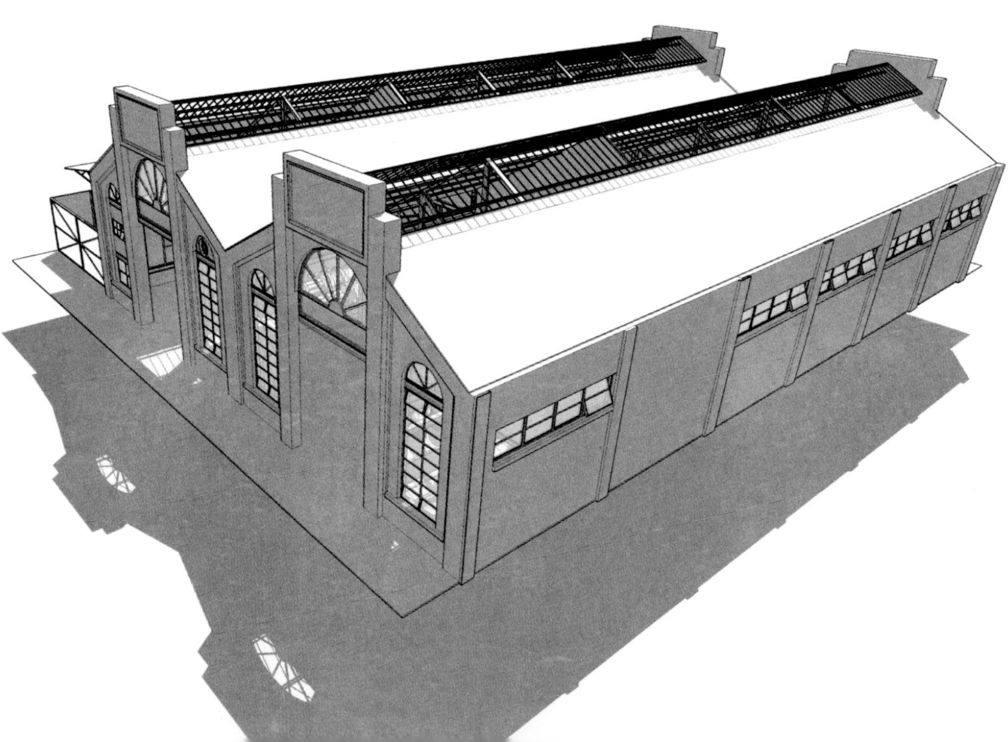

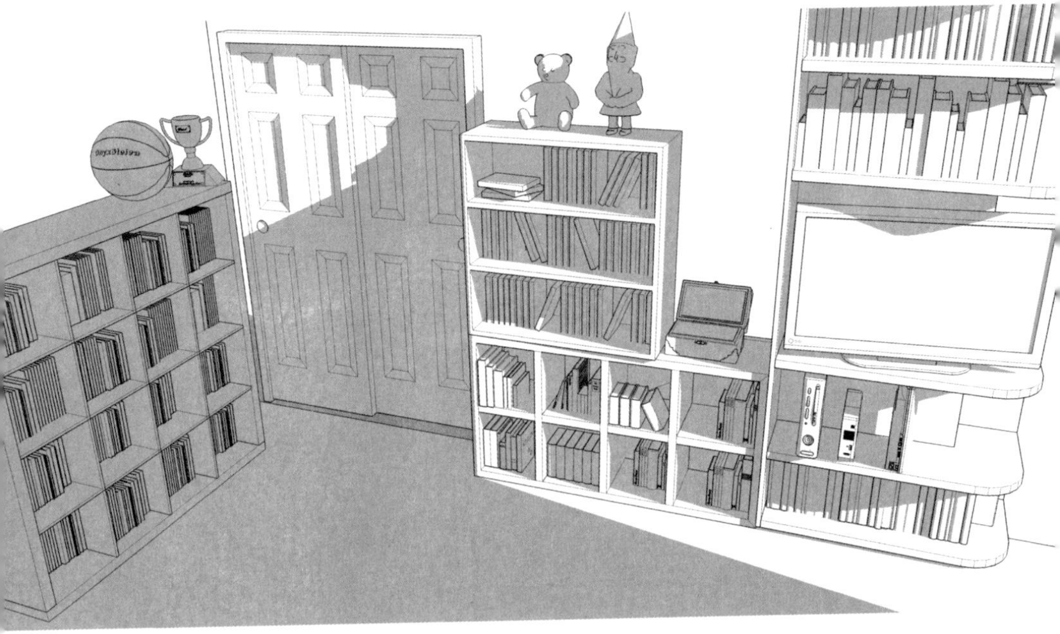

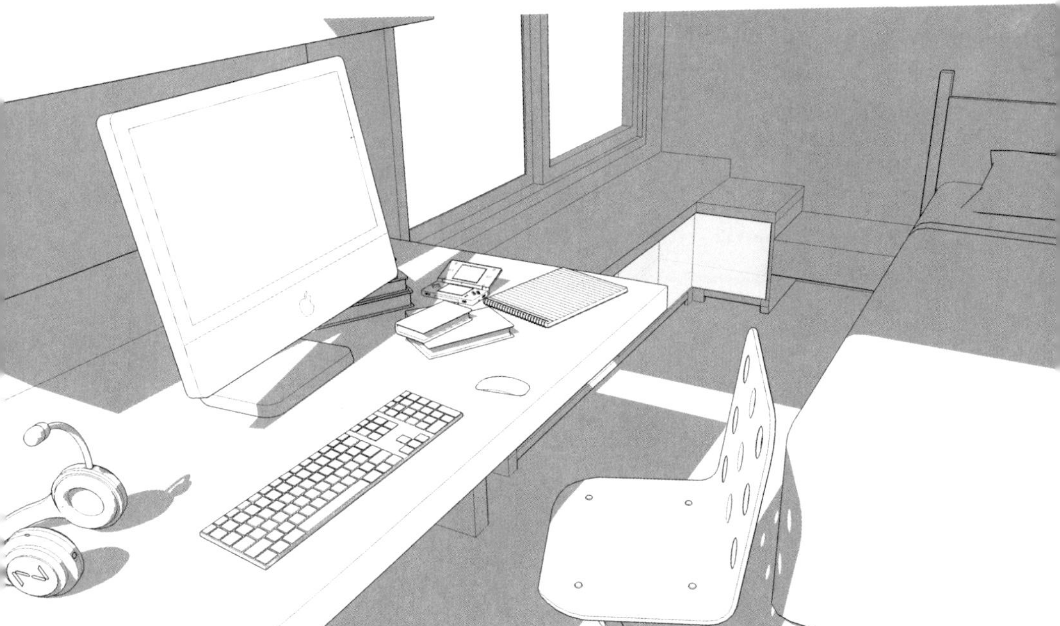

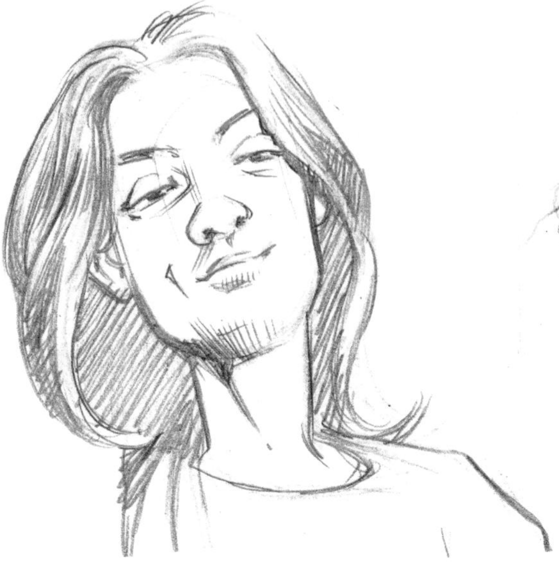

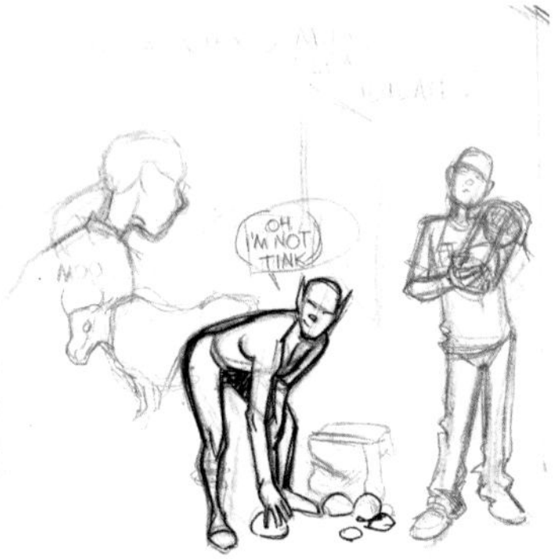

OH I'M NOT TINK

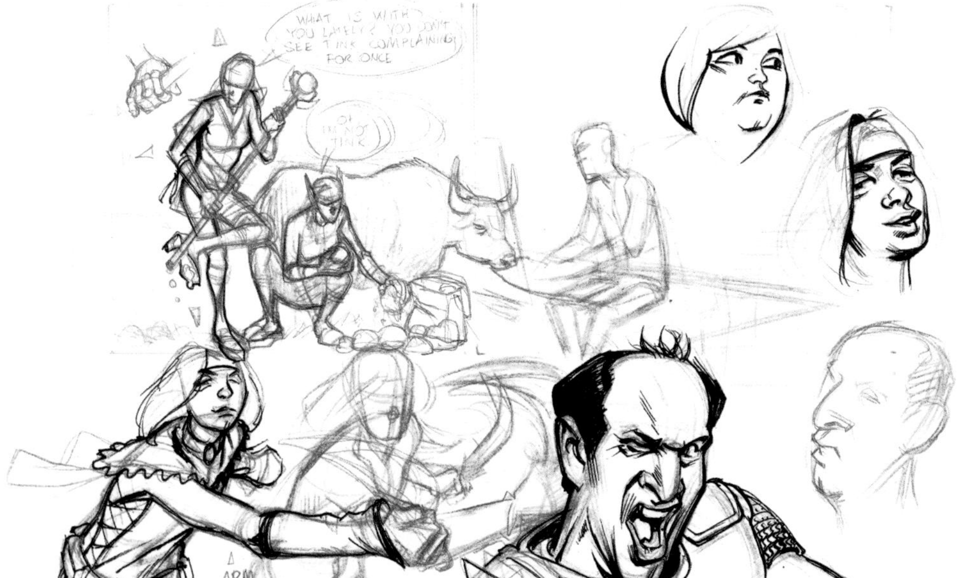

WHAT IS WITH YOU LATELY? YOU DON'T SEE TINK COMPLAINING FOR ONCE
OH I'M NOT TINK
ARM SHORTER

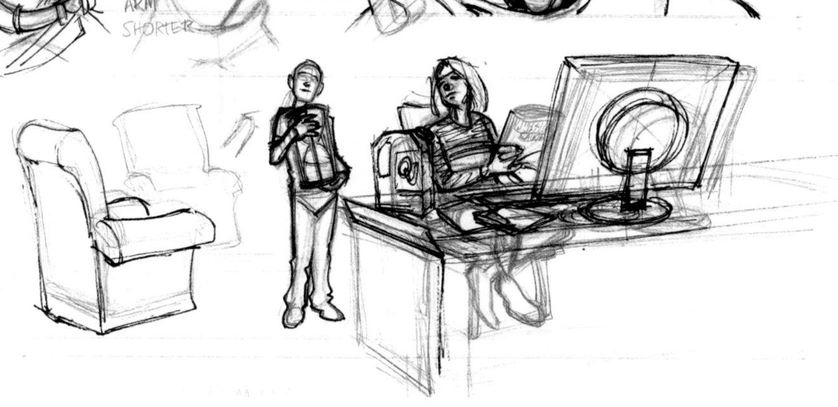

Facing: Andrew Currie works out various details and characters for *Bladezz*.

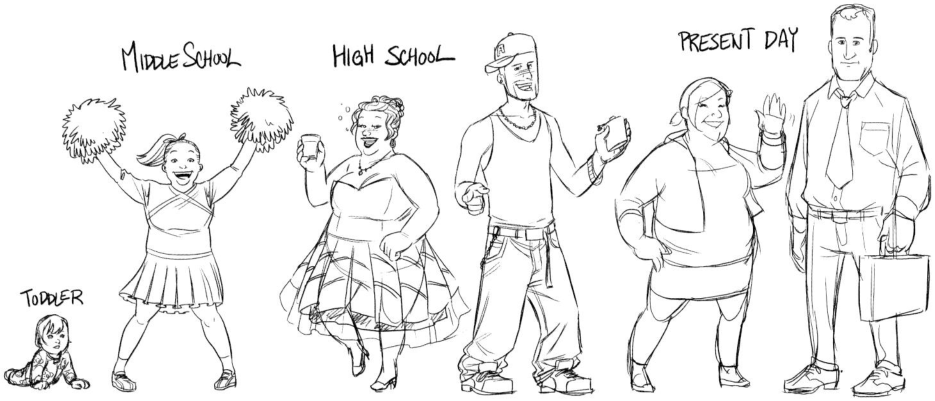
MIDDLE SCHOOL
HIGH SCHOOL
PRESENT DAY
TODDLER

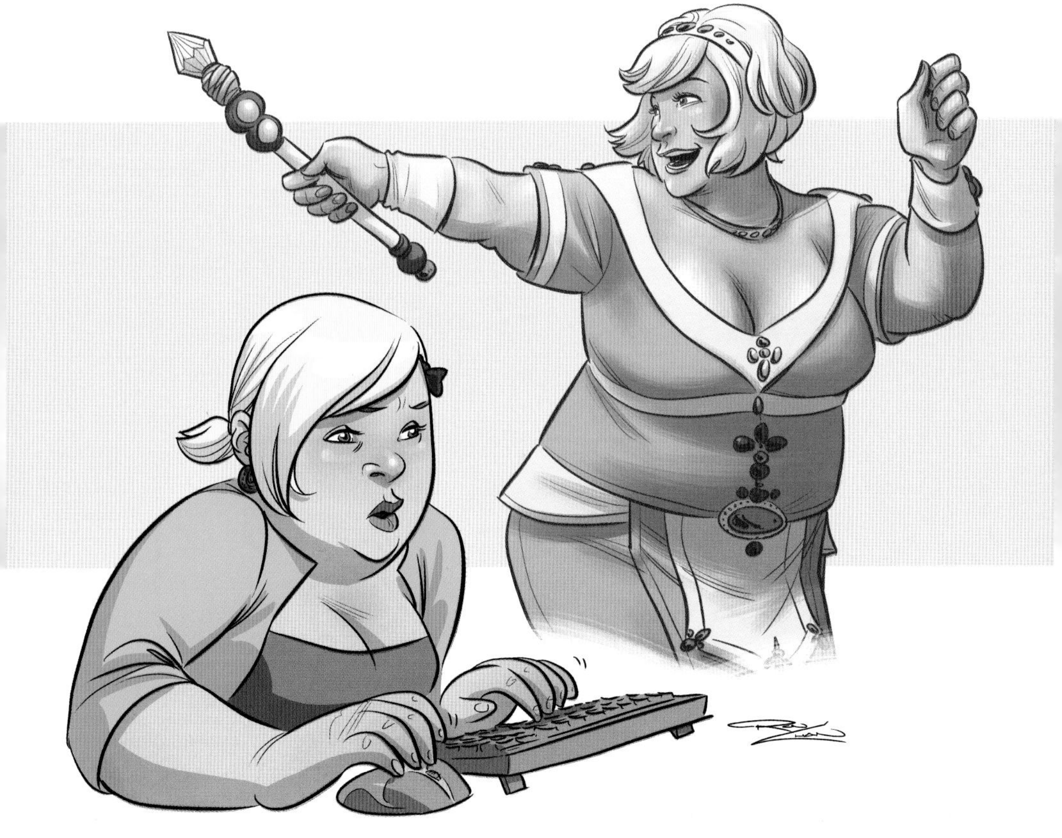

Above: Ron Chan defines Clara's and George's appearances through the years.

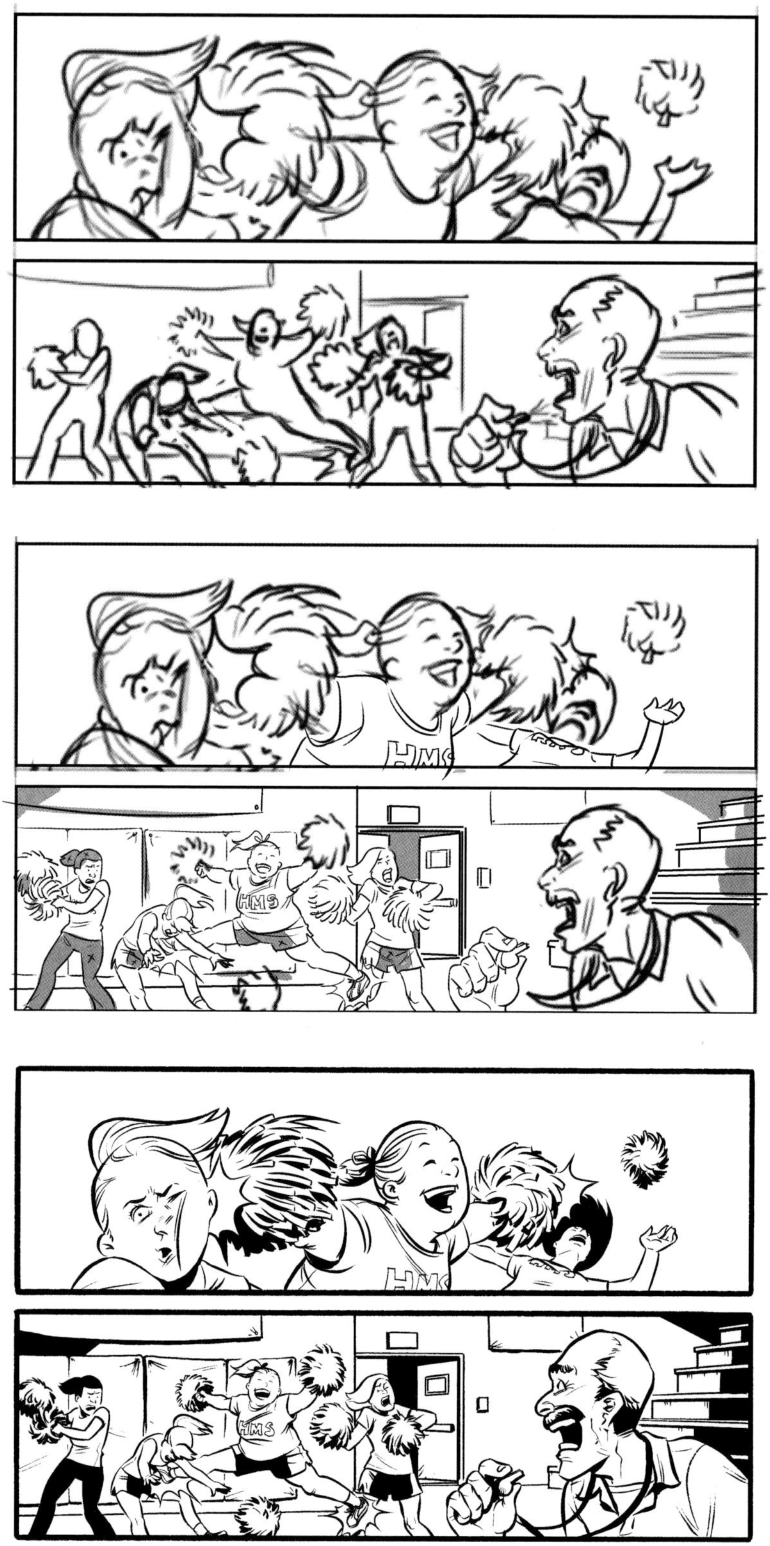
HMS

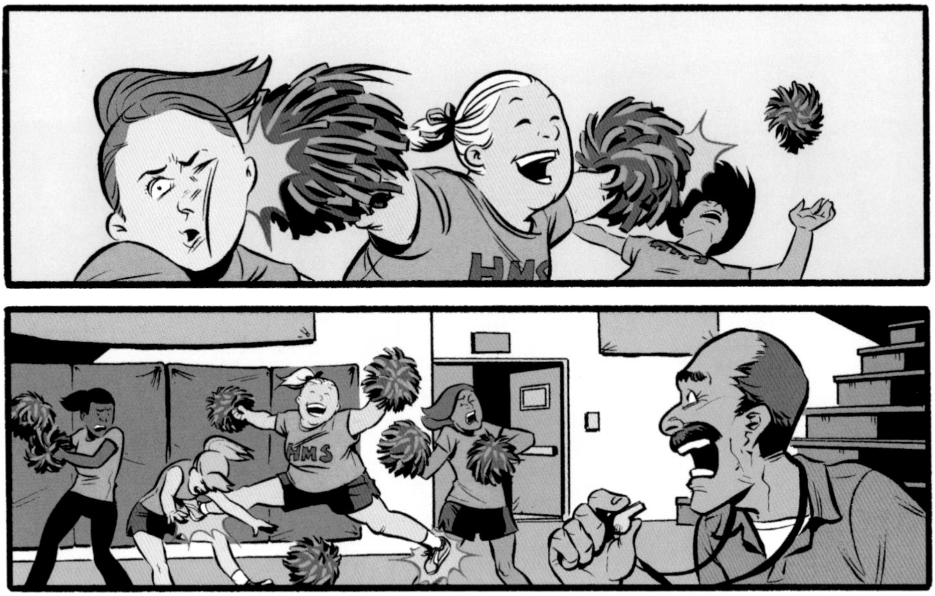
HMS

Ron Chan's process from layouts, through pencils, inks, and colors. Ron did everything except letter the book himself.

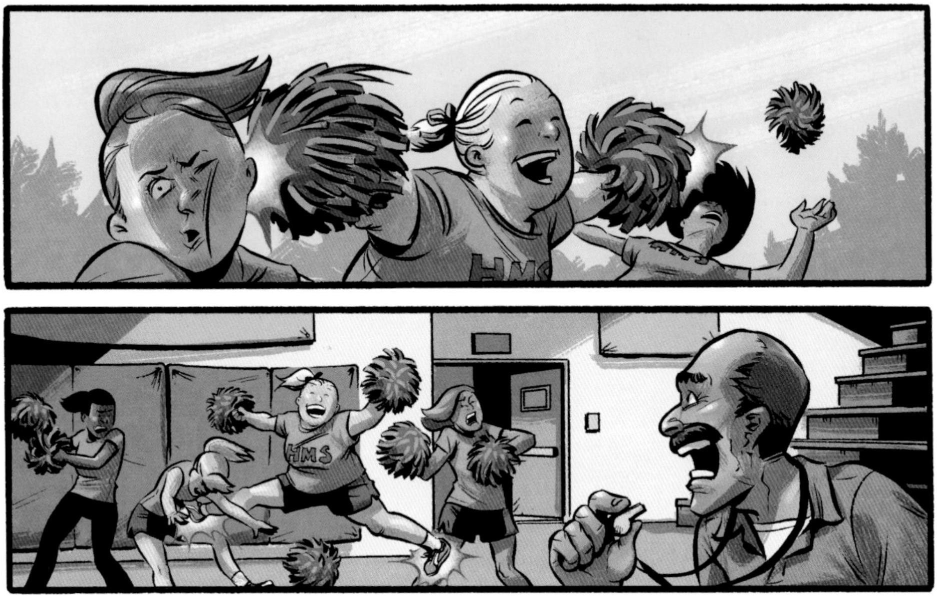
HMS

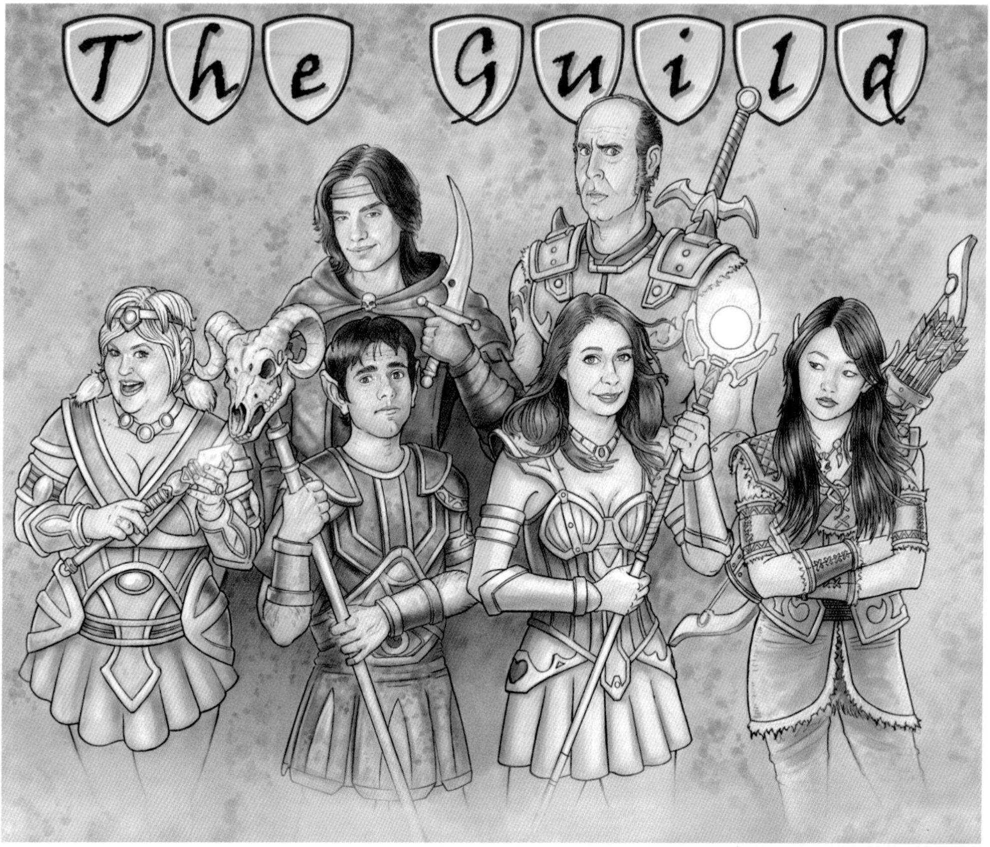
The Guild

This page and following: Pinups by concept artist Jeff Carlisle and *Wet Moon* creator Ross Campbell, and a variant cover celebrating Dark Horse's twenty-fifth anniversary by *Criminal* and *Fatale* cocreator Sean Phillips.

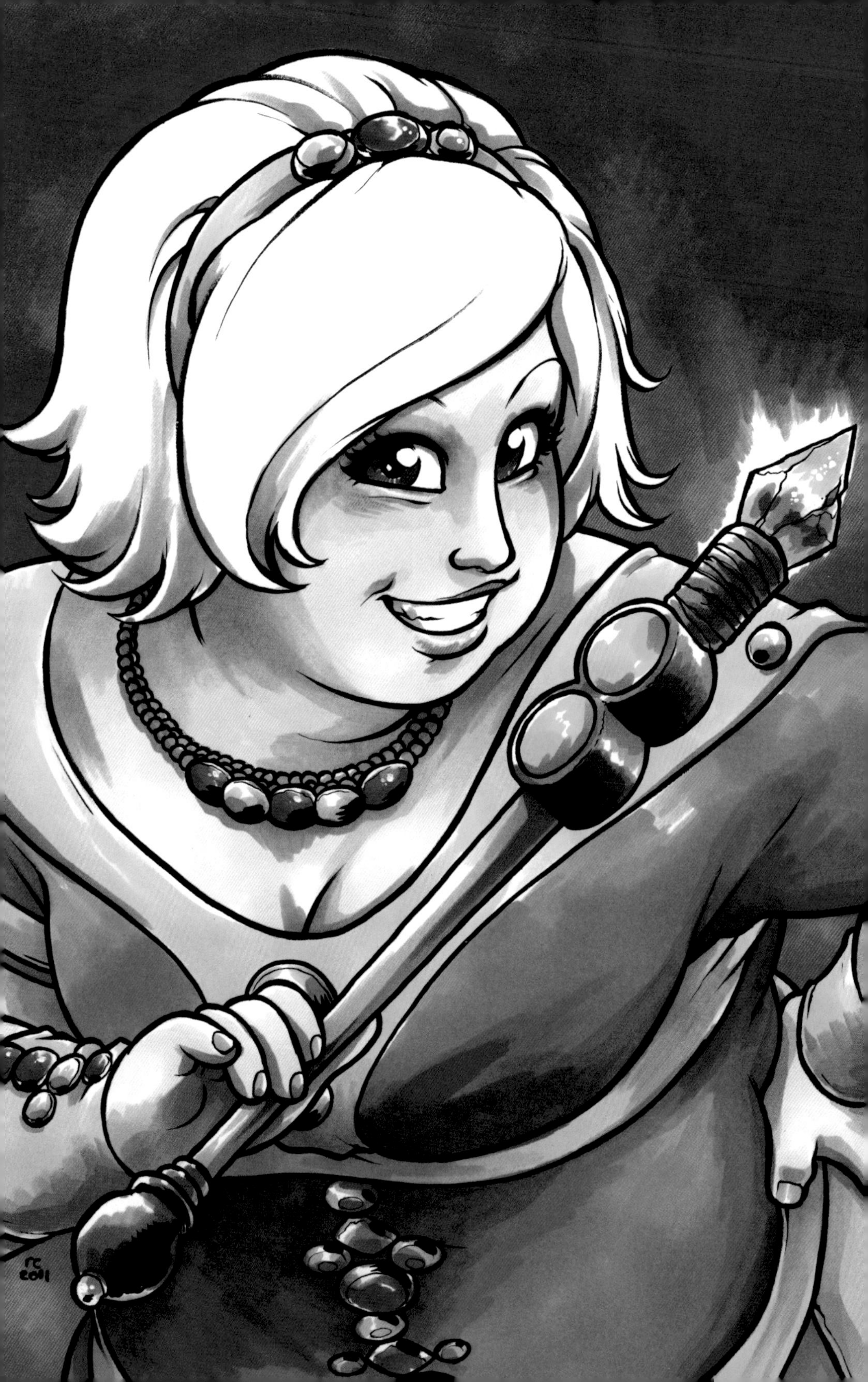
rc
2011

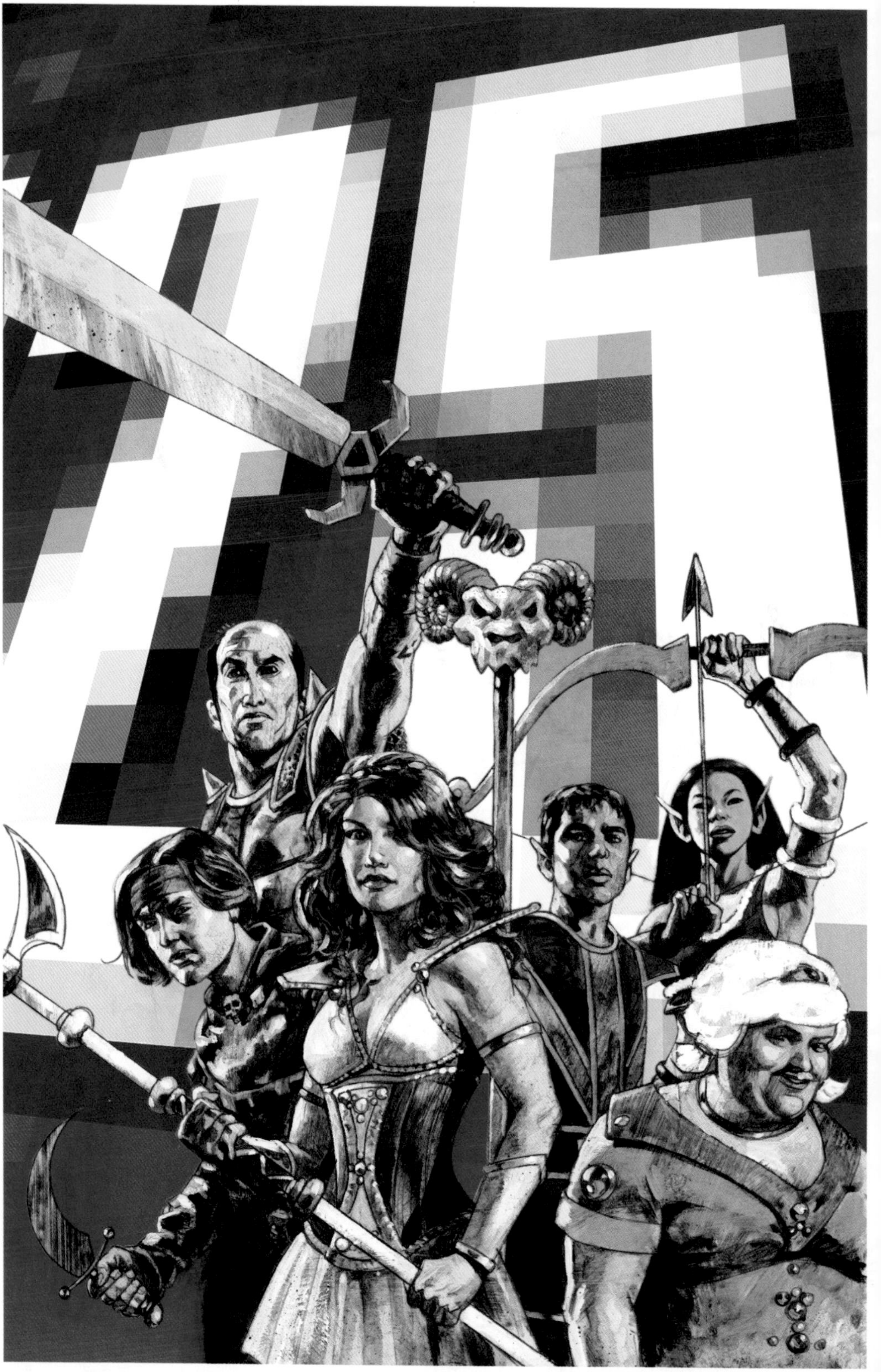

ALSO FROM DARK HORSE BOOKS . . .

THE GUILD
FELICIA DAY & JIM RUGG

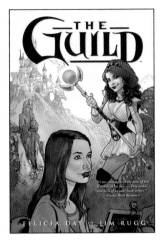

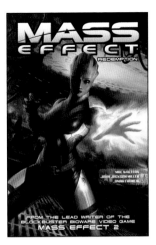

THE GUILD VOL. 1
Felicia Day and Jim Rugg

From the creator and star of the cult web series comes this prequel story, chronicling Cyd Sherman's life before joining the guild and revealing the origins of the Knights of Good.

ISBN 978-1-59582-549-0 $ 12.99

MASS EFFECT
REDEMPTION
MAC WALTERS
JOHN JACKSON MILLER
OMAR FRANCIA
FROM THE LEAD WRITER OF THE BLOCKBUSTER BIOWARE VIDEO GAME
MASS EFFECT 2

MASS EFFECT VOL. 1: REDEMPTION
Mac Walters, John Jackson Miller, and Omar Francia

From the lead writer of *Mass Effect 2* and *3*! Commander Shepard's companion Liara T'Soni undertakes a deadly mission of extraordinary importance in the lawless Terminus Systems.

ISBN 978-1-59582-481-3 $16.99

Buffy
WHEDON VAUGHAN JEANTY LEE RICHARDS

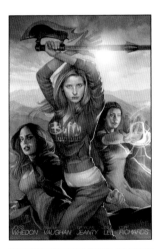

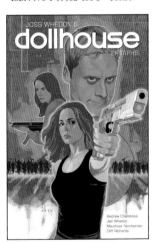

BUFFY THE VAMPIRE SLAYER SEASON 8 LIBRARY VOL. 1
Joss Whedon, Brian K. Vaughan, and Georges Jeanty

Series creator Joss Whedon brings his beloved series back to life with his comics-only follow-up to season 7 of the television show. This hardcover edition contains the first two arcs, plus two one-shots.

ISBN 978-1-59582-888-0 $29.99

JOSS WHEDON'S
dollhouse
EPITAPHS
Andrew Chambliss
Jed Whedon
Maurissa Tancharoen
Cliff Richards

DOLLHOUSE VOL. 1: EPITAPHS
Andrew Chambliss, Jed Whedon, Maurissa Tancharoen, and Cliff Richards

Joss Whedon's television series continues in comics, as the Dollhouse technology goes viral, turning people into mindless killers. Echo and the others who have retained their minds must fight to survive the sudden apocalypse.

ISBN 978-1-59582-863-7 $18.99

AVAILABLE AT YOUR LOCAL COMICS SHOP OR BOOKSTORE!
To find a comics shop in your area, call 1-888-266-4226. For more information or to order direct, visit DarkHorse.com or call 1-800-862-0052 Mon.–Fri. 9 AM to 5 PM Pacific Time.

DARK HORSE BOOKS
DarkHorse.com

DARK HORSE BRINGS YOU THE BEST IN WEBCOMICS!

These wildly popular cartoon gems were once only available online, but now can be found through Dark Horse Books with loads of awesome extras!

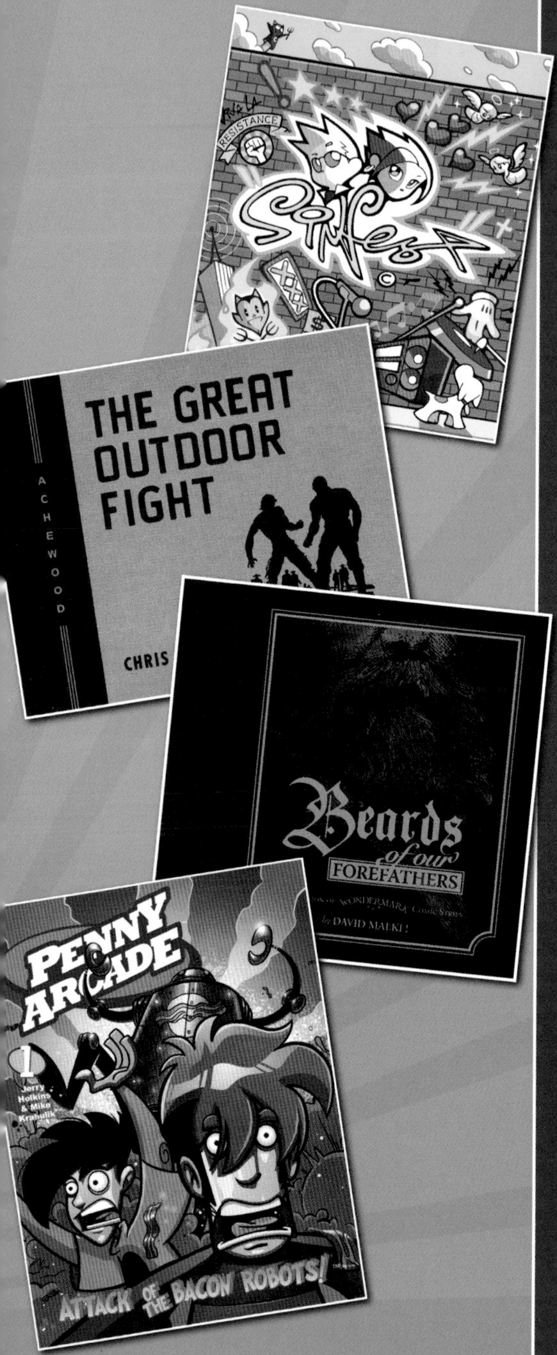
RESISTANCE
Sinfest
THE GREAT OUTDOOR FIGHT
ACHEWOOD
CHRIS
Beards of our FOREFATHERS
by DAVID MALKI!
PENNY ARCADE
1
Jerry Holkins & Mike Krahulik
ATTACK OF THE BACON ROBOTS!

SINFEST

By Tatsuya Ishida

Sinfest is one of the most-read and longest-running webcomics out there, and explores religion, advertising, sex, and politics in a way fleen.com calls "both brutally funny and devastatingly on-target." What other series has had the chutzpah to make characters out of God, the Devil, Jesus, Buddha, Barack Obama, Sarah Palin, and corrupt Wall Street CEOs? If your comic-strip craving hasn't been satisfied since the nineties, deliverance is finally at hand.

Volume 1 TPB
ISBN 978-1-59582-319-9 | $14.95
Volume 2: Viva La Resistance TPB
ISBN 978-1-59582-424-0 | $14.99

ACHEWOOD

By Chris Onstad

Since 2001, cult comic favorite *Achewood* has built a six-figure international following. Intelligent, hilarious, and adult but not filthy, it's the strip you'll wish you'd discovered as an underappreciated fifteen-year-old. "I'm addicted to *Achewood*. Chris Onstad is a dark, hilarious genius." –Dave Barry

Volume 1: The Great Outdoor Fight HC
ISBN 978-1-59307-997-0 | $14.99
Volume 2: Worst Song, Played on Ugliest Guitar HC
ISBN 978-1-59582-239-0 | $15.99
Volume 3: A Home for Scared People HC
ISBN 978-1-59582-450-9 | $16.99

WONDERMARK

By David Malki!

Dark Horse Comics is proud to present these handsome hardbound collections of David Malki's Ignatz-nominated comic strip *Wondermark*. Malki repurposes illustrations and engravings from 19th-century books into hilarious, collage-style comic strips. More than just webcomic collections, the *Wondermark* books have been praised for their magnificent design and loads of extra content for casual readers and superfans alike.

Volume 1: Beards of Our Forefathers HC
ISBN 978-1-59307-984-0 | $14.99
Volume 2: Clever Tricks to Stave Off Death HC
ISBN 978-1-59582-329-8 | $14.99
Volume 3: Dapper Caps & Pedal-Copters HC
ISBN 978-1-59582-449-3 | $16.99

PENNY ARCADE

By Jerry Holkins and Mike Krahulik

Penny Arcade, the comic strip for gamers, by gamers is now available in comic shops and bookstores everywhere. Experience the joy of being a hardcore gamer as expressed in hilariously witty vignettes of random vulgarity and mindless violence!

Volume 1: Attack of the Bacon Robots! TPB
ISBN 978-1-59307-444-9 | $12.99
Volume 2: Epic Legends of the Magic Sword Kings! TPB
ISBN 978-1-59307-541-5 | $12.99
Volume 3: The Warsun Prophecies TPB
ISBN 978-1-59307-635-1 | $12.99
Volume 4: Birds are Weird TPB
ISBN 978-1-59307-773-0 | $12.99
Volume 5: The Case of the Mummy's Gold TPB
ISBN 978-1-59307-814-0 | $12.99

DARK HORSE BOOKS

AVAILABLE AT YOUR LOCAL COMICS SHOP OR BOOKSTORE | To find a comics shop in your area, call 1-888-266-4226

For more information or to order direct: •On the web: DarkHorse.com •E-mail: mailorder@DarkHorse.com •Phone: 1-800-862-0052 Mon.–Fri. 9AM to 5PM Pacific Time.